Who I am

MELANIE C

Who I am

MY STORY

WELBECK

Published by Welbeck
An imprint of Welbeck Non-Fiction Limited,
part of Welbeck Publishing Group.
Based in London and Sydney
www.welbeckpublishing.com

First published by Welbeck in 2022

A CIP catalogue record for this book is available from the British Library

ISBN
Hardback – 9781802793352
Trade Paperback – 9781802793369
eBook – 9781802793376

Typeset by seagulls.net
Printed and bound in the UK

10 9 8 7 6 5 4 3 2 1

To each and every fan – thank you for everything x

Contents

WARNING

This book discusses frank and frequent feelings and experiences around mental illness, anorexia and binge eating disorder, as well as anxiety and depression, and may trigger or evoke trauma for some readers. If you are experiencing similar feelings and need someone to talk to, here are some recommended services:

Calm – Support for those feeling suicidal as well as those worried about someone.
Thecalmzone.net or call 0800 58 58 58 (from 5 pm until midnight, 365 days a year)

Mind – For information and advice on mental health problems.
Mind.org.uk or call 0300 123 3393 (from 9 am until 6 pm, Monday to Friday except bank holidays)

Shout – Free, 24/7 mental health text support.
Text Shout on 85258 (24 hours a day, 365 days a year)

The Samaritans – If you're having a difficult time, feel suicidal or are concerned about someone.
Samaritans.org or call 116 123 (24 hours a day)

As an ally and advocate for LGBTQIA+ people, here are some fantastic organisations I'd like to recommend for those that may need support:

Akt – For LGBTQIA+ 16–25-year-olds facing or experiencing homelessness or living in a hostile environment.
Akt.org.uk for live chat (Monday to Friday)

Stonewall – Help and advice for lesbian, gay, bisexual and transgender people.
Stonewall.org.uk or contact freephone 0800 0502020 (from 9.30 am to 4.30 pm, Monday to Friday)

Mermaids – Charity and advocacy support for transgender, non-binary and gender-diverse children, young people and their families.
Mermaidsuk.org.uk or call 0808 801 0400 (from 9 am to 9 pm, Monday to Friday)

FOR AUSTRALIA:
Lifeline – Crisis support line (24-hour) 13 11 14
Beyond Blue – Mental health support line (24-hour) 1300 22 4636
QLife – Counselling for LGBTQIA+ people (3pm – midnight) 1800 184 527

FOR NEW ZEALAND:
Lifeline Aoteaoa – Crisis support line (24-hour) 0800 543 354
Outline New Zealand – Rainbow specialist and trans peer support (6pm – 9pm) 0800 688 5463

Introduction

Summer 2021 and I'm getting a few bits down the shops. I'm just beginning the process of thinking about whether or not I should write this book. This very one that you currently hold in your hands.

The decision, alongside the COVID-19 pandemic that has dominated all our lives for nearly 18 months, is leading me to reflect on my life in a way I haven't had the time, or space, to do, until now. The restrictions put in place due to Coronavirus have started to lift in my part of the world. I'm in North London – my adopted home since the early nineties – and there's a sense of expectation, of new beginnings, in the air.

"Are you finally getting some normality back in your life now?" said the man behind the counter as I pay for my shopping. "To be honest," I replied, the thought striking me quite suddenly there and then in the middle of my local greengrocers, "since I was 22 years old, my life has been far from normal."

As I started to seriously think about telling my story, the nerves and doubts continued, tapping into a lot of my insecurities.

Who wants to read about me? I'm not interesting. Why would anyone care? Who am I to think I've got something to say?

I was also very wary about exploring and explaining my life in such detail, because there was a lot of painful stuff to unearth. I had recently begun a phone hacking case against certain parts of the British tabloid press and as part of that process I'd had to read through hundreds of old press clippings. Going back over what was written about me in the nineties and noughties sent me into a dark space for several days. I knew that even thinking about writing certain chapters of my memoir could do the same. Did I have it in me to face it, to confront it, to recover from it?

The tabloid attention that surrounds the release of an auto-biography is another type of scrutiny that I had to consider. At best, the intrusion over the last three decades has made me unhappy; at worst, it's contributed to me being very unwell. Do I want to re-live those levels of attention? Do I want to open myself up to headlines, hypotheses, attention and analysis once more?

Then I started to think about what could be gained from this, about the positive effect that writing a book could have, not only on me, but on other people too. One of the most rewarding aspects of being a songwriter and musician is the impact you can have on other people. I receive the most amazing messages from people who tell me a certain song I've written has made them feel understood, made them feel a bit less lonely. I'm not a therapist, a healer, or a doctor but I thought that maybe this book could bring people a bit of comfort, a glimmer of light in the dark.

If that's the case, it would be worth it for that alone.

Getting back onstage with the Spice Girls for the *Spice World* tour in 2019 was a huge catalyst in changing the way I think about many things and was another big part of why I was starting to open up to the possibility of writing an autobiography. Standing onstage each night and looking at the hundreds of thousands of people who had turned up to see us play, I was finally able to recognise and appreciate what we had achieved. What *I* had achieved. Prior to the *Spice World* tour, I had very real worries about becoming Sporty Spice again. I feel differently now, but back then I wondered whether I could pull it off. For nearly 20 years I had a very complex relationship with the name that was given to me, and the band that brought me so much yet took away a great deal.

But as we played each show, it hit home how hard us five had worked to make the Spice Girls a success. What we achieved despite it all. When we first formed the band, we were told girl groups didn't work, girls wouldn't buy music by girls, magazines wouldn't put us on covers, we couldn't possibly sell out an arena, let alone a stadium. We knew it was a load of rubbish and if anything, it propelled us to work even harder to prove people wrong. We played arenas *and* stadiums, appeared on the front of countless magazines. We broke records and made history. We didn't invent "Girl Power", but I think we were successful at catapulting the phrase, the ideology, and the culture to a whole generation of young people who have gone on to build on that movement by creating #TimesUp and #MeToo. That makes me incredibly proud.

The Spice Girls were a global phenomenon and I'm profoundly grateful that I was a part of that. The *Spice World* tour gave me an opportunity to celebrate our accomplishments and accept every aspect of myself: Sporty Spice, Mel C, Melanie C, Melanie Jayne Chisholm. I realised it was time to celebrate every part of myself. Even the rubbish bits!

The tour showed me that I don't become Sporty Spice, she's not an outfit or a costume. She is a part of me, and she's never gone away. Sporty is part of me because she *is* me. And she has been me since I was a kid bombing around the estate on my little blue Raleigh, risking life and limb in the playground doing tricks on the bars, and holding my own against the boys. I came from very little and once my parents divorced there was even less. It made me tough, and it made me ambitious, but it made me a little lonely too.

As far back as I can remember, I set my sights on being someone. Someone that mattered. Someone that stood out.

I wanted, *needed* attention and I worked out at a very young age that the stage was the place to get that.

But the attention and adoration came at a price. I got everything I had ever wanted but I had never felt so lonely. I became ill – physically, mentally, and emotionally.

And yet I survived.

Maybe, I started to think, this is a story that should be told. Despite the things I may feel I *might* lose from the experience, perhaps the gains will far outweigh the losses.

Who I Am is the story of a broken girl from a broken family who patched herself together with sticks and glue and an over-whelming desire to succeed. It's a story about how that girl, an ordinary girl from an ordinary town, achieved extraordinary things, against all odds. This is the story of the many highs associated with those achievements, but the lows too. It's a tale of reward and regret, of love and loss, and of both confusion and clarity as I've learnt to understand and accept myself through the many twists and turns of my life.

It's been a very bumpy road to get to a place of self-acceptance and self-love, and I'm aware that life can pull the rug from under me at any moment. I'm still on that journey and I know I'm not alone in my struggles. I don't claim to have all the answers, but I think I've worked a few things out. Not everything, but some things.

What you read within the pages of this book is what I want people to know about me, Melanie Chisholm, because I want them to take away strength and positivity from this book (and I hope we have a laugh on the way too because, bloody hell, it's important to laugh, isn't it?).

To understand me, you must understand the truth. Or, certainly, my truth. And this book is my truth. It's my story.

This is who I am.

It's taken some time for me to own it, to be proud of this life that I've experienced and to realise that my story is a compelling one. This book is about that life, a life that's been far from normal. It's the story about who I am and how I became who I am. And, most importantly, it's about how *I* decided who I am, rather than allowing other people to define me.

It is, I believe, a very human story at its heart; it's about how we can be surrounded by people yet feel totally alone. We can be rich in material wealth but poor in emotional wellness. We can achieve everything we've ever wanted but be without anything we really need.

So, yes, it looks like I've decided to tell my story.

I hope I've made the right decision.

I guess we'll find out.

Prologue

1988. It's springtime. I'm 14 years old and I've got a dance competition tomorrow, the Allied Dancing Association Kirkby Comps. The big one at the Kirkby Suite, a Brutalist style community centre near my nan's house, where all our major competitions take place.

Winning this would mean so much to me. More than the Liverpool FC and Madonna posters on my wall. More than INXS's *Kick* cassette I play constantly. More than my gold Tomahawk bike. More even than my absolute pride and joy, my bright red Toshiba tape-to-tape boombox that sits proudly on my bedroom windowsill.

I know I'm capable, I just have to put the work in.

So, I practise. But I don't *just* practise. I do the moves over, and over, and over again. There's barely room to swing a cat in this living room, but I carry on, squashed in the small square of space between the sofa and the armchair. Slowly, painfully slowly, I perfect each hand gesture, head tilt, foot placement.

Smile, look up, blink and breathe, twist there, turn here, smile wider, lengthen those lines.

Friends call for me to go out, my little brother Paul tries to come in to watch *The A-Team*. It's a Saturday so I'm babysitting him while Mum is out at a gig. But I won't stop. I can't. He rolls his eyes and walks off, defeated.

I spend hours in the living room repeating the steps until they're perfect.

6 pm comes and goes. 8 pm. 10 pm.

Finally, I flop into bed, exhausted.

Sunday. I win the competition. I grin my widest grin, proudly holding up my medal as people clap and cheer. Something clicks, instinctively, as I stand there celebrating my victory: when you put the effort in, you get what you deserve. Put in, get out. Cause and effect.

This is the earliest memory I have of how perfectionism permeated my life. For both good and, well, not so good.

This extreme sense of discipline can quite literally make you. And it can break you.

It did very nearly break me. Nearly, but not quite.

CHAPTER ONE

Never Be The Same Again

There are these photos of me. They're taken at a street party to celebrate the Queen's Silver Jubilee. It's Monday 6th June 1977. I'm three and a half years old.

In one, I'm wearing a short, red coat with white lapels and white buttons, knee-high white socks with white shoes and, perched at an angle on my head, a small, pointy, red plastic hat. I'm holding up a flag, with a picture of the Queen's face in the middle. Behind me, my mum and my Nanna Alice look on from the front porch.

I've got this big, lovely smile on my face.

In the next picture, I'm in someone's garage, sitting next to lots of other little kids at a long table heaving with crisps, vol-au-vents, and sausage rolls. I'm at one of 4,000 street parties being held that day to celebrate our sovereign's 25 years on the throne. The paper plates and cups are themed red, white and blue. God Bless the United Kingdom. If we could zoom out of that picture a little, we'd see Union Jacks hung from windows and bunting strung up across lampposts. There would be cans of Skol for the dads, and warm bottles of Blue Nun for the mums. Cherryade, Dandelion & Burdock and cream soda for the kids.

The seventies: A packet of crisps and a flat, warm Coke in a pub car park. Ford Cortinas and Ford Capris. Pick 'n' mix and packets of football stickers from WHSmith. Benny from *Grange Hill*. *The Benny Hill Show*. *Jim'll Fix It* and *Top of the Pops*, Choppers and Space Hoppers, *Star Wars* and *Star Trek*. Punk and Disco. Danny and Sandy. Luke and Leia. Yoyos, hopscotch, hula hoops, marbles, conkers, a Mr Whippy '99, daisy chains, landlines, shag pile, Atari. *The Beano* and *Blue Peter*. Bell bottoms, platform shoes and lava lamps. "Night Fever", "Dancing Queen", "Don't Stop 'til You Get Enough". "Can you dig it?" "Cool." "Far out." Margaret Thatcher. The Cold War. The decimal system. No seatbelts in cars or helmets on heads. Miners striking, dockers too. Smoking outdoors, indoors, in cars, in offices, in schools, and on the bus. Smoking everywhere, all the time. The summers were hot in the seventies, especially in '76 and we played outside, even when we were tiny, even when it got dark. They were hard times, but they were good times. Innocent times, for me at least.

I love seeing how happy I am in those photos, taken in a world without filters or image sharpening tools. But I can see, clear as day, that wide, innocent, uncomplicated smile beaming back at me from all that way, over four decades ago now.

I sometimes look at those pictures when I want to remind myself what I looked like when I was truly safe, secure, and happy. When I was Melanie Chisholm, three and a half years old, who lived with her mum and dad at 13 Kendal Drive, Rainhill, Merseyside.

The Silver Jubilee is the last time I can remember me, Mum, and Dad being together. It was the last time I would experience something that was, for most people back then, completely, and utterly normal: a family. No separation, no divorce, no half, or step siblings. Just Mum, Dad, and Melanie.

That kid in that picture didn't know it then, but life was going to change beyond all recognition. And she was about to change with it.

• • •

I like to think that before I was even a twinkle in my mother's eye, I had an auspicious start in life. My mum, Joan Tuffley, and my Dad, Alan Chisholm, met on 1st November 1969 at Number 10, Mathew Street, Liverpool.

Any Scouser can tell you straight away what's there: The Cavern Club, the birthplace of The Beatles, the home of Mersey-beat. That damp, dark cellar with its low brick ceilings and sticky floors made stars out of Paul, Ringo, George, John, Cilla and Gerry, and later saw legendary performances from Mick and Keef, Elton and Freddie.

The Cavern was *the* place to be in the Swinging Sixties when Dad and Mum got their glad rags on and headed there for a night out. As they danced to Elvis, Sly and the Family Stone and the Fab Four, a mutual friend of Mum and Dad's, who had previously dated Dad, introduced them to each other.

Joan and Alan hit it off and got engaged on the 25th April 1970.

In June 1971, they bought a small, three-bedroom, semi-detached house in Rainhill, an area considered to be quite posh, especially compared to where they were from, the small satellite towns of Liverpool. Dad was raised in Kirkby and Mum's family, although originally from Toxteth, lived in Huyton. They both could be tough places.

Both of my parents were from solid working-class stock. My mum's dad, Grandad Vincent, was a groundsman, Nanna Alice worked in Littlewoods. Mum's older brother, Victor, and younger brother, Alan, worked for Liverpool Council and as a car fitter, respectively.

Dad's family were Catholic Scousers, some of whom worked on the docks, or in shops. My nannie, Nannie Kay to us, managed Kirkham's County Bakeshop in Kirkby until she retired, although she got bored being a retiree and decided to work in a stationery shop in Liverpool, taking the train into town every day until she was 75. My Grandad William (or Billy), who died of cancer when he was 54, worked at English Electric in Netherton. He worked seven days a week to make ends meet. My Auntie Lynne ran a hairdressers opposite Goodison Park, Everton's home ground (boo, hiss, etc). She still has the shop today, even though she's well into her seventies.

All my family were, are still, hard workers simply because they had to be, to get by. I've inherited that same mentality.

My Nannie Kay was very religious and one of eight siblings. I think she found solace and comfort from the Church after losing my grandad so young. She never had another relationship. My mum's side went to church occasionally, and I'm not sure how comfortable the families were about a "Proddy Dog" and "Cat lick" union, but my dad had already shown a rebellious streak by supporting Liverpool when the rest of his family were Evertonians.

The football stadiums Anfield and Goodison Park are also places of worship in the city of Liverpool.

Despite their far from prosperous backgrounds, Mum and Dad were doing well for themselves. Dad worked as a lift engineer at the factory of the manufacturers Otis, and Mum worked as a secretary for an estate agent in Liverpool city centre.

Mum may have spent her days doing admin, but what she loved best was music. What Mum *did* best was singing.

A few weeks before they met that night at The Cavern, Mum had been in Germany, performing with her soul band, Exemption, for the troops on the American base in Karlsruhe. By the time she and Dad got married, she was in a new band called Petticoat & Vine, who looked like they might be quite successful. They were being compared to The Mamas & the Papas and had signed a record deal with Philips Records, who had Dusty Springfield and Donna Summer on their books, and a publishing deal with Feldman & Co, who had the rights to classics like "The White Cliffs of Dover" and "It's a Long Way to Tipperary".

The band got booked to perform their first single on *The Harry Secombe Show*, and people were saying they might be the biggest thing out of Liverpool since The Beatles.

The Petticoats performance happened to be shown again on *Harry Secombe* the day Mum and Dad married and held their reception party at the George Henry Lee Social House, West Derby, where Grandad Vincent was the gardener. The entire wedding party crowded into the television room to watch it, Mum in her wedding dress, crouched on the floor watching herself on the box.

It was a big deal, a working-class girl from Huyton being on the telly, making it as a musician.

Well, almost making it.

It didn't quite work out for Mum. She ended up leaving Petticoat & Vine and later joined a new band called Love Potion. They also looked like they might do well. They signed to Polydor Records and were managed by a guy called Tony Hall, who had worked with everyone from Jimi Hendrix to Joe Cocker. It felt so promising, like she was on the periphery of success. Mum had toured with Harold Melvyn and the Bluenotes and the Manhattans and The Real Thing, and was kept busy with various bookings, but maybe things didn't progress as much as she'd hoped.

That didn't stop her though. She refused to give up on music, and still sings to this day. Joan O'Neill is a well-known and much-loved singer in and around Liverpool.

Mum was playing gigs until two weeks before I was born at 9.32 pm in Whiston Hospital on Saturday 12th January 1974. Dad was working that day; there were power strikes across the country at that time, and there was only electricity on certain days of the week. Can you imagine that now? Mind you, who knows what future this crazy world holds, so let's not jinx anything, shall we? Anyway, because of the cuts, Dad worked Friday to Sunday, but luckily, he finished by 5 pm so arrived in plenty of time to see me being born with my thick head of black hair.

My birth was ordinary in many ways, but auspicious in one. The midwife that delivered me was delivered by Paul McCartney's mum, Mary, who had been a midwife when Paul was a child. Another Beatles link... however tenuous it might be!

Saturday's child works hard for a living, so the poem goes. Combine that with my being the archetypal hard-working, self-reliant, disciplined Capricorn, and it's not surprising how some things turned out. I was never going to do things by half measures.

My earliest memories of Kendal Drive are all soundtracked by sixties and seventies music: Stevie Wonder, Tina Turner, The Rolling Stones and, of course, The Beatles, but also to the sounds of Mum's bands too. Various bearded blokes carrying guitars would be in and out to rehearse, to audition, or to talk about the set later that night. They'd squash together on the black leatherette sofa in the living room with its dark red curtains, dark mustard wallpaper and pride of place, a vase of dried flowers in front of an imposing brown brick fireplace.

With all that music around me, it's no surprise that I was drawn to performing too.

Singing wasn't my first love though; it was dance that did it for me. I was straight into ballet and tap almost as soon as I could walk. Mum would drive me 20 minutes to Prescot each weekend for dance lessons. I have no memory of my first performance, which I'm told featured me playing a bunny rabbit. I'm sure it was where I got the taste for those bright lights, but possibly no more, or less, than all the other kids that naturally gravitated to dance classes back then.

Those first few years, they were happy. Mum, Dad, music, dance. That kid in those pictures, her life was pretty good.

A few weeks after the Silver Jubilee, we went to Corfu on holiday, which was unusual back then because people didn't have money for "foreign" holidays. Dad was doing well and Mum had a five-night-a-week residency, so we could afford it. There was lots of swimming in the sea and making new best friends, never to be seen again once we came home. But while I was living my best beach life, there were serious conversations happening between my parents.

It was in Corfu during the summer of 1975 that Mum and Dad discussed divorcing.

Dad was reluctant and they tried to make things work for another year but sadly the marriage was over, and so too was the childhood that, until now, seemed idyllic to me.

"We're going to live with Nanna Alice," said Mum, in June 1978 as we left Kendal Drive forever. One minute I lived in a semi-detached in Rainhill with Mum and Dad and the next I was living on the Stone Hay Estate in Whiston with Mum and my grandparents. Without my dad.

I would never again live with my dad. I would never again live with both parents. In fact, I wouldn't be in the same place with Mum and Dad for another 13 years.

I couldn't possibly have understood it at that point, but, like I would later say in a song of the same name, things would never be the same again. *I* would never be the same again.

• • •

Nanna's house backed onto a graveyard, and we would go to the church there for carol concerts, which I loved. They had a proper stereo system too, a dead stylish sixties home music console that was set into a low coffee table. Nanna used to love crooners like Perry Como and Glenn Miller – "A String of Pearls" and "In The Mood" – and I loved dancing around the living room to her music.

Nanna spoiled me rotten, though being back at home was tough for Mum. Her parents weren't happy that she'd left the marriage. It wasn't the "done thing" in the seventies and no doubt they were bothered about what the neighbours were saying. "Oh, that Joan's back at home with her little one, I wonder what's going on there." You can imagine the curtain-twitchers having a field day.

Mum's parents were very strict, especially on Mum who was the middle of three and the only girl. She always called herself the odd one out because she wanted to sing which, back then, was not something "nice" or "good" girls did. Music was only for lads, you know. Back then, it wouldn't be uncommon to hear people compare singers and actresses to sex workers. But Mum didn't care what people thought, she had fallen in love with singing when she was a young girl, and she wouldn't let anything hold her back. She started performing in bands when she was 14 years old. Grandad Vincent went mad when he found out. He found her this one time rehearsing in someone's garden shed, and cycled over there, raging, and made Mum run home alongside his bicycle.

But she never gave in, she was a bit of a rebel. When she was 19, she went to Germany on tour to perform for troops on army bases. Things over there didn't go well, though. The other band members ended up leaving her and an asthmatic drummer in shitty, damp digs with no money. She had to call home to ask for help to get back to Liverpool. She returned with her tail somewhat between her legs and a bollocking, no doubt, from her dad.

A love of music and performance wasn't the only thing I inherited from Mum. I've got her same spirit of adventure, her determination to succeed, whatever the cost. Like her, I would end up leaving home at a young age to follow my dreams too.

We lived with my nanna on the estate in Huyton for about four months until the council eventually gave us our own place. "It's a flat about 20 minutes' drive from Nanna's, across the River Mersey," Mum said, excitedly. "We're going to live in a place called Runcorn." I was sad to leave my Nanna Alice and Grandad Vincent and they seemed upset too. I'd loved the adventure of being in a new place, sharing a room with Mum and getting to spend loads of time with her.

We couldn't stay at Nanna and Grandad's forever, though, and on 30th September 1978, we packed up the few belongings we had – a small bag of clothes, my toys, Mum's guitar – and headed off to Runcorn where a whole new life, and many more changes, awaited us.

Not least of all, our new home: 274A, Falcons View, on the Southgate Estate, in Runcorn.

It was a world away from Kendal Drive. We went from a three-bed, semi-detached house in a good area to a two-bed council flat in a, well, not so good area.

Designed by a famous architect called James Stirling, the Southgate Estate was described as "a Modernist Public Housing Project". It was brand new when we moved there in late 1978, alongside the 6,000 other people living in the 1,500 flats and houses. Bloody hell was that place ugly! The design was based around boxes of grey concrete with multicoloured cladding in LEGO-like blue, yellow, and orange and these big round windows, like a ship's porthole, on each floor. We called it the estate, the Washing Machine or LEGOLAND.

It was a sprawling, rough, council block with walkways running across the top of the estate called Streets in the Sky, which connected us to the nearby Runcorn shopping centre and the rest of the town. Like lots of estates built around then, the walkways became a haven for drug dealing and drug taking, and a convenient place to rob people. It got really bad during the eighties, and they eventually started demolishing the estate in 1990.

It must have felt like a very different world to me, but when you're a kid you get on with it, don't you?

It's during that time that little Sporty Spice began to emerge, as I fell in with the other kids who lived on the estate. I made friends quickly. We were right scallywags, running around, snot streaming out our noses, clutching onto our white paper bags of penny sweets.

"Watch me, watch me," I'd shout in my no-name-brand trackie (no way could Mum afford adidas or "adeeeedus as we say up there), jumping up on the parallel bars in the playground out the front. Parks were made of solid concrete then too – there were no such things as soft play or sprung floors. The sandpits were full of dog poo and cat wee. Not that it bothered us, as we spun ourselves around and around, just one slight slip of our enthusiastic amateur gymnastics between us and a trip to A&E. "I bet you can't do this," we'd laugh, clutching onto the bar with just one leg and propelling ourselves over and over in terrifyingly fast somersaults, sometimes backflipping off the bars and onto those brutal concrete floors. We'd make up whole routines and then walk to school with bright red friction burns on the backs of our knees!

The estate kept me entertained. I learnt to ride my beloved blue Raleigh with stabilisers and a white plazzy lunch box stuck on the back, going as fast as I could over the concrete pavements of LEGOLAND. Once the stabilisers came off, I'd wobble along, often crashing to the ground and scraping my knees and hands.

I was always outside. There were no computers or phones to distract me. The telly only had three channels anyway, until 1982 when Channel 4 came along. That's if you could get a picture on the crappy, tiny, black-and-white boxes we called televisions back then. You'd spend half your time hitting the side of it to try and get the lines to disappear and the other half twiddling with the aerial to get a picture.

Even then, the only kids' programmes you could watch were between 4 pm and 5.30 pm weekdays and on a Saturday morning from 9 am before the sport started at 12 pm. Not like now with whole channels of kids' telly and streaming on demand. I have to say thank goodness CBeebies and YouTube existed when my daughter, Scarlet, was little. But I think about what we've lost too, because of the constant access to swiping, scrolling, and staring at screens.

Other than Saturday morning telly and *Top of the Pops*, I didn't watch a lot on the box. I had my mates, I had school, and I had dance. Well, I'd *had* dance.

At a certain point, Mum couldn't afford dance classes; money was tight enough as it was, so I'd had to say goodbye to my ballet and tap lessons when we left Kendal Drive. It wasn't just the cost of the classes themselves but getting there on the bus or in a car. Also, you needed to buy ballet shoes, leotards, and pay for exams. It was too much for Mum. As much as I wanted to be at dance, it wasn't possible.

When I started at Southgate Infants, Mum had so little money that I was entitled to free school dinners. We never went without but for a time, anything considered extra (such as dance classes) was off the agenda. I had my school uniform and a couple of other outfits I'd wear at home or out to the shops; a denim skirt and dusty pink cropped sweatshirt with shoulder pads (could I have dressed more eighties?) and later, my favourite look of all, a Liverpool FC trackie. I rarely took it off. Is it a surprise that my nickname would later become Sporty? I think not!

I never felt like we were poor or that we lived hand to mouth because we were the same as everyone around us, but I was aware that we didn't have a lot. We fixed and made and mended almost everything.

But running outside with my new mates and making up routines on the bars reminded me how much I'd loved those lessons in Prescot. Being out on the estate was my only physical outlet at that time. I was desperate to go back to dancing.

"If I could just get Mum and Dad back together," I'd think, countless times over the coming years, "everything would be okay."

We may have lacked money, but, as I mentioned, we were rich in music. Even as young as five, I can remember going to sleep to the sounds of the bass thumping from the living room next door as Mum's band rehearsed. Music was always around me.

And I remember there was one specific moment when a singer really took my breath away.

Every Saturday morning, me and Mum would do the weekly shopping. She would drag me around Kwik Save (R.I.P.) before, finally, we got to the best bit, the cake shop. It was a local one, like your Greggs today (not fancy like Paul). It was sometime around February 1978, one of the coldest winters on record at that point, and I'd not long turned four years old. We hurried into the shop out of the bitter cold where, as we waited, a song came on the radio. A very striking grand piano rang out, staccato, and then this voice – a voice that I'd never heard before – began to sing. It was almost childlike but very theatrical, completely different to anything I'd heard Mum play, and totally different to how she sang. "Out on the wily, windy moors, we'd roll and fall in green..." I stood, transfixed, in front of the "chocolatey eclairs" (as I called them) barely aware of Mum shaking me to ask what I wanted while "Heathcliff, it's me, I'm Cathy/I've come home, I'm so cold/Let me in your window" filled my ears.

I'd no idea what this person was singing about but I was totally absorbed as Mum dragged me out of the shop. What was *that*, I wondered, and, more importantly, *who* was that?

Later that week, on Thursday at 7.30 pm, I sat down to watch *Top of the Pops*, just as 15 million others around the country did back then. I was allowed to stay up as a treat to watch *TOTP* on the condition that I went straight to bed afterwards. I sat on the floor, eyes glued to the box, and here she was again. *Heathcliff*! She was wearing a long white dress, her dark hair a halo in the bright white light, her strange voice telling an eccentric story.

If I hadn't heard anything like Kate Bush before, I'd certainly never seen anything like her either. I was mesmerised. It was as though the music was a part of her, it flowed through her body.

Until then, music was what Mum did. It was soul and Motown and rock, and it was something that involved adults. Kate Bush, albeit 21 years old (and therefore ancient to my young eyes), was something new. Something more recognisable and reachable.

I started to explore other music. Adam and the Ants, Michael Jackson and, later, Madonna. They all seemed to have one thing in common: they weren't just singers, they were *performers*. Performing was what I did when I danced. That was interesting to me. I didn't want to do what Mum did. I liked the music, but it wasn't *my* music, it wasn't what us kids listened to. Madonna and Michael weren't just singing in front of a microphone with a band. It was dancing, moving, theatrics, stage sets, incredible costumes.

I didn't think about becoming a pop star for many more years, but through the likes of Kate, Madonna, and Michael, the seeds were starting to be sown.

Melanie Chisholm, dancer. Yeah, I liked that. Melanie Chisholm, pop star. I *really* liked that!

• • •

November 1978 and there was a knock at the door. I heard Mum take a deep breath and go to answer it. When she came back, there was a man standing behind her. He was quite tall with long, shaggy, brown hair, and a big, scraggly beard. He smiled at me, uncertainly, and I looked back at Mum, confused. "Melanie, you remember Dennis, don't you?" she said, a huge if not slightly nervous smile across her face. "Call him Den."

I didn't know who this Den was, though he looked like a lot of the hippy musicians Mum sang in bands with. Den seemed to have a suitcase with him. And bags. This was weird. Even more strange, he brought them all in and didn't leave after he'd had his coffee.

In fact, Den didn't leave at all.

At four years old, it's hard to comprehend a lot of things, especially adult relationships. I didn't know who this bloke was, but I didn't want him living with me and my mum.

Mum had met Dennis O'Neill a few years back when he joined the Ken Phillips New Era Band, and they had been in a couple of other bands together since.

It was at bedtime that I'd get the most upset. "I want my dad, I want my dad," I would scream, stomping my feet on the gloomy brown carpet, tears streaming down my face. I'd wake up in the middle of the night, push open the bedroom door, and slip in beside Mum. Eventually she took to locking the door. I'd push and push against it until, exhausted and unable to get in the door, I would eventually go back to my bed.

Den wasn't the only new person I had to get used to. He also had two boys from his previous marriage, Stuart and Jarrod, who were seven and three years older than me. We didn't say much to each other at first. With so much going on in my tiny world, these new people just added to the confusion. If they were hanging about at ours all the time, how was I ever going to get Mum and Dad back together? I looked on quietly as these two older boys would play.

Slowly, though, I joined in.

"Jarrod, put Melanie down," Den would quietly sigh from behind his newspaper as the boys flung me around playing hide and seek or tag. We'd run off screaming, popping plastic guns in the air as we raced through the living room. If Den or Mum got mad, we'd know to clear off outside. Although I wasn't happy about Den living with us, having our Jad (what everyone called him) and Stuart (aka Stu) around some weekends became quite fun.

Playing with Jad and Stu added to this increasing persona that was – I really don't like the word "tomboy" – not particularly "girly", whatever that might mean. It wasn't until 2017 when I first worked with the amazing drag queens and non-binary people of the club collective Sink The Pink that I started to think about gender and how crazy it is that we tell children they should be more (or less) "feminine" and "masculine". It was such an education for me. When I grew up, girls were supposed to wear dresses, play with dolls, and be friends with other girls. But I liked dresses *and* dolls and I liked ballet *and* bikes. I loved being around boys as much as girls. I wasn't afraid to get dirty, and I loved running and jumping and climbing.

We live in much more interesting times now where the gender lines are less binary, and gender is much more fluid.

None of us are just one thing, are we? It's something I feel we should hold onto today; that we're all many things, and that's to be celebrated. Our complexity is what makes us so normal/brilliant/unique/interesting!

I wonder now if part of how I dressed and mucked in with the boys was about trying to harden up, to close off my feelings (without gendering "strong" and "tough" as masculine!). There were so many changes at that time; perhaps I was trying to feel invincible physically so I could feel the same emotionally. There was so much going on at home that it's not surprising my feelings started to manifest in other ways.

I had a lot to deal with.

· · ·

I was five years old when Mum left me with someone they barely knew for five months.

When an opportunity came up with the Roy Stevens band, who'd been booked to do a summer season at a nightclub called The Showboat in the seaside resort of Rhyl, both Mum and Den were excited. They would be performing the day's biggest hits to decent crowds from April through to September. It was solid work and well paid. They would initially do three nights a week, starting in April 1979, and then six nights a week from June.

It did pose one problem though: me. It tended to be a less-than-two-hour drive home and, a fair number of times, they would not make it back.

When we lived in Southgate, Mum and Den were in their late twenties and so they had their own dreams to fulfil, as well as put food on the table. It wasn't uncommon for me to go stay with family while Mum and Dad worked all week and then performed at weekends. As a parent and performer, I appreciate how hard it is to find the balance between raising a child and building a career. On one hand, you want to always be there with, and for, your child. But then in comes that need to succeed and, alongside that, a desire for your kid to see you as an independent person with ambition, drive, and the ability to provide for yourself. In Mum and Den's case, they were trying to fulfil their dreams while making sure there was enough money to live. They were professional musicians and had a passion to perform.

It's a tricky one to get right and I'm not sure it always works out well for the child. I say that as both a daughter and a parent.

In this case, Mum and Den were dead set on making Rhyl work. Given how long they were away for, I couldn't just be sent to an aunt or my nanna's, and I couldn't stay with Dad because he was too far from school and was working every day with no one around to help him out. Instead, they found someone who would live in with me while they were away. She was a young woman in her late teens. She came over to the flat with her mum to meet me and my mum. We said hello and Mum asked her about her life, and her experience with children.

It was quickly agreed that she would take the job. The plan was that she would come and live in our flat with me while Mum and Den went away for the best part of five months.

She had the credentials of a nanny, but it turned out, in my experience, that she was barely a babysitter. I had, in fact, been left in the care of a very young, very inexperienced and emotionally immature woman. I wonder if it's meaningful that neither Mum, Den, nor me can remember the girl's name, what she looked like, or how they'd found her. But let's call her Claire, for now.

So, in April 1979, off they went and my life with the baby-sitter began. Initially they did three nights a week, and from the June it went up to six nights. Mum and Den would come back every Sunday overnight and I'd be so happy to have Mum home. She'd do a big shop to make sure me and Claire would have enough food for the week, and she'd let me stay up late with her and watch telly.

In truth, living with Claire wasn't great. In fact, it was terrible.

I didn't tell Mum this until years later, but I'd often come back from school, and Claire wouldn't be home. I'd walk up those cold concrete stairs that smelt of wee and wait on the freezing-cold steps outside our flat for Claire to come home. Hungry, frightened, and desperate for the loo, I remember once having to wait for so long that I wet myself. A neighbour took me in and changed, fed, and comforted me.

Mum quit the job in August. She was five months pregnant at this point. Somehow, she realised that I was being passed from pillar to post and that Claire had moved her boyfriend in and moved me out. Perhaps the neighbour finally told her what had been going on.

I never said a word. Mum would come home every week, and I didn't tell her anything.

But after that, I'm not sure I ever returned to myself, not really.

There's another photo of me, around five years old. If I compare that picture with the Jubilee photos, do I see any difference? Not really. On the outside, I was the same sweet, smiling, little girl. I don't think I ever told anyone, including even myself, the extent of the impact that time had on me. But there were physical manifestations. It wasn't long after this that I began to get heavy nosebleeds. Sometimes they would be so bad that they'd have to get an ambulance out to the estate in the middle of the night. The nosebleeds eased off as I got into my teens, although I still, occasionally, get them now.

It breaks my heart a bit to look at that kid, at me, and think what must have been going on inside my mind. The security, safety, and comfort of a normal childhood had vanished over those 18 months since I posed for that picture at the Silver Jubilee.

I can only imagine how terrible my mum must have felt when she realised. It was actually she who, while I was writing this book, reminded me that this had happened.

Now I can rationalise the impact that stemmed from what feels like a blip in my memory but was of course a seismic event in my very young life. I realise that times were different back then, that Mum was trying to provide for the family while following her own dreams, that she thought she'd left me in safe hands. But, consciously or unconsciously, I'm sure that period heightened my feelings of insecurity within my own family. I spent years quietly trying to figure out where I fitted in, while at the same time also wanting attention. It was a case of "nobody notice me... but also everybody look at me". That duality, that confusion, hasn't always benefited my mental wellness.

There was so much upheaval in my young life. Mum leaving Dad, Den moving in, me being left alone with Claire. I saw Dad but only on weekends and holidays. I'd go over and we'd watch *Match of the Day* and we'd eat tinned ravioli. Or he'd cook me his one speciality meal: chilli con carne. A Dad classic in the seventies. I remember falling asleep on the couch watching *Starsky & Hutch* snuggled up to him. I should've probably been in bed by then, but I guess we both wanted to have as much time together as we could.

Then, when I was seven, my dad went off too. "I'm going to go away for a bit, Melanie," he told me when I was over at Kendal Drive (he'd remained in what was the family home) one weekend. Dad had taken the breakup hard, and even though it had been a couple of years, he was still feeling it. He'd decided to take voluntary redundancy from Otis, sell the house, and go travelling for several months around the US, Canada and South America.

I was so excited when he rang me every week from exotic-sounding places like New York and Los Angeles. When he did come back, he'd brought me a dress from a shop in San Francisco. It was navy blue with white polka dots and a red carnation. I treasured that dress.

As an adult I can understand why Dad felt he needed to get away, to find himself, to seek out peace and so on. But coming after our abrupt departure from the family home, Den moving in, the arrival of new siblings, the impact of being left with a childminder, this further news impacted me deeply, albeit subconsciously.

It became another event I learnt to suppress.

I really hero-worshipped my dad and put him on a pedestal, yet when he left it seemed not to affect me at all. I must have just blocked it out, got on with life. Mum doesn't remember me ever crying for my dad, and I don't remember feeling this huge loss, despite the fact I was so close to him.

I was young and I adapted, which is to say I learned to freeze my feelings – something, as I now know, that isn't the healthiest thing to do. And it impacted my relationships in later life. I ended up being drawn to men who were fun but unreliable. They wouldn't commit and they would often let me down.

I understand now it was something my dad had to do. I believe he needed a change of scenery to figure out which path to take next in his life.

And that he did. On his return, he had a career change and became an operations manager at holiday camps in France and Spain, which meant he was away for months at a time. I didn't get to see him as much as I would've liked but I did have great holidays with him.

• • •

My parents' divorce filled me with guilt. I always felt like it was my fault. When they separated, I took on this idea that I wasn't enough to keep them together. When Den and Mum got together and had my little brother, Paul, and, later still, when Dad met his wife Carole and had my brothers, Liam and Declan, I felt like a spare part. Everyone had their mum and dad, why couldn't I have mine? Why was I always the one that needed to be looked after, babysat, or sent off somewhere so the adults could get on with their lives?

It made me feel different. It made me feel like a burden.

This thought started popping into my head, around the time that all this happened. It's a thought that persisted for years: "Maybe it would be easier for everyone if I wasn't here".

It wasn't that I wanted to end my life, but more that if I were to magically disappear, maybe everyone else's lives would be easier.

I was very much alone in the world because I couldn't share these feelings with anyone. I didn't have any siblings or friends in the same position. It was just me. Everyone else had their nuclear family. I yearned for a sense of belonging and a family of my own because so often I felt like I was outside, on my own, looking in at these happy families that I wasn't fully a part of.

It makes me emotional writing this, to think that I felt so out of place, so different to everyone else. I know how much Mum and Dad loved me. I'm very close to them both. I was very loved as a child, it's important that I stress that, but all these things had a huge impact on me, how I saw myself, how I related to other people.

It's made me the person I am, for worse, but also for better.

I do think the turbulence of those formative years is a big part of my success. It's what made me so determined to succeed. It gave me a hunger for acceptance and attention. I wanted, *needed*, people to notice me, to like me, to be entertained by me, impressed by me. I wanted to have a place of my own and to belong.

I found that onstage. Even though back then the stage was a small dance studio with an audience of 10 mums, it filled me with joy, warmth, security, and safety when I performed. When I think of being onstage, that's what I feel. It's the place where I'm totally myself and where I feel utterly happy.

When I am performing, I feel unobtainable, like people can't reach me, my problems can't get to me. I can be quite shy in social situations, I don't like being looked at, but when I'm onstage, I want people to look at me, to enjoy my performance. I feel so much safer performing than just being... me. I feel stronger, more resilient, powerful.

I might get nervous or suffer stage fright, but I'm still at my absolute best onstage. I feel totally safe.

It was there that I finally got the attention that I wanted and needed. In real life, both of my parents were so distracted with all they were going through: the divorce, finding work, having more children. For a few moments though, under that beautifully warm spotlight, it was all about me. I had everyone's focus and the only person that could give that away was me.

The solution I thought I'd found to combatting my isolation came with its own issues – chasing that feeling can lead you to dark and unpredictable places as you try to replicate the high when it, inevitably, disappears. I often think that people who become famous are the ones least well equipped to deal with it. We are too vulnerable, too in need of that attention that we feel is lacking elsewhere. When we find it, it's intoxicating, it's addictive. But it's not sustainable. The screaming stops, the bookings slow down, and the venues shrink.

You're left with a vast, gaping hole.

We fly too close to that sun that shines so brightly because it feels so warm, so safe. Of course, sometimes that means we get burnt.

This I was to find out for myself later in life.

CHAPTER TWO

If U Can't Dance

One minute it was the three of us in Southgate, the next there were four.

I was a couple of weeks off turning six years old when our Paul was born. We'd just had Christmas and a few days later, Mum came to kiss me goodnight. Which was weird because she'd already done that. "You be a good girl for Nanna and Grandad, won't you?'" Mum whispered as she leaned over. I looked up, puzzled. "Your little brother or sister is on the way, I'm off to go and have the baby now. You'll get to meet them very soon." I shrugged and went back to sleep, wondering what shop Mum would be getting the new baby from. It was 31st December 1979.

My very favourite toys were Tiny Tears and my Sindy dolls so when Mum and Den came back a few days later with this tiny, scrunched-up thing I was excited. "A new doll," I thought, looking at Paul, all wrapped up in a swaddle.

I was besotted and fascinated with this tiny being. I'd spend hours watching him in his cot and, when he was older and able to sit up, I loved making him smile and laugh. As he got bigger, Mum let me hold the bottle and I'd watch his face intensely as he guzzled down the milk, his hazel eyes staring into mine. I felt an instinctive protectiveness towards this little human who had arrived on this strange planet of ours.

But he couldn't do much. Eventually I'd get bored and go back outside, setting up makeshift ramps for our bikes and generally causing harmless mischief with my mates on the estate. During those early years, Paul was a cute thing to play with, but not much use.

He was also another mouth to feed. After her divorce from Dad, Mum went back to square one financially. Den was no better off, having left his wife and two kids. When he wasn't performing with Mum in whatever band they were in at the time, he was an HGV driver and, later, a taxi driver. He wasn't getting a huge wage and that had to be shared between two households with four kids.

Mum would do bits and pieces here and there, usually in offices, but paying the bills and getting food on the table was a constant source of worry for her and Den. We didn't have a lot. Mum always knew, to the exact penny, how much she had in her purse. Before we went to do the weekly shop, she'd bang around the cupboards and fridge writing her shopping list. I'd watch, crushed, as she crossed off *biscuits* or *crisps* if we couldn't afford them.

Growing up without much made me very conscious of money. Even now I'm financially stable, I'll still drive to get cheaper petrol, yet sometimes I'll spend 50 quid on a candle, which I'm fully aware is ridiculous. Money distorts things – it's like looking through a kaleidoscope. I'm always mindful of what I'm spending, and then I'll chuck a huge amount away on something frivolous.

Expensive candle addictions besides, while I'm a very generous person, I can be quite careful. Call it a working-class mentality.

With Paul's arrival, the council agreed that we had outgrown the two-bed flat on the estate. Now we were a family of four, they moved us to 68 St Austell Close, Brookvale, Runcorn, a three-bed place just a few minutes' drive east from Southgate.

I went to the local primary school, Brookvale, a short walk from the house. My own daughter would be 10 before I allowed her to walk across the road to get the school bus, in our very nice, posh part of North London. And even then, I secretly followed her.

We weren't in Brookvale for long. We had one more move before, finally, this new family put down some roots.

• • •

Back in the sixties, Paul Simon sat on the platform at Widnes train station, nostrils overwhelmed by the smell of chemicals and wrote the song 'Homeward Bound' about returning to his girlfriend in London. "If you know Widnes, then you'll understand how I was desperately trying to get back to London as quickly as possible. 'Homeward Bound' came out of that feeling," he is quoted as saying.

Over the years, there have been several plaques above Widnes railway kiosk commemorating this magical moment of musical history. Unfortunately, they kept getting nicked.

A mess of factories and power plants, Widnes was renowned for a, well, shall we say unique smell that permeated the air. (I should clarify in case they don't ever let me back up there again that the smell has long gone.)

So, one day in February 1982 that's where me, Mum, Den, and our Paul were headed. It's not classed as Merseyside, even though it's literally on the side of the River Mersey.

Dad had given Mum some of the money from the sale of Kendal Drive. It was just enough for her and Den to put down a deposit on a three-bedroom terraced house at number 15 Ireland Street, Widnes. There was a living room and kitchen downstairs and two bedrooms and a box room upstairs. It would be the family home for the next 15 years until I became a Spice Girl and helped to buy Mum and Den a new place.

Despite the surrounding factories spewing out their toxic waste, our corner of the world was quite green. We were perched on the edge of a big stretch of greenbelt called The Bongs, an expanse of fields that covered a couple of square miles. It was idyllic in some ways, although there was a huge chemical works just behind my school and a brook that ran through it, which was a minging bright orange from God-knows-what chemicals. There were graffiti-covered bridges with rope swings over parts of the brook and the odd burnt-out car that would appear from time to time.

Think Hampstead Heath but make it Northern.

Number 15 was in the middle of a long row of Victorian terraces. Den pulled up outside our new house and Mum went ahead and opened the front door. I raced through, running around the house, taking it all in, bagsying my bedroom.

In contrast to Runcorn, Widnes was almost posh. Okay, that's overstretching it slightly, but certainly it wasn't as rough as the estate had been. There was lots of space and nature, and no crime. Well, no *serious* crime.

The house was a bit of a dump when we first moved in, but Den and his brother did the place up. They built everything from scratch: cupboards, wardrobes, and they even made a shed from pallets for the narrow garden outside.

A garden! Now that we had a bit of green out the back, I was allowed my first pet. We kept Fluffy the rabbit in a hutch (which I never cleaned out). When I first got her, I treasured the cute little thing, but she turned into a bit of a monster. Fluffy was huge and would scratch you to bits if you tried to pick her up. The reason I never cleaned out the hutch was partly out of laziness, but I was also terrified of that giant, angry, mutant, moody rabbit!

Have you ever worked out your porn name? – the name of your first pet and your mum's maiden name – mine's Fluffy Tuffley. I think it kind of works!

Grandad Vincent, our very own Mr Greenfingers, came and did us a vegetable patch, where we grew runner beans, potatoes, and raspberries – very self-sustainable before it got trendy. Nanna and Grandad would visit every Sunday. Mum would push the boat out with tinned salmon sandwiches on granary bread cut into triangles and Nanna would bring ready-salted Marks and Spencer's crisps, which were the absolute height of decadence back then.

Almost as soon as we got to Ireland Street, I was outside playing. I'd upgraded my blue Raleigh to a gold Tomahawk, the kids' version of a Chopper – I was the bloody bee's knees on that bike.

Once again, I quickly made mates and we'd spend hours jumping off the nearby garages, swinging off ropes under the bridge, playing out on The Bongs and getting up to other less savoury pastimes such as putting out fires. Kids would start fires and we'd put them out. It all seemed totally normal back then. "Melanie, teatime!" Mum would yell, and I'd reluctantly return home for turkey drumsticks and beans. Mum often laughs about once overhearing me threatening to kick a boy in the goolies. I still get a bit embarrassed when she mentions it.

I might have been years away from becoming Sporty Spice, but a sporty spice I was, running in and out of dance classes, pegging it to gymnastics, bombing about on my bike or, as I got older, our Paul's BMX. As I mentioned, I lived in my tracksuits and trainers. When, years later, Peter Loraine at *Top of the Pops* magazine gave each of us our Spice Girls nicknames, he was spot on with mine.

I was really close to my cousins, especially Neil, who I knocked around with all the time. He was the son of Lynne, my dad's elder sister. There were only 11 months between us, and he was like a brother to me. There was me, Neil, and sometimes his older brother Roy, and then Paul and my maternal cousins, Jennifer and Yvonne. We'd dress Paul up, make up random plays, and force everyone to watch.

Roy was a body builder (maybe I was inspired by him in later years). He would chug raw eggs and do his posing routines for me and Neil in my Auntie Lynne's garden. This was after his New Romantic phase when he painted a huge picture of Phil Oakey from Human League on his bedroom door and wore kilts and makeup. Ah, those teenage years of trying to find yourself!

My bedroom was my sanctuary. It was tiny, mind. Me and our Paul had bunk beds (I was the top, obviously) and I had my dolls lined up on one wall with all my *Look-in* and *Smash Hits* magazines shoved under the bed. I had a massive Adam and the Ants poster, from the "Prince Charming" video, at the foot of my bed. Like loads of kids in the eighties I was inexplicably obsessed with Pierrot the Clown, who was a fictional character from the sixteenth century. Think white face, pom-poms, and a really creepy expression. I've no idea why we were all into it, but I had the Pierrot bed cover and a wallpaper border along the wall. Mum bought our beds out of the Bensons catalogue, and she had to pay two pounds a week for however-many months or years to pay them off. Later, they were joined by an MDF wardrobe and desk, where I'd pretend to do my homework as a teenager.

The thing I loved best was my red Toshiba boombox, which was a present for Christmas from Dad one year, followed by my Casio keyboard which, let's be honest, I rarely played. It looked cool though! The first cassette tape I bought was Wham!'s *Fantastic* and, yes, I do still know all the words to "Wham Rap! (Enjoy What You Do)". My mate Lisa McNaughton, who lived up the road, loved Andrew and I loved George. Obviously, I was barking up the wrong tree there!

I'd always get something amazing from my dad for birthday or Christmas. He would always go big. I got the Liverpool trackie one year and the next the Toshiba tape-to-tape boombox, which was a very big deal. Dad got me my first computer too, a ZX Spectrum. I'd spend hours playing *Horace Goes Skiing* (once the bloody thing had loaded, no super-fast broadband then, kids!). Our Paul always played a racing game, and he learnt some of the Formula 1 tracks that he has since gone on to race in real life!

Going to my Auntie Lynne's for Boxing Day was a yearly tradition and I loved it because Neil would be there too. He had this thing about disappearing under the table and I'd feed him like he was a dog. Kids are weird! We'd all spend hours at the table eating, then us cousins would go off and watch *The Muppet Show* or play with our new toys until later that night when there would be more food to get through. Frustration was our favourite board game, but it would soon get confiscated when the arguments inevitably kicked off!

I loved those times. I felt like part of a family.

• • •

Now we were more settled, and with Den and Mum earning a bit more money, Mum asked me if I wanted to start dance classes again. The answer was immediate and enthusiastic: "Yes!" I started to do ballet and modern dance every Saturday.

I may not have danced properly for several years, but I picked up where I'd left off. I seemed to have a natural ability and I was really good at it, among the best in the class. I didn't start doing exams or entering competitions at first because it was all a bit beyond Mum's budget, but my teacher, Olwen Grounds (who ran her own dancing school), persuaded Mum that I was pretty good and so we found a way.

Olwen Grounds Dancing School was brilliant. It was really respected in the region – we were among the best out of all the dancing schools. Miss Grounds gave me the fantastic training that enabled me later to go to one of the best Performing Arts colleges in the UK.

My best friend from school was (and still is) Alison George, and she used to go to dancing too. She was (and still is) especially amazing at ballet. With Mum and Den out gigging, Alison's Mum and Dad – Hazel and Dave – would take me and Alison to and from dance class. Alison lived close to Fairfield Juniors, and we'd go back to theirs for tea after school and then on to dance class, and her parents would drop me home after.

It was proper English tea too: white bread and butter with a cup of tea on the side.

Alison was a real music head like me, and we'd listen to Fleetwood Mac's *Rumours* album up in the loft. Her dad, to this day, makes us all laugh so much. He's hilarious and can be pretty outrageous. They're the perfect pair because Hazel is very nurturing and softens the blow if she thinks Dave's gone a bit too far, but in a very loving way! They were like my surrogate family and I'm still so close to them. Ali is a very dear friend, and I always go back and visit her mum and dad when I'm home. We've all been on holiday together a few times too.

Ali and I went to dance class a couple of times during the week and on Saturday mornings and for a time we went to gymnastics on Saturday afternoon.

I worked hard, maybe too hard. Now I'd figured out that the stage was a place of safety, and comfort, I focused all my attention on it. I loved being at dancing school, it was like a second home. I would practise for hours and hours, doing and re-doing routines and choreography. I'd shut everyone and everything out and go over and over my steps to make sure I got nothing wrong.

I was unaware at the time but this sense of needing to be perfect began to slip into obsession. I didn't stop moving. If I wasn't dancing, I was at gymnastics. If I wasn't at gymnastics, I was out in my trainers, cross country running. I loved it all – dance, gym, netball, football, rounders (except cross country, which no one ever wanted to do, but they made us).

I wonder if I was keeping my body busy so my mind wouldn't get the chance to stop.

I wasn't in the slightest bit jealous of the kids on my street who got to play outside all weekend while I was up and out early to learn routines and rehearse for competitions. When I danced and did gymnastics, I felt this wonderful feeling of warmth. As the trophies, certificates and ribbons built up, I felt good about myself. When I was performing, all was well with the world. I'd started to accept that Den wasn't going anywhere, and I still longed for Mum and Dad to get back together, that never really went away. When I danced though, I could forget about all that.

The realities of the world slipped away. It was just me and the choreography, the moves, and the performance.

I felt safe.

. . .

In some ways, I felt like a parent to Paul. We were, and remain, very close. When he was injured in a car crash in January 1985, just after his fifth birthday, I felt like my world had stopped.

Paul and Den had gone to fill up the car, up near Fiddlers Ferry, a power station in Widnes about five minutes from our house on Ireland Street. They should have been gone for 20, 30 minutes max. It had been nearly an hour and there was no sign of either of them.

"Don't worry, Melanie," said our neighbour, Elaine, putting her arm around my shoulder. "Everything will be fine."

I could sense this wasn't quite true, that Elaine, despite having a smile on her face, was worried. Mum had been looking anxiously out of the window for a while when she told me she was popping next door to Elaine and her husband Ste's house. "Won't be a minute, love," she said, pulling on her coat against the cold January air. A few moments later, the three of them came back in. "Elaine's going to sit with you for a bit," said Mum as she and Ste headed back out the front door. I heard Ste's car engine rev up. "They're just gonna have a look for Paul and Den, make sure the car hasn't broken down or anything," said Elaine with that same tight smile.

You sort of know, don't you, when something isn't right. Mum knew and even though Elaine did her best to reassure me, I knew too.

Me and Elaine sat there, *ThunderCats* playing in the background, but neither of us were watching it. The phone rang and

Elaine sprang up to answer it. I heard her talking in a low voice but couldn't hear what was being said. A couple of minutes later, I heard the door open and rushed to the hallway expecting to see Den and Paul. Instead, it was a very anxious-looking Mum and Ste.

"Joan," said Elaine, as Mum's eyes went to Elaine, who was holding the telephone. "There's been an accident."

As Den and Paul were driving towards the Fiddlers, a car on the opposite side of the road overtook another one, misjudged the distance, and went straight into the front of their car. A head-on collision.

Ste drove me and Mum to Warrington Hospital, where the police met us to take us to Paul. He was battered and bruised with a bandage covering a deep cut on his forehead. His left eye was hugely swollen and puffy. It was Den, however, who had taken a lot of the impact on his side of the car. He lost all his teeth, among countless other injuries, and would be in hospital for nearly three weeks.

Paul was just five years old when the crash happened and although his injuries weren't too serious, it did really knock him psychologically. After the accident, he not only shared my bedroom but often he'd share my bunk bed too. As well as the crash, he'd experienced seeing, very randomly and very horrifically, a cat killed in a separate incident with a pellet gun. It made him, understandably, a bit fragile as a little kid. We stayed in the same room together until I left home at 16.

I've always looked out for my little bro. Later, as adults, I helped to diagnose his Type 1 diabetes when he was clearly unwell on a family holiday. We were in Mauritius for my thirtieth birthday, and he was tired all the time, he had blurry vision, was losing weight, and he was constantly thirsty. I'd seen similar symptoms with someone I'd worked with and said to him, "Get to a doctor, you've got to sort this out."

Although I was his sister, I did mother Paul in some ways. With Mum and Den out playing gigs, it was mostly the two of us at the weekends when we were kids. We spent a lot of time together and, being that bit older, I assumed a role almost of a parent rather than big sis on those Friday and Saturday nights. I probably drove him mad, bossing him about!

You can see how close we are, I think, when you watch us on Channel 4's *Gogglebox*.

Paul is such a big part of my life, and I'm a big part of his too. We've been through so much together and I like to think we've been there for each other, especially when times get tough. He could also be a little shit, but I'll wait a few more pages before I fully throw him under the bus...!

When the Spice Girls became famous, he was around 16 years old and at college. Turns out, it's not just the person who becomes famous that is affected by fame. Life changes for everyone around them too. Me, Victoria, Emma, and Mel B had younger siblings the same age as Paul when things kicked off for us in 1996, and they all found it hard. It's so lucky that all our younger brothers and sisters happened to be the same age because it meant they were able to tell each other about what was happening.

With Paul, it started out with other kids teasing him, but that quickly turned into full-on bullying. Everywhere Paul went, he was never just Paul O'Neill, he was "Mel C's brother", "Sporty Spice's sibling". He still sometimes gets shit from people, "Oh, how many cars has your sister bought you this week?", "Your sister's a slag," and stuff like that. Sometimes people can be so bloody horrible.

In the end, he decided to drop out of college. It was just too much for him and he was quite depressed for several years. Not that he ever let me know that at the time.

I'm so proud of him. He's such a lovely, brilliant guy. He laughs about it all now, he'll say, "Oh, life was never the same once you got famous, it was so difficult… until you got me a PlayStation and then I was fine." Paul is always first for a joke, he's so funny. But I know it was hard on him and he was changed by the experience.

Some of that change was for the better though, and as he would say himself, it's made him the person he is today. These things are so hard at the time, but you can grow a lot and learn a lot. As horrible as it is, it's all temporary.

Paul loves to point out that Mum spent all of our family allowance on my dance and gymnastics, classes, competitions, and costumes, which in all honesty she did. But I think it paid off!

When I was asked to do *Gogglebox*, I knew it had to be our Paul to do it with me. We get on so well and have a laugh. He's such a funny fucker. We just get each other.

He's not just my little brother, he's one of my best mates.

· · ·

Paul and I loved nothing more than eating our tea off our laps. There was one person, however, who wasn't such a fan. "Peg it," I shouted, turning back to Paul, who, like me, was scoffing turkey burgers on the sofa. I'd heard the unmistakable grind of a lorry's engine, heaving as it turned into Ireland Street. Sure enough, when I looked through the blinds out onto the street, there was Den in his massive HGV.

Ordinarily, tea-time in our house was archetypally *Royle Family*, as we laugh about it now. Me and Paul would get in after school, butter a couple of white slices of bread, grate mounds of cheese, and then fry it all up in a pan. Not too long after that, around 6.30 pm, Mum, often knackered from work, would chuck some bright orange Crispy Pancakes or turkey burgers in the oven. Actually, let me be fair, Mum was, and still is, a great cook. Tea during the week might have been an oven job because she was so busy, but on a Sunday, she'd cook everything from scratch. She used to make Chinese food, which was unusual in the eighties. If you wanted Chinese, you'd ring the local takeaway. But Mum read up on some recipes and made us Sweet and Sour Pork, Sesame Prawn toast, and whole Chinese banquets sometimes. Watching her make food from scratch gave me the confidence to cook in later years.

But back then, like all kids, we loved processed and, even better, fast food. Hunched over and crushed together on the sofa in the tiny living room, plates balancing precariously on our knees, we'd scoff our faces while watching telly.

But Den wasn't a fan of this casual dining arrangement. He was quite strict and insisted we sit at the table for our tea, every night. As the HGV pulled in, chips, beans, and Crispy Pancakes would go flying as me and Paul raced to the dining room (aka the makeshift and slightly wobbly lean-to that Den and his brother built) just in time as Den walked back into the house.

He'd chuck his keys down, take off his coat, and poke his head around the door. "Hmm," he'd grunt, seeing us at the table, like butter wouldn't melt in our mouths. Or on our jacket spuds…!

The living room was so small, you could barely get through the door to the kitchen. The couch was along one wall, next to which was a small stack of shelves where Mum kept her nail kit. She'd fetch the nail varnish out the fridge and sit in front of the telly doing her nails. I'd cosy up next to her and she'd stroke my head as we watched *Dallas*. We had a fireplace, made by Den's fair hands, next to the shelves and then the stereo and the telly squeezed in beside each other.

Every Friday and Saturday night Mum and Den would be working, out playing gigs wherever they were booked. Around 5 pm, their bandmates would start piling in, heading through the kitchen to the cupboard under the stairs where the instruments and equipment were kept. "Shush," me and Paul would cry as they'd come back through the living room carrying bass guitars, a PA system and bass amps, as we tried to watch our favourite TV shows, *The Dukes of Hazzard* and *The A-Team*.

Often, they'd be auditioning someone for whatever band they were in at the time, so you'd get some bloke called Graham or Derek with his guitar come and sit down, his wife balanced on the arm of the sofa, and they'd interview him and then have a jam session.

When there were no babysitters available, we would spend Friday nights in various working men's clubs in some far-flung corner of the North West. We'd each get a bottle of warm, flat Coke with a straw and a packet of Golden Wonder cheese & onion crisps. We'd be plonked in the corner, told to keep quiet and not fidget, as Mum and Den performed "What's Love Got to Do with It" or "Superstition".

We had no idea that this wasn't normal, to have a travelling circus in and out the house, or to spend weekends watching our parents perform. To me and Paul, it's how life was, but it was very unconventional.

When I was old enough I got £1.50 a week pocket money for babysitting Paul, which I'd save and spend on music and, later, shopping trips to Warrington with my mates. We tried on loads of stuff in Miss Selfridge, Etam and Top Shop but bought very little! It would be a Maccy D's for lunch then if we were particularly flush a little trip to Superdrug to buy some spectacularly crispy Constance Carroll lip gloss teamed with frosted pink Rimmel lipstick, aqua blue eyeliner, and matching mascara. To complete the look, I got a corkscrew perm done, by Den's ex-wife, Marlene. I'd moaned at Mum to let me get it done for months. She finally let me when I turned 16. But I hated it! As soon as I got home from the hairdressers, I washed my hair four times trying to get the perm out or at least make it a bit less curly (it doesn't work, by the way). It just didn't look the same as when I'd had a sleepless night in my Clairol wavelengths, another trick we tried to make our hair look like eighties pop icon Taylor Dayne.

Those trips and other such extravagances were few and far between though, partly because I was at dance most weekends and partly because £1.50 wouldn't get you far, even back then. Compared to what my daughter gets these days for an allowance, we got a bloody pittance!

As I got older, I'd have to beg Paul to keep quiet about the various mates (I mean boys, really) who'd been in and out, and the cans of cider or Mad Dog 20/20 that would get drunk. We were quite well behaved, considering, but I wasn't a total angel. Paul was addicted to chips and chocolate, and so I'd bribe him with money for the chippie and a Marathon (before the Snickers rebrand!). Paul would say now he was a little shit (which he was), breaking my toys and being annoying. His favourite thing to do would be to burst into my room, let out a massive fart and then run off. He was always into mischief. He would shit-stir with my mates, telling my other bestie Zoë (Curlett) I'd said this-and-that about her, which I bloody hadn't. He was a right terror.

Younger brothers, who'd have 'em!

. . .

As I said, pride of place, next to Den's homemade brick fireplace was the hi-fi stacking stereo system. Record player on top, radio below that, double tape player next (perfect for taping the charts every Sunday) and stacked in the cabinet below was the precious vinyl: Gladys Knight, Stevie Wonder, Fleetwood Mac, The Stones, The Beatles, Carole King, Hall & Oates, Dire Straits, the Average White Band, and Jimi Hendrix offered up a world of magic as I clumsily put the needle on the record and listened, transfixed, as "Walk of Life" played.

I don't think there was a single household in the eighties that didn't have a copy of Dire Straits' *Brothers in Arms*.

Stevie Wonder's *Songs in the Key of Life* and *Innervisions* were the most influential on me. *Songs in the Key...* is my favourite album of all time. I remember listening to that record and being immediately swept up. "*Wow, New York, just like I pictured it*! *Skyscrapers and everything*!" I'd get lost in this world, hearing about all the places that I'd never experienced. I could imagine being in America, which is where all of us British kids were obsessed with back then. Stevie took me to the heart of New York City. To this day, "Sir Duke", Stevie's dedication to Duke Ellington and Ella Fitzgerald, can still pick me up if I'm feeling down.

I was such a music nerd. I'd really get into the stories of the songs and study the sleeve notes, the lyrics, and the journey of the album. I'd think about why the artist had put this song there, or what I thought the artwork was about. Carole King's *Tapestry* was one of those. I'd sit on the living-room floor surrounded by vinyl, learning the lyrics and studying the album credits.

It's interesting comparing song credits from now to then; these days, a song could conceivably have up to 12 writers working on one track. Back in the seventies, Carole wrote every song with maybe four other writers across the album, in total. There's nothing wrong with other people writing music for an artist (and that's happened for decades, through Elvis and the Motown years), but 12 people writing one song? There's so much pressure to have quick success that artists don't have time to develop their own skills, their own voice. Now you get "writing camps" where acts are thrown into a succession of rooms with teams of hitmakers and where the emphasis is on churn, rather than creativity.

I haven't done it, so maybe it is a worthwhile process, but I think a lot of artists find the writing camps quite disheartening. Not to mention, you're now sharing the profits with 10 other people which, in streaming terms, really means you're all getting very, very little. What's half a penny divided by 10? Because that's what you're looking at per stream.

Although I write with other people all the time (just maybe not five of them!), I must admit that you can't beat the purity of musicians like Prince or Stevie Wonder, who wrote, produced, arranged (and even played) across the entirety of their albums. Those guys are on another level.

Several years later – on 9th June 1998, to be precise – I would get to meet the legend Stevie himself via the late, great Luciano Pavarotti, or "Maestro", as he was called. We were invited to join the annual *Pavarotti & Friends* concert in his hometown of

Modena, Italy, for a War Child concert to raise money for the children of Liberia. Geri had just left the band, and although Pavarotti himself called her and begged her to come and perform, she politely declined. So it was just us four and we sang "Viva Forever" with Pavarotti. Can you imagine?!

He must have just marked his performance in rehearsals and soundcheck because when he sang those first lines "*Lo si caro* (I'll be there)" live, it *boomed*. You can see on our faces that we're all wowed by the depth of his voice. He really let rip and we all nearly jumped out of our skins! It was an incredible thing to get to do. We jokingly named the great tenor the fifth Spice Girl and he became known as "Mel High-C" for the day.

We met Stevie in his dressing room before the show and there's a great picture of me and Emma looking absolutely gobsmacked. She was a huge fan of Stevie too, so the pair of us are just buzzing in this photo. "It's great to see you," he said by way of introduction. We were a bit speechless really. It was often the way with being a Spice Girl; we'd all be thrilled to meet our heroes, but they were all excited to meet us too.

There was a big finale at the end of the concert where we're all gathered around Stevie on the piano: us Spicies, Pavarotti, Celine Dion, Jon Bon Jovi, Spike Lee, and The Corrs. Can you believe that line-up? I think you can see me mouthing "Oh my God," at one point, because I can't believe I'm onstage with Stevie, who then starts ad-libbing around the song, singing, "Spice Girls, Spice Girls." What?!

If I think about sitting on the living-room floor, reading through the lyrics of *Songs in the Key of Life* to years later being onstage, next to Stevie, singing with Stevie... It's magical.

• • •

Less magical was starting a new school. I'd been at Fairfield Juniors just a few days when the teasing started. "Go home, Scouser," snarled Stuart, a great big lad three years ahead of me in school. I looked away, pretending not to know who he was talking to, but I knew full well those words were aimed at me.

As someone brought up just outside Liverpool and later Runcorn, the kids in Widnes labelled me a Scouser. Something which I was incredibly proud of before, but at that very moment, a new kid in a new school, I wished I was anything but. The irony was that Liverpudlians classed me as an outsider too because I wasn't born there. I never seemed to fit in wherever I was.

I often felt confused and uncertain. Where was my place in the world? Although I had loads of friends, I always felt somehow different, not quite like everyone else.

Out of all my friends I was the only one of divorced parents. Nowadays, a lot of my daughter's friends have parents who are divorced, but in the seventies and early eighties, I was the odd one out among my mates. They all had normal families. No one else had to visit their dad and his girlfriend in the summer holidays. No one else had stepbrothers and half-brothers (even though I've always thought of Paul as 100% my full brother).

As much as I hated being different to the other kids, I also felt special because Mum was a singer. Every Friday and Saturday night she'd get her makeup on and get dressed up and go onstage to sing and be fabulous. Because my mum *is* fabulous. And then Dad worked in Spain, which was also unheard of.

I fluctuated between feeling vulnerable about my differences yet proud of them too: a Scouser who wasn't a Scouser; the only child of divorced parents but the daughter of a glamorous mum and dad. Why couldn't I be normal? But also, how cool was it that I wasn't like everyone else?

Although I had loads of friends (Ali, Cathy and Zoë were my closest), I could be quite a solitary kid. I found too much noise or too much interaction overwhelming. I still do sometimes. So, as sociable as I was, I was quite a loner back then. In many ways I still am. I've never really admitted that to anyone, including myself before now, but I'm someone who not only enjoys but needs solitude. I require space away from people to reflect and think, just like I did as a child.

I was happy alone in my room pottering around with my dolls. I'd cut their hair, give them a felt-tip makeup job, and sew their clothes. If Mum popped her head in, I would have looked like the typical little kid lost in a world of toys. But there was a lot going on underneath. I spent hours ruminating on how I wasn't like my friends, as I drew makeup all over my Sindy or rearranged the teddies on my bed.

As I got older and became a teenager, the phone would ring off the hook with people wanting me to go out with them down the park or, as we got older, to a pub. I was always popular, but the reality was that sometimes I was much happier in my bedroom by myself, thinking my thoughts. I had many conflicting feelings as a young person, and I spent a lot of time contemplating my life, my family, and my future and where I fitted into everything.

"Oi, Scouse, why don't you go back to Scouseland?" laughed Stuart, turning to all his mates, who were doubled over laughing. I stared at him for a moment. A long moment. What should I do in this situation?

Blam! I jumped up and pushed him in the chest. He didn't see it coming. "Shut up, stop saying that," I shouted, hitting him in the arm. He just stared at me in shock. "Stuart got hit by a girl," teased one of his mates as I turned on my heel and walked off, flicking my ponytail triumphantly behind me as I went.

It didn't stop the teasing, but it helped. Every time he started on me, I'd jump on him, and we'd scuffle. In the third year of Juniors, I got into it with Anthony Mullen (though we ended up making friends and were mates all the way through secondary school). I would often get into physical fights in the playground, pushing and shoving the boys and having little scraps.

I think I was probably holding a lot of unresolved anger in that little frame of mine.

We didn't have things then like counselling or therapy, we just had to get on with it. Although I became increasingly non-confrontational as I got older, when I was a little kid, I seemed to have no fear.

I was ready to fight anyone and quite often I had to fight for my place. I was up for that. I refused to be teased or bullied by anyone.

It was something I'd do well to remember later in life.

CHAPTER THREE

Northern Star

The eighties: "Rock on Tommy!", "What you talkin' 'bout Willis?" and "I love it when a plan comes together". "Just Say No!", "Choose Life", and "Relax!", Pac-Man, pencil cases, Etch A Sketch, Rubik's Cube, Subbuteo, breakdancing, moonwalking, and Top Trumps. My Little Pony, Girls World, Space Hoppers, Space Invaders, flying saucers, Wham Bars and fizzy cola bottles. Wishing you could afford satellite telly so you could watch the new music channel, MTV. *Jaws, E.T., Back to the Future, Ferris Bueller's Day Off, Top Gun, ThunderCats,* and *Fraggle Rock.* Our Price, Wimpy, Woollies and the tuck shop. Leg warmers, mullets, leotards, bum bags, and aerobics with Jane Fonda. The Sony Walkman, VHS tapes, and TDK cassettes. *EastEnders* vs. *Corrie.* Barbie vs. Sindy. *Dallas* vs. *Dynasty,* Duran Duran vs. Wham! *Now That's What I Call Music!* Michael Jackson. Prince. Madonna. President Reagan and Maggie Thatcher. Charles and Diana. The fall of the Berlin Wall. Live Aid.

The whole world almost came to a halt on Saturday 13th July 1985 for Live Aid. For months, the news had been full of horrific images of starving people in Ethiopia, where a famine had devastated the country between 1983 and 1985. Over one million people died during the famine, while double that number became displaced, and 200,000 children were left orphaned.

Bob Geldof of the band The Boomtown Rats had decided to do something about it, seeing as no one else seemed to be doing much. Alongside Midge Ure from Ultravox, Bob put together the charity single "Do They Know It's Christmas" featuring Phil Collins, Duran Duran, U2, Boy George, Banarama, and lots of others. It was released on 3rd December 1984, and Geldof hoped to raise a few thousand pounds. Within the year, the single had made over eight million pounds.

Bob then very ambitiously staged Live Aid, a televised concert beamed across the world from Wembley Stadium in London and the John F. Kennedy Stadium in Philadelphia. The idea was to raise as much money as possible and donate it directly to those in need. Nearly two *billion* people across the globe tuned in – almost 40% of the world's population – with donations reaching nearly £130 million dollars for famine relief.

Live Aid will stay with me forever because it helped shape how I wanted to move through the world in later life, both professionally and personally. It only takes one person to make real and meaningful change.

The line-up was ridiculous. Living in a musical household meant the VHS tapes were lined up (on Long Play, not Short Play, obvs), so not a minute of the 16-hour concert was missed: George Michael, Elton John, U2, Duran Duran, Simple Minds, Queen, Elvis Costello, Sting, Bryan Adams, Bowie! Macca! The list was endless. The mad thing to realise now, looking back, is that I've met, if not worked with, almost every single one of these legends.

Imagine little old me knowing that would eventually happen – it would have blown my mind (and still kind of does)!

There were two performances that day that really stopped me in my tracks: Madonna and Queen.

Freddie Mercury is my number one favourite performer of all time, thanks to the voice, the stage presence, the *drama*. He's the person I most regret not having had the opportunity to meet. The crowd participation at that show was just incredible. That performance re-launched Queen: it was considered not only the best at Live Aid, but one of the greatest live performances of all time. It's a masterclass in stagecraft. Queen totally got the assignment that day. After they came offstage, Elton John apparently rushed into Freddie's trailer joking, "You bastard, you stole the show!"

The most impressive thing about Freddie's performance on that day is the sense of physicality. He didn't just sing with his voice, it was from the pit of his soul. Every single cell of his body delivered those words.

While I never got to meet Freddie, I have had the opportunity to work with both Roger Taylor and Brian May. Brian is the sweetest man, he's so gentle and so unique in his style of playing guitar. In 2011, I was invited to do "POP Goes the Musical" for *Children in Need*, where musicians would come in at the end of the show and perform a couple of songs for the kids. I went into the Queen musical *We Will Rock You* at the Dominium Theatre in London's West End. I performed "We Will Rock You" and "We Are the Champions". Brian May not only came, but also played with me. He's just the most wonderful person and full of stories. Through him, I feel like I've gotten to know the essence of Freddie, as Brian talks about him a lot. He often says, "Oh,

Freddie would do this or say that." We've stayed in touch since that first day we met.

Back in 1985, there was another performer I was very excited to watch because I'd not seen her perform live with a band before. At that time, she was quite a newbie among all these highly success-ful artists, but she had completely captured my imagination.

It was, of course, the one and only Madonna.

I first became aware of Madonna Louise Ciccone in 1984 when she appeared on *Top of the Pops* to perform "Holiday". Like Kate Bush, she was young, and she was cool. And she was making pop music that I could understand a bit more easily than Kate and her highbrow Emily Brontë references!

For the Live Aid performance in Philadelphia, Madonna had dyed her hair red and was wearing bright red lipstick in sharp contrast to her floral, lace green suit. She had on more clothes than usual, but she was covered in rosary beads, crosses, a CND (Campaign for Nuclear Disarmament) chain, bright flowery bracelets and huge hoop earrings. She was so cool. I watched, mesmerised, as Madonna moved across the stage with two dancers. She commanded the audience with ease.

Live Aid was big for a lot of people, but something very special happened to me on that day: I had an epiphany. I knew what I wanted to do, what I wanted to be. Seeing the perfor-mances by Madonna and Freddie Mercury completely enthralled and inspired me.

I didn't get to see Madonna live until her fourth concert tour, *The Girlie Show* in September 1993. I was in the nosebleeds at Wembley Stadium and bawled my eyes out when she walked on stage. I couldn't believe that tiny little dot miles away from me was her, Madonna. My hero.

I didn't so much watch those Madonna videos but *study* them. I'm surprised I didn't wear out the tape watching her set over and over, learning the moves, melody changes, and every word she spoke and sang.

It was a perfect mix of performance, choreography, theatrics, spectacle, and great pop music. It was ground-breaking and it set the stall for future pop concerts. Madonna was so innovative. Pop stars didn't play stadiums back then, let alone female pop stars. Places like Wembley were for rock bands. Male rock bands. Madonna paved the way for all of us, especially female performers: the Spice Girls, Britney Spears, Beyoncé, Ariana Grande, all the way through to Billie Eilish.

She didn't just push the boundaries, she flat out broke them: fashion, music, feminism, sex positivity, body positivity, philanthropy and even politics were all in her wheelhouse. Madonna was a vocal supporter of the LGBTQI+ community and did so much to raise awareness around HIV and AIDS at a time when not many other people did.

Whether I was able to process all that information at 10 or 11 years old, I can't say. But what I am sure of is the impact she had on me as a musician and performer. Watching Madonna at Live Aid that day and as I continued to follow her career throughout my teens, I took on board all the many amazing things she stood for. Not only was she an incredible entertainer, but here was a woman who broke the rules, a woman who smashed through the glass ceiling.

In that tiny bedroom, lying on my bunk bed, I'd sing my heart out to Madonna, Annie Lennox and the Eurythmics, and Whitney Houston. I would imagine myself onstage, performing to thousands around the world, signing autographs and doing interviews on television.

Those formative performances crystallised within me the first stirrings of what it might be like to be a pop star. Not a dancer, a West End star, or an Olympic gymnast. A pop star.

Without Madonna, who knows how anything, including in my own life, might have turned out. She changed my world, and she changed *the* world.

. . .

It's funny what the body does to you, isn't it? Until senior school, I was very at ease around the boys. I had no problems scrapping with the lads if they tried to tease me, I could stand up for myself no problem. I was as happy outside doing bunny hops on Paul's BMX with the boys as I was in Ali's loft listening to her dad's very well-worn records.

But then, you turn 12, 13 and the dreaded puberty begins. As if I wasn't already, I became very self-conscious. Mum dragged me to M&S to buy a training bra, the cringiest experience ever. Both of my parents tried to talk to me about the birds and the bees and my form teacher made us watch a film featuring an explicit and traumatic birth that was supposed to educate us, somehow, about safe sex.

We got our real information though from books. Me and my bezzy mates would gather in secret to read Judy Blume's *Forever*. There was "the page" that we would read repeatedly where Katherine loses her virginity to Michael. Anyone who grew up in the eighties can't hear the name "Ralph" without thinking of that book! It was far more educational than the one sex-ed lesson we had. We'd walk down to the lower school bathrooms, where the girls' gym was, huddle together, and pull out our well-worn copies, giggling our heads off as Blume described the fictional couple's first sexual encounter.

As soon as I became aware of boys and kissing and sex and babies, I went from being confident and outgoing around boys to very shy and very awkward almost overnight. It wasn't made any better by a boy called Ryan Wilson, who had decided in the second year of senior school that he fancied me. I was mortified! And not only mortified, but I wasn't interested. I was still into dance classes and pop stars: I'd barely grown out of my Sindys at this point. He was also a little bit of a bad lad; he'd swagger around school and mess about in classes. I didn't know much, but I knew it was best to keep away from Ryan.

The thing was, someone else liked Ryan. I'd gone to Fairfield Junior School with this one girl, and we'd been pretty good mates. But when she heard that Ryan had scratched "Raz 4 Mel" on his desk, joining the generations of other scrawls and old chewing gum forever attached to the battered old wood, she wasn't best pleased.

I was walking back home from school one day and took my normal shortcut across The Bongs. At the time, I was in the fifth year, so around 15. I was in my own world, thinking about an upcoming dance competition the next weekend and what I needed to rehearse more. Then I became vaguely aware that someone was behind me. I could hear her, this girl who used to be my mate but had recently taken a clear dislike to me, talking to her cousin, slagging someone off: "She's such a fucking slut," I heard, realising that they were talking about me. *"You're not going to intimidate me,"* I thought, deliberately slowing my pace to show them I wasn't bothered.

I had dead-long hair at that point in a plait down my back and I was wearing, very proudly, a blue trench coat from M&S.

Then I hear: "She thinks she's so fucking good, look at her." But I just kept walking calmly even as I felt her getting closer and closer. The next thing, her breath was on my neck – "Slag!" – and my head flew back as she grabbed my plait and pulled me down to the ground. There was a short pause while I considered my options: stay down and see if she gets bored and leaves or get up and see where things went.

I scrambled to my feet and looked her dead in the eye. She was shocked to see that I wasn't crying and that I was ready to fight back. As I got closer to her, she started to back away.

"And your mum's a slag who sings in nightclubs!" she screamed.

Well, that's when I went for her. I threw myself at her, arms and legs flying. She really didn't see that coming. Mind you, neither did I. I think I was more surprised than anyone.

It seemed to be over in seconds and I can't really remember how it ended but I pulled myself together and got myself home, covered in scratches and bruises.

Mum was furious. She comforted me as I cried my eyes out, asking who had done this to me. Paul, bless him, nearly ran straight over The Bongs to confront the girls. I think he holds a grudge to this day.

It was a silly incident in theory, but it really shook me. I was always popular at school, I never had "enemies" or fights with people. Apart from Stuart back in Juniors. Okay, fine, and Anthony. But generally, I was everyone's friend. After all the upset at home, I'd learnt to keep everyone happy and that extended beyond my family to my friends. I was the good girl, the peacekeeper.

I think, perhaps, that Ryan liking me, in addition to being known as a talented dancer, made people envious. They didn't like seeing me get attention. I'm not the first person that's happened to, and I won't be the last, but it knocked me. To add insult to injury, quite literally, when the school found out they threatened to take my prefect's tie off me. That really upset me because it was just so unfair.

A couple of months later, just before Christmas, I asked my dad for a weights bench from the Argos catalogue. I think that the fight made me start to look differently at my body. As a kid, I didn't question if I could dance and do gymnastics, I just did it. My body was always there for me, it did what I wanted, and it did it really well. I spent my time running around school, dance lessons, gym class, and playing out with my mates so I was always slim; there wasn't a pick on me.

But after that fight on The Bongs, I wanted to change my body. I wanted to be strong. My body became a place of defence, a kind of fortress, in a way. I thought, *"No one's going to get the better of me again, physically."* If I was strong physically, no one could touch me.

I knew I wanted, *needed*, to be strong.

There are things that happen to us in our formative years that impact us in both subtle and more obvious ways. After that fight, I became more wary, my senses were on alert for potential danger in a way they hadn't been before. I was set on changing my body but only through exercise —I had no issues with food at this point. I didn't even think about my weight or go on diets, like some of my school friends. Thank goodness. I was naturally very lean and, because my life was so physical, I could eat what I wanted. But the fight very slowly, very subconsciously turned a cog in my mind that I needed more from my body. The way that it was, wasn't quite enough.

• • •

Olwen Grounds School of Dance, on the other side of town where I lived, was your typical dance studio. Wooden floor, full of splinters, loads of mice bopping about, damp up the walls, shabby curtains clinging to the windows. We'd spend hours there doing classes, exams, and performances.

There were certain competitions we'd do every year. The big one was Kirkby Comps, part of the Allied Dance Association, which was for the North West. We'd do Ballet, Tap (not my strongest), Modern, song and dance, duets, trios and troupes (when the whole class would perform together)! I won Modern Solo, which was a big deal to me. Modern is essentially dance that originated from American Musical Theatre – think lots of leaps, high kicks, and pirouettes. They also had National, which is traditional folk dancing, and then Greek dance, which was quite classical – I even played *The Tempest* one year, which involved me tearing around the stage as the raging storm. They kept us very busy learning multiple disciplines and half the time we didn't really know the origins or meanings of what we were doing, but we enjoyed it whether it was the Scottish lilt or traditional Hungarian folk dance.

The Comps were our highlight of the year, the big event. It's funny thinking about it now; they'd stick on a fuzzy old tape, invariably cued up to the wrong song, the auditorium would be full of feedback and on we'd prance about in blue eye makeup with pink cheeks and red lips, doing our best dancing. At the end, we'd line up in a crescent, legs bevelled to the left, kids picking their knickers out their bums, and we would hold up our scores (often upside down or back to front). And your smile would widen and hopes lift as they'd call out whoever had taken third place. You'd think, *"Ohh, I could get second or first!"* It was all brilliantly *Blades of Glory.*

The Comps were held in Kirkby, the satellite Liverpool town where Dad and all his family are from, and where they all still live, apart from him. Whenever we were there doing dance competitions, I'd take my mates down to Kirkham's (my nan's bake shop) and Nan would give us all free cream cakes. That was our little ritual.

Those times at Kirkby Comps and in those stuffy, stinky rehearsal rooms were formative years for me. I grew as a dancer and my personality, informed by my abilities as a dancer, developed too. Our house was full of trophies and medals. I was even in the local paper once, when I won Gold in the Modern Solo (which, of course, Mum has still got!).

I wasn't a singer though. At least, not publicly, yet. I loved to sing, but I didn't think I was any good. I was alright, I could hold a tune, I could sing a *bit,* but I didn't think I had vocal talent. Yet it gave me a lot of joy to sing. I was in the school choir, and I'd get the odd solo here and there. I was 14 when I did my very first singing performance and I chose to do Whitney's "Greatest Love of All", which was mad because it isn't the easiest song to sing. I couldn't have picked a tougher challenge. What was I thinking?! My boyfriend at the time (Ryan – yes, I did eventually give in!) was sitting in the first or second row and I sang the whole of the first verse flat. It was such a cringe moment. I could see Mum in my peripheral vision, wincing. I think I managed to redeem myself by the end, thankfully.

I sang with Mum a year later for my GCSE Music. As part of the exam, you had to perform a solo piece and a duet. I got Mum to do it with me, right there in the music classroom, and we did Annie Lennox and Aretha Franklin's "Sisters (Are Doing It for Themselves)". Our Paul was there, I don't know why – he didn't start at Fairfield until the next year – but he remembers being surprised because until then all I'd banged on about was wanting to be a prima ballerina!

I loved singing, but I thought dance would be the direction I'd go in. I had such a passion for it, even though I occasionally found I would get frustrated with my body because it didn't always do what I wanted it to do. I always felt freer when I sang. It felt like it came more naturally to me. But I knew, from watching Mum, how hard it was. It felt impossible to become a singer. Mum was playing social clubs and working men's clubs – she really had to work hard. I wasn't sure that's what I wanted.

What I was certain of was that I wanted to perform and I slowly started to connect the dots: my dance performances, Madonna at Live Aid, Mum singing in a band, Kate Bush on *Top of the Pops*. They were all different versions of entertainment and there wasn't a single doubt in my mind that that is what I would be doing with my life.

I wanted to entertain. I *needed* to.

• • •

I wasn't unhappy about leaving school. I didn't hate Fairfield High, but my mind was always on the dance studio, a performance at the weekend, or the career I was trying to figure out how to achieve.

I wasn't that into studying. My strengths were more physical and creative, so school for me had been about keeping my head down and getting it done. I did okay in English and languages, but I struggled with maths, and I really couldn't be arsed with science. I'd sit at the back in those lessons and act up a little, but I was never the class clown, a loudmouth or a troublemaker. School was just something I had to do. Simple as. I did okay in my GCSEs – well, by our standards back then. Nowadays a kid thinks they've failed if they only get an A rather than an A* (or should that be an 8 rather than a 9 these days?!).

I got four Bs and five Cs – one of which was for music. Yup, they gave me a C for music – what a cheek!

There came a point in secondary school where I was forced to choose between dance and gymnastics. I was serious about both, but they weren't complementing each other. Eventually, gymnastics directly clashed with dance, and I had to pick one. It was a no-brainer. As much as I wanted to be an Olympic gymnast, I knew I wasn't good enough. Not really. I decided it was dance. I wanted to get on that West End stage. I got more pleasure out of dancing and I knew that I was good at it.

After years of dance classes and competitions, there was no doubt in my mind what I wanted to do when I left school. I'd spent the last 10 years drawing "Melanie C Superstar" on all my schoolbooks. It was time to make this dream come true. I wasn't about to go to college and do A-levels, was I?

"Dance school," I told Mum. "But it has to be in London. I need to be in London."

Everyone knew that if you wanted to make it in this business you had to be in the capital. People from outside of London, of course, broke through – The Beatles, Oasis, Take That – but one way or another, you ended up in London because that's where the music, film, TV, and theatre industry was, and mostly still is. If you were serious about making it as a dancer, a West End star, or a musician, you had no option but to head South.

I was 15 when I auditioned for dance school and 16 when I left home. That feels very young now – I can't imagine my own daughter leaving home at that age. But I was so focused on what I wanted to do, and being a dancer is such a youthful career, that taking a year out wasn't an option. It's such a competitive world and I knew I had to get on with it. There were no second thoughts. Not a single doubt. In fact, it was really exciting. I saw it as the next part of my journey to get to where I wanted to be.

I auditioned at three places down South, but what made that trip more memorable was because both Mum and Dad came with me. It was the first time since 1977 that I'd been in the same place with the two of them, just us. I was excited but also nervous. Yet if there was any tension between them, they hid it well. It felt special that they were both there for me at that time.

The three of us got the train down from Liverpool Lime Street and walked from Euston to the college on York Way, near King's Cross, which back then was dead rough. Before the huge regeneration project of St Pancras and King's Cross the area was pretty edgy. There was lots of drug use and homelessness, and blokes looking for sex workers.

I'm not sure it calmed my dad's nerves about me leaving home at such a young age and he was really worried about me going to a performing arts college. "Have you got anything to fall back on?" he fretted as we walked around London. Mum was the opposite. "Melanie, you go for it," she said, "Just give it a go and see what happens." Dad was always a bit more worried than Mum about my chosen career; dance and performance is of course an unstable line of work and so many people don't make it. But Mum understood that I had to try, whatever happened, just like she had.

Even though I was just 15 years old, I had a lot of self-belief. I really thought all of this was my destiny. There was no Plan B. There was nothing to fall back on. Having no back-up plan, emotionally or literally, means that this thing, whatever that thing is, must work. I would find out that all five of us Spice Girls shared that single-minded attitude, and I still wonder if having that complete belief, but also a need to succeed because that's the only option, is part of what makes you successful.

I auditioned for the London Studio Centre (the well-known dance and theatre school that was then on York Way in King's Cross) and got in. It was my first choice, so I was absolutely over the moon until I realised the course was to start in September 1989, rather the following year when I would finally have done my GCSEs and finished secondary education. So I carried on with the auditions we'd already organised at the Doreen Bird College of Performing Arts down in Sidcup and for Laine Theatre Arts in Epsom.

The day I found out about Doreen Bird, me and our Paul were still in bed, and the post must have come, because Mum came into the bedroom waving an envelope.

"Oh god," I groaned.

The envelope was thick so I knew it couldn't be a simple "No, thanks".

"Don't be soft – open it," urged Mum so I carefully tore it open.

I burst out crying.

"I got in!"

I'd gotten into Doreen Bird!

I was so excited to be starting the next part of my life and the path that I felt so sure would lead me to West End success. That was my plan at the time. Get into a show and from there, somehow, I'd become a pop star. It was vague but it felt right to me.

I'd always had the odd job here and there, and so had saved up a little bit of spending money before I left home. As kids, me and my cousin Neil worked in my Auntie Lynne's hairdressing shop. We'd sweep up all the hair, and all the old ladies with their blue and purple rinses would press 50p into our hands. We loved it. Sometimes you'd get the odd scally coming in selling knock-off gear. I remember this one lad flogging a load of shell suits once but my 50 pences didn't add up to enough – gutted.

I got a job in a chippy for the six weeks before I left for college to build up my savings a bit more. I was on £1.50 an hour, which was below minimum wage, even back then. I stank of fish and chips and grease. My hair was greasy, my skin was greasy, *I* was greasy. Loads of lads from school used to come in before they went to the youthie disco, and I'd be mortified. I hated it. On the upside, my mates loved me because I used to give them massive portions of everything and charge them 20p.

Needless to say, given how many potatoes I had to peel, I wasn't afraid of hard graft. And I was glad I had a few quid in my pocket for when I headed south to live on my own.

I also managed to save some cash for college by working with Dad during the summer holidays. From the age of 14, I volunteered to work in holiday camps in Spain, or France, depending on where Dad was that year. Me and this local lad, David, would collect the hotel bed sheets that British holidaymakers had spent their summer sweating and doing God-knows-what-else in. I dread to think.

The time I spent with Dad over these years was a bit limited. I'd get to see him for weeks every summer and winter, which was great, but he was away each year from spring to mid-autumn. The time we did get to spend was always fun. He has a big group of Scouse friends who are right characters. When he was still an engineer at Otis, he played for the factory's eleven-a-side and he'd take me along on football tours with him and his mates, Blancy, Maca and the Walshies, to places like Torremolinos and the Butlin's in Minehead. I remember running on the pitch in Fuengirola on the Costa del Sol when I was four years old, either trying to get the ball in the net, or maybe trying to get my dad's attention.

After returning home from his travels, Dad decided on a career change, and began managing various campsites around Europe, so I'd spend the whole six-week summer holidays in places like Cap d'Agde near Montpelier or Playa Bara in Spain. We sometimes still go back as a family to Bara, because Dad remained good friends with the owner. I love those holidays; they're always very chilled and they bring out plenty of nostalgia for us all. They're all strolls down to the beach, barbequing every night, sitting out under twinkly lights, drinking Rioja. There's always loads of different nationalities camping side by side. It's a wonderful place.

It was a great place to spend time in as a kid, and later a teenager. I'd have the summer outside in the sun, running about and making friends with the kids on the campsite. This one time, someone Dad worked with, Debbie, took me shopping and we ended up spending the whole of Dad's week's wages on a top and a denim skirt for me.

Another time, my dad was on security detail for the night, so I went to stay with his friends, Lorraine and Annette, in their tent. Dad remembers patrolling the camp and suddenly smelling smoke and seeing that a fire had broken out in the campsite, in the area where I was sleeping that night. In fact, he thought it could be the same tent. Heart in mouth, he rushed over – there was thick smoke and people running around, trying to get water to put the fire out – frantically looking for me.

I was there, being looked after by Lorraine and Annette. It was the tent next door that had caught fire; all I remember is being woken in the night and dragged out of my sleeping bag and suddenly there was this incredible heat and huge flames right by me. In a daze, I saw my dad appear from nowhere and spot a gas bottle, dangerously close to the flames. Without thinking, he rushed in to move it and suffered terrible burns on his feet in the process. He must have been in a lot of pain, but he immediately came over and picked me up in his arms.

He was white as a sheet; we'd all had a real fright that night.

I can still hear it now; being woken from a deep sleep to the crackles and commotion of the fire. We were on another campsite in France years later and a bar caught fire. That sound of crackling, popping, and people panicking. I think anyone that has experienced being close to, or affected by, a fire will know what I mean.

The fire brigade eventually came and put the fire out, and I was given loads of fuss. But what I remember most was Dad suddenly being there and scooping me up. My dad felt like a real hero to me that night.

I was well looked after by everyone Dad worked with; it was a lovely community of people.

Dad had various girlfriends over the years until he met Carole, then that was it. They met in France, where she was a holiday rep for the same company, and have been inseparable ever since. I was a bridesmaid at their wedding in 1988. I remember going shopping with Carole for my bridesmaid's dress in C&A. I loved it.

Carole is from Leeds and they moved back there not long after their wedding. It was a shame my summers in Spain and France had come to an end because I loved that time with my dad and Carole. I loved the late dinners out in the warm night air, listening to my dad's stories and snuggling up in the caravan to watch movies.

Was I a big fan of the communal showers? Well, no, but that's camping!

It was good to have Dad back in the UK full-time though and they had a lovely house – 33, Winterbourne Avenue – with a big garden and a conservatory. I used to love spending time with Carole's mum, Winnie, and her brother, Mick. They were both real characters that kept me entertained and welcomed me with open arms.

Spending time in Leeds meant lots of treats – we'd have lunches out and trips to the movies. Dad and Carole would often have M&S food, which was a real luxury. I loved the minced beef and onion roll we used to have. I had a lovely bedroom at their house, up in the loft. Carole decorated it so nicely – it was all floral, pastel, peaches and cream. She has a real eye for interior design. There would always be lots of magazines waiting for me on the bed and I remember blasting out Kylie's *Rhythm of Love* album while trying to emulate her eyeliner wings (and failing). I still love that album.

Dad and Carole still live in Leeds today with my two younger brothers, Liam and Declan. Liam and Declan were so young when the Spice Girls happened, which is probably a good thing but strange to think they never really knew me before. In fact, I was in Leeds with the girls when Declan was born – that's how little they were at the time. I'm really proud of their achievements. Also, looks like they inherited the family travel bug; Liam worked in Tokyo and Declan recently got back from Australia.

For years Dad was like a mythical figure; when I told my friends he worked abroad and spoke French and Spanish it sounded very glamorous. I really idolised Dad, I put him on a pedestal. He was a very loving parent and he made sure I felt loved by him. I knew even if he wasn't there physically, he would be there if I needed him.

As I've got older, I realise how hard things must have been for Den, though. He's the strong, silent type and was pretty strict when we were growing up. Because of yearning for my own dad I don't think I've ever given him the respect he deserves. I have now had my own experience of being a stepparent and I know it isn't easy.

The divorce continued to have an impact on my relationships through my teens and twenties. It wasn't the only thing that held me back from having a serious relationship, but I think it's why I've always resisted the idea of marriage. Although my parents went on to have long and lasting relationships with other people, their own failed.

• • •

When you grow up in, or near Liverpool, football isn't just a fun sporting event that you casually participate in.

I was born supporting Liverpool FC and have seen the team play at Anfield countless times. When I hear the theme tune to *Match of the Day*, I'm instantly transported to being six, seven years old and staying up late with my dad to watch the highlights of that week's games. I'd get to eat sweets and crisps and fall asleep to that lovely sound of the ball being kicked and the roar of the crowd as their team scored.

Even now when I go home to Mum's and football is on the telly I feel instantly comforted. It's a part of me.

There were two big events in the late eighties that really shook Liverpool and the football community: the Heysel Stadium disaster in 1985 and, of course, Hillsborough in 1989.

I was 15 when Hillsborough happened, and I can recall that day so clearly. I remember I had bad hay fever, and it was April, so it was from the tree pollen. It was Saturday, and I was at dancing with Ali. We'd taken a break to go to the shop; Ali got a Balisto and I got two bags of pickled onion KP Meanies crisps. Those details have always stayed with me.

I'll never forget holding the crisps as we heard what was happening over the radio.

At home later that night we watched in silence at the horrific images on the television.

Ninety-four people lost their lives that day at Hillsborough stadium in Sheffield for the FA Cup semi-final between Liverpool and Nottingham Forest and up to 776 people were also injured. There was overcrowding in the pens, which led to a huge crush and an awful loss of life and dreadful injuries. In the end, 97 people died as a result of the disaster; the last person, Andrew Devine losing his life in 2021 after suffering severe and irreversible brain damage at the game 32 years earlier. It was the highest death toll in British sporting history. It shook the city to its foundations and the repercussions of that terrible tragedy is still felt today.

One thing that made what happened even worse was the coverage by *The Sun* newspaper over the following months. *The Sun*'s coverage of Hillsborough was disgusting; they blamed Liverpool fans for causing the disaster. It took until 2016 for the second set of Hillsborough inquests, found that the (then 96) victims had been "unlawfully killed" and that the supporters' behaviour had no part to play in the disaster. The inquest laid blame at the South Yorkshire police and ambulance services for failing to fulfil their duty of care and found that the design of the stadium was a contributing factor in the disaster.

The people of Liverpool were, rightly, furious with *The Sun*. To this day you will struggle to find a single copy of that newspaper sold in the city. No one will buy it.

Throughout my career I did a lot with the Hillsborough Family Support Group, including press and charity support runs. Anything I could do really to raise money and awareness for a cause that is very, very close to my heart.

Not long after Hillsborough, I headed off to Doreen Bird in Sidcup before joining the Spice Girls in 1994. Since then, I've rarely been back home for any length of time and the citywide ban of the paper escaped my attention.

When we started doing press, *The Sun* was one among many tabloids we did interviews with. I'd never put two and two together. And nothing was ever said to me, although of course this was before social media.

In 2016, I released *Version of Me*, my seventh solo album, and did an interview about it with *The Sun*. There's a picture of me with a huge *Sun* logo behind me. Understandably, people were upset.

It really got me down, I had a tough time for a few months, and I was terrified to go to Liverpool. I've not been back to Anfield since because people were so upset.

I know it's naïve, I know the buck stops with me, but I just did not know. I should have known. I wish more than anything that I had.

A local paper printed that I refused to apologise, which made it a million times worse.

This is my opportunity to unreservedly apologise in print, so there can be no further misunderstanding. I will never, ever do anything with *The Sun* again. I can only apologise and hold my hands up. I should have known, but I just didn't.

I hope that people can forgive me.

To all those who lost their lives at Hillsborough, you will never walk alone.

CHAPTER FOUR

Goin' Down (South)

I was 16 years old in 1990 when I left Ireland Street and headed 250 miles south to Sidcup. I was off to become a dancer. A real-life dancer. The West End, Broadway, *Top of the Pops*, the BRITs, the Grammys. Fame and fortune, here I come.

It was the nineties. "Hasta La Vista, Baby!", "Eat my shorts!", "Not!", "Big mistake. Huge!", Pringles, The Prodigy, Kurt and Courtney. "You Can't Touch This." Acid House and house parties. "Just Do It". Chokers, bling, Maharishi's and Mitsubishis and crop tops. Microwaves. *The Fresh Prince of Bel-Air* and *Twin Peaks*. Jason Priestley and Luke Perry. Blur vs. Oasis. Motorola vs. Nokia. Biggie vs. Tupac, Robbie vs. Gary. Opal Fruits vs. Starburst. The Internet, Hotmail, Ask Jeeves!, Cindy, Christy, Naomi and Tatjana. Kate Moss. Thelma and Louise, Leo and Kate, Pam and Tommy, Monica and Bill. "I did not have sexual relations with that woman." *The Real World*. The whole world read *Harry Potter* and played Sonic the Hedgehog. We all got lower-back tattoos and belly button piercings. The

Rachel. Lads and Ladettes. We were *Home Alone* and *Wild at Heart*. Grunge, rave, and rap. CDs and DVDs. Tamagotchi. Nintendo 64. "I Wanna Sex You Up", "Now That We Found Love", Vanilla Ice and TLC. Leah Betts. Rodney King and the LA riots. The Channel Tunnel. Clinton and Blair. New Labour. Girl Power.

… but we're getting ahead of ourselves, aren't we?!

It was the early nineties and it felt like a huge adventure to leave Widnes. I'm sure Mum and Dad fretted about me, but I didn't have a care in the world – it's what I knew I had to do to start my dream life.

I shared my digs, a lovely big house set back off the road, with seven other girls and the family of four who owned the house. The wife was also a childminder, so there were usually lots of little kids running around. It was total chaos most of the time!

We were known as the Heskett posse after the name of the family who owned the home. There was Emma, who was from Scunthorpe, and Susan Wright (who is now Susan Hallam-Wright and who went on to marry David Essex). Freya and Ruth were from Cambridge, and they were the poshest people I'd ever met. Well, they were the *only* posh people I'd ever met! Me, Rachel and Claire were in the dining room with their two single beds side by side and my single bed at the bottom of their bed. They squashed us in. It was basic but that's what I was used to, what I'd come from.

Because my parents were divorced, I got a full grant, which paid for everything from tuition, board and shoes (dancers get through a lot!), and even a bit of spending money. I didn't have to get a job to supplement myself, but a lot of my friends worked in the Sidcup McDonald's or in local pubs. The college was small, around 140 people, about 45 of us in each year, so you got to know most people well.

Living in Sidcup and studying dance meant we had access to the West End, which we made the most of. Someone always needed a pair of pointe shoes, so every Saturday we'd take the train into town and go to Freed on Drury Lane. Being from the North, spending time in the West End was so exciting. I went to see so many shows. Some of my mates would get jobs as ushers in the theatres and they'd sneak us in, but students could get in free to some shows, or for very cheap and we'd stand at the back. We always found a way in, one way or another.

We were determined to find some fun after classes too. We were still underage of course, but Claire looked a lot older than us. She was tall and had long blonde hair, so we'd send her into the offy to get bottles of White Lightning, Mad Dog 20/20, or whatever rot we drank. That was rare though, especially in the first year of college, where we would be dancing 12 hours a day. We wanted to make a good impression and do our best, so we didn't go to pubs much.

I grew up in a binge-drinking culture so if we did drink, we thought it was fine to drink until the point of obliteration. I was never a massive boozer back then though. I got drunk a few times with my mates from school in the park, or at the odd house party. On my seventeenth birthday, we did drink a load of Diamond White, which resulted in me spending the night with my head in a bucket! That put me off for a good while – I still can't drink cider.

I was having the time of my life in Sidcup, but it was also a bit of a wake-up call. For a lot of people coming from the regional dance schools, you've been the big fish in the little pond, one of the most talented people in that environment. Then you get to a

"Grown-Up" respected performing arts college with the cream of the crop. I was still full of confidence, but I was never a favourite of the teachers. And I think this knocked my belief in my abilities a little, those three years that I spent at Doreen Bird.

I was never troublesome, but I wonder if there was a bit of prejudice because of my background. There were lots of girls from wealthy families who had been to the Royal Ballet School or to Elmhurst Ballet School. They were well spoken; they knew the rules. I wasn't naughty but I was a bit of a scrappy Northerner, you know. I was working class and I didn't speak "properly".

I was frustrated because I really did believe in my ability, and I didn't feel I was given a fair crack of the whip. On the other hand, I wish I had taken advantage of all the opportunities, worked a little bit harder, and raved a little bit less in those later years. While we were very well behaved in the first year, there was a bit of going out all night in the second year. I think if the teachers had encouraged me more, I might have buckled down more. But because I wasn't a favourite, my attention strayed, which is a shame.

It was in the second year that me and Rachel moved out of the Hesketts'. We ended up renting a room from a professional couple who were never there, so we really lucked out. They had this lovely house with a fancy kitchen, and we had this amazing place pretty much to ourselves.

During the summer break after our first year, me, Rachel, Ruth and Jo (another good mate) went on our first holiday without any parents. It was the summer of 1991 and Dad arranged for us to go stay in L'Estartit at the northern end of the Costa Brava. Being broke students, we didn't have the money to fly to Europe, so it was a lovely 27 hours squashed in a coach from somewhere up North to Spain, with a ferry break in-between. We didn't care though; the hellish journey was all part of the fun.

It was there on the Costa Brava that we discovered rave and house music. There was a square where all the clubs and bars were, and everyone was outside dancing all night to this weird, mad music. Rachel and I fell in love with it. We had the best time, and really bonded during that holiday. We're all still good friends although we don't get to see each other much: Rachel lives in Ibiza and these days is a very Zen and brilliant yoga teacher. Ruth is in Canada and Jo in Berlin.

By this point, the music was quite commercial, so we missed the years of raving in fields, sadly. I remember The Prodigy's "Charly" and Felix's "Don't You Want Me" playing in the clubs then. I was a massive fan of The Prodigy, which is funny because one of my mates, Natalie Appleton from the band All Saints, went on to marry Liam Howlett from The Prodigy. And bizarrely, we beat them and The Chemical Brothers at the MTV Awards in New York 1997 for Best Dance video! I still love that band. I saw them at Ally Pally, at one of the last gigs they did before Keith Flint, the band's frontman, passed away. His death in 2019 was incredibly sad. I'm so grateful I got to see them play with him again. The first time I'd seen The Prodigy was at the clubbing Mecca Mr Smiths in Warrington, around '91 or '92. I was right near the front with my mates and Keith grabbed my hand. It was my claim to fame for years to come.

They're an amazing band. Alongside Faithless, The Chemical Brothers and Fatboy Slim, they took dance music from being a bloke with headphones behind some turntables to full live band, festival-headline acts. They were so entertaining, so theatrical, and high-energy and punk.

As soon as we got home from Spain, we found the hotspots around London and Essex and spent most of our weekends there, dancing all night long in our trackies, Fila boots, and long-sleeved striped t-shirts.

Somehow (our age, let's face it!), we were up and at the ballet barre at 8.30 am every Monday morning. We had a great jazz dance teacher called Adrian Allsop, who always used current dance music in class. We thought he was the coolest teacher ever! There's a promotional video from college that was unearthed by *TFI Friday* many years ago. It shows me ferociously practising the isolation section of one of his dances while my other classmates just sit there.

I was at it again: practice, practice, practice.

It was around this time, in my second year of college, that I started to think seriously about the possibility of singing. Until then it had been a vague fantasy, an idea without shape. I knew I wanted to be like Madonna, but I hadn't really thought through what form that might take, or how I might do it.

That year we entered an inter-college competition, and I chose to perform a song called "Chief Cook and Bottle Washer" from Broadway's *The Rink*, originally sung by Liza Minnelli.

I rehearsed hard. The performance on the day, at Palace Studio, was in front of my college mates and a line of stern-looking judges. There's a part of the song where it goes into a kick-line and, for the first time as a performer, I felt and saw the audience sit up. I felt this profound connection, suddenly. I'd never, ever had that with dance. Perhaps it's because as a singer you're facing the audience, you're looking at them, you're almost seeking out their souls! With dance, you have something similar, but it's more… internal somehow. I felt as though I'd been electrocuted, almost, so strong was this energy between myself and everyone watching.

I can pinpoint that as the *exact* moment when I thought, wholeheartedly, *"I want to be a singer"*. Until then, I'd thrown about various ideas around dance, the West End, Madonna, and Kate Bush. It all seemed to come together at that moment. Dancing. Singing. *Performing*. There's something about connecting with people in this really special way when you sing that began there and has stayed with me throughout my career. I got an incredible feeling when I danced, but this was something new, something deeper, and somehow richer.

It's the goosebumps, hair on the back of your neck moment. It's magical.

Before long, I would find out just how magical.

. . .

A couple more weeks, and I might not ever have been in the Spice Girls. I graduated from Doreen Bird in 1993 and I was suddenly out in the big wide world. I was full of excitement and optimism for the future. "This is it, life is about to start," I'd say to Rachel as we dashed around London to various auditions.

I'd managed to get myself an agent, albeit one based in a not particularly salubrious office above a shop in Streatham, South London. A major league player this person was not! I did some very random auditions. Me and Lee (my friend in the year above at college) once got sent out for a musical written by an Elton John impersonator. Yes, it was as weird as it sounds. We had to drive miles outside London to meet this person who had written a show about Elton and was looking for dancers and singers.

It didn't come to anything.

My plan had been to do something, anything on the West End, and I tried out for numerous roles. I had yet to find success though. Zoë, my friend from home, ended up getting cast in *The Phantom of the Opera* – she was the youngest ever person to play Christine. But for me… nothing.

I'd been recalled for *Cats* several times, which was always a buzz because you'd audition in the theatre itself on Drury Lane. It was exciting just to stand on that stage and dance to "Jellicle Ball", which is one of the mad T.S. Eliot-based songs in the show. If you were recalled, you'd get to sing, which I did once or twice.

But I was still waiting for that, "You've got the part" call. I hadn't heard anything yet and I was getting increasingly nervous. College was over, which meant no more grants, no more rent, no more dance classes. I needed to nail an audition. I needed some money. I did the odd bit of session singing and a bit of cabaret here and there, though it was badly paid, if it was paid at all. I took any scraps I could, but I was hungry for so much more.

I was living with a bunch of dancers from college in a three-bed in Sidcup. I had the box room, which was tiny, with a single bed, a chest of drawers, and a poster of Robbie Williams on my wall. I didn't have a telly. Or anything much. I didn't own anything really, apart from my trusty old red Toshiba boombox and my bootleg cassettes that I kept in an old box: Madonna, Five Star, Terence Trent D'Arby (who now goes by the name Sananda Maitreya) and Eternal, as well as older classics by Dusty Springfield and Gloria Estefan and Miami Sound Machine. They were my worldly possessions.

The flat was basic. We bought scabby plates and cups and cutlery from the charity shop, and we'd handwash everything. If we had classes or auditions, we'd handwash our skanky old leotards then dry them off a bit with a hand-spinner. We'd put them out to dry on the radiators and because everyone (except me) smoked, our clothes absolutely stank. So gross!

We were all signing on. The Sidcup dole office was full of trained students trying to get work, so they were used to us coming in. Because nothing was happening for us, there was pressure to give up and to go and get a "proper" job.

There's nothing wrong with that, but that wasn't an option for me.

The challenge of a dancer once you leave college is to maintain your ability by continuing to dance. But you're so broke you can't afford classes, so now you *really* need to book a job. And it's expensive. Travelling into London from Sidcup costs a fiver, plus buses, lunch and so on. If you break your pointe shoes, you need new ones, which are about 30 quid. You'd need new ones around once a month. When you're on the dole, you're getting £35 a week so there was nothing spare. We'd get to Sidcup train station, sidle up to the ticket machine, and buy a child's ticket because it was so much cheaper. We'd run through dead quick in case anyone spotted us. Did I pay for *every* fare on those old London buses where you jumped on at the back? Maybe not. We had to make ends meet however we could.

And, despite having many auditions, I couldn't seem to book a job. It was so frustrating. Before college, I'd been the star of the show, completely self-assured in my talent. College took me down a peg or two, and now real life threatened to do the same. I don't remember being anywhere near feelings of depression, but the foundation was perhaps a little shakier than it had been. I started to wonder, right at the periphery of my consciousness: *"Am I good enough? Can I do this?"*

Dance and performance had always been a safe space for me, the safest part of my life. When I was sometimes insecure in my home life, I put on my pointe shoes and headed to the studio.

I won so many competitions and prizes, I lost count. It was a clear exchange for me: if I felt sad or isolated at home, dance made me happy and confident.

Now, here I was, auditioning in London and nobody wanted me.

. . .

One cold February day, Rachel and I went to Danceworks to audition for a cruise. For the last couple of months, I'd seen a lot of my mates do the same thing, which was to try out for various auditions, get none of them, audition for a cruise ship, get that and quite literally head off into the sunset. I was out of money, signing on and with no prospect of any cash or work on the horizon. I *still* hadn't heard back from *Cats*. The foundations were starting to crumble a little more. "Fine," I said to Rachel, "I'll do a bloody cruise audition."

I was vaguely aware of someone walking around, handing out pieces of paper that appeared to be an ad photocoped from *The Stage*. They chucked one down on our table and Rachel slid it across to me:

WANTED

R.U. 18–23 WITH THE ABILITY
TO SING/DANCE
R.U. STREETWISE, OUTGOING,
AMBITIOUS & DEDICATED

HEART MANAGEMENT LTD
are a widely successful
Music Industry Management Consortium
currently forming a choreographed, Singing/Dancing,
all Female Pop Act for a Record Recording Deal.

OPEN AUDITION
DANCEWORKS, 16 Balderton Street,
FRIDAY 4TH MARCH
11.00am – 5.30pm
PLEASE BRING SHEET MUSIC
OR BACKING CASSETTE
Heart Management Ltd – (0276) 476676 / 476526

"That's it," I exclaimed immediately, "that's what I'm going to do." It sounds mad to say now, but as soon as I saw that audition notice, I knew I was going to get it. "This is destined to be," I told Rachel, who laughed and said, "Well, go for it!"

The foundations plastered themselves back up, the doubt sidled away, my confidence returned.

The morning of the audition, I woke up (stinking of fags) and turned to my picture of Robbie tacked up on the wall. "Melanie," I said to myself decisively, "you can do this. You *have* to do this."

I got dressed in my smartest outfit, a knitted lilac crop top and some tight black trousers. That was very dressed up for me back then. Not only was I a dancer, but as a raver, I still lived in trackies, as was the style of the day.

There were some butterflies that morning as I walked up to the train station, which took me into Charing Cross. But the nerves started to settle as I felt this weird calm running through me. I heard myself saying, *"This is the one, this is what you want to do, and you can do it."* It was the exact same feeling I'd had when Rachel first slid the audition notice over to me. I was nervous but confident that it was going to happen. It's a feeling that I almost can't explain. I just *knew*.

The audition was packed. Danceworks has several floors and there were girls queuing all the way up and down the stairs. There was nothing to do but wait.

There was someone else there on the stairs that day that I recognised, a girl who I first met at an audition for *Oklahoma!* in 1993. When I say we'd met, we'd gone to the audition, been given some choreography to learn, and were then asked to perform it in groups.

As we were breaking into our own spaces to rehearse, there was this noise. Remember, this is 1994, so no one had phones then, apart from city boys who carried around those huge Motorola brick phones. Everyone's looking around, wondering *what's that noise?*, and here's that girl. "Sorry, excuse me," she says. She pops open her bag and heaves the phone to her ear, "Hello? Oh yes, hello, how are you?"

That's how I first met Victoria Adams, as she was known at the time. The funny thing is, I had an audition for Laine Theatre Arts, the college Victoria went to, but after I got into Doreen Bird I didn't attend it because the expense was too much for Mum and Dad to go back down South again. We could have been college mates!

After an hour, perhaps more, I finally got called into studio three. Me and 40 other hopeful young girls.

The audition was being run by Chris Herbert and his dad, Bob, who had a management company called Heart. Chris was in his early twenties and was a tall, slim, young guy. His dad was a cross between a gentleman and a geezer, very *Miami Vice*: all tanned, casual suit and smart loafers, yet well spoken.

Chris and Bob were there and so was Shelley, Chris's stylist girlfriend. It was the cliché audition scenario – think *X Factor*.

There's three people sitting behind a desk, silently appraising you and occasionally taking notes or murmuring to each other. You try to ignore the fact that people are judging you, your ability and talent, how you look, your body shape and size, your hair, your clothes, and your personality. Every bit of you is exposed and while you do get used to it, and you learn to control the nerves, it's still something that fills me with dread. When I auditioned for *Blood Brothers* in 2009 it had been years since I'd had to put myself in that position. It was terrifying.

For the first round, they played Eternal's hit single, "Stay" (luckily, I knew the track well, thanks to my bootleg tape!) and we had to dance. "That's it," said Bob, or maybe Chris. "We want to see you move, just freestyle."

That initial audition was very superficial. It was about how people looked and a little bit how they moved. I chucked myself around and when they pointed to the people who were staying, I was one of them. I was through the first round!

So now I got to sing.

The ad had said to bring sheet music or a backing cassette to sing along to. Being at a performing arts college, all the songs we learnt were musical theatre, so the only sheet music I had was for *Cats* and other shows, which hardly screamed streetwise pop star (mind you, Victoria performed "Mein Herr" from *Cabaret* at hers, and she still got in!).

In a panic, I had rung Mum. "I've got an audition," I told her, "but I need sheet music. What have you or Den got?" She had a load from being in bands, so she ran through what she had. "That's the one," I said when she got to "I'm So Excited" by the Pointer Sisters. "I'll sing that."

I went in and sang "I'm So Excited" and then they asked me a few questions. "I was originally gonna go into the theatre," I said, sitting on a chair with my arms folded, "but I'd much rather do this."

"Thank you, we'll be in touch," said Chris and I smiled and left.

That was it.

I tried to put it out of my mind but that feeling kept coming back. I was confident I'd get a call-back.

Around this time, I had recurring bouts of tonsillitis that would strike without warning and put me in bed for days on end, sometimes over a week.

After the audition, I was struck down again with a severe bout. I couldn't get out of bed, I couldn't speak. I was sweating under the sheets one day when the landline rang. It was someone from Heart Management, telling me I had a call-back for the girl band.

I was ecstatic, but also... ill. I took down the details of the next audition and rang Mum in a panic. "I've got a call-back for that band, but Mum, listen to me, I can't sing." "Have you got a number for them?" she asked me, and I read it out to her, croaking and sweating.

She told me she'd ring them, and I staggered back to bed, drifting in and out of sleep in a hazy fog. She finally called back a few hours later: "I told them you're sick, that you can't do another audition this week, and asked them to wait a few days. Melanie, I'm sorry, they said no, they said they can't wait."

They told Mum if anything changed, they'd be in touch, but not to hold my breath.

I was so upset. I'd been absolutely certain that this was the one, this audition was going to lead somewhere. I'd felt it in my gut, but clearly my instincts had let me down. It had all come to nothing. I was back to square one and I felt complete and utter despair.

I moped around for a while, but eventually I dug deep and got myself back on the circuit, going back and forth to London for more auditions.

I couldn't believe it when the phone rang a few weeks later. "We'd like to see you again," said the person on the other end of the line. Another girl hadn't worked out and so they'd like to see me, if I was better. I couldn't believe it! I had a second chance.

The audition was held in the late spring at Nomis Studios on Sinclair Road in Hammersmith, West London. After fretting about what to wear, I went with a black top, black skirt, and trainers. Hair tied back. I took a deep breath and walked in. Chris and Bob were there with another man and four other girls. "I'll introduce you to the others, Melanie," said Chris. "This is Geri, Michelle, Victoria, and Melanie – another Melanie. This one is Melanie Brown."

Melanie Brown was really cool. She was wearing a red Varsity jacket with white leather sleeves and a Kangol hat, backwards with all her hair out. "Hiya Melanie," she grinned, in her broad Leeds accent. We were both from up North. My dad had lived in Leeds for a few years by that point, so I immediately felt an affinity with her. I liked her straight away. Between us, we somehow settled upon me going by Melanie or Mel C and Melanie became Mel B.

Victoria, I recognised from the audition, but she was more low-key than Geri and Mel B, who from that first moment were both clearly very outgoing, very confident young women. Victoria had been recalled after another Mel – Mel Coloma – was swapped out because it was felt her vocals were too overpowering.

Victoria was a bit more middle-class compared to me, Geri and Mel B. Victoria's dad, Tony, had done well with a building company. They were far from landed gentry, but they did have a pool, unimaginable at the time. Victoria was quite quiet initially, but she soon came out of herself. She's a very funny person with a sharp sense of humour. She would also be the one who would keep us down to earth a bit, because she was ambitious but practical with it. She was the anchor of the band in some ways. I always forget this, but when we first met her, we always called Victoria "Tor" right up until the end of the nineties. I can't imagine her being called that now. She's very much a Victoria, although Mel B always calls her Vic, which I'm sure is just to annoy her!

Geri was immediately brilliantly eccentric. She had her hair in bunches and this pink mohair jumper. She was wearing a fifties-style bra that made her boobs all pointy. She struck me as being quite wacky which, it turned out, was the case! She'd missed the first audition and somehow blagged it onto the next. She talked ten to the dozen. She barely took a breath.

What to say about Michelle? I'll put it this way: if she'd stayed in the band, she would have been Posh Spice because she actually was posh!

Bob and Chris had some experience in the music industry. Chris had gone to school with Matt and Luke Goss, and it was Bob who saw potential in the twins and financed the beginnings of Bros (or *Gloss*, as they were then known). They parted ways from Bob, however, when the twins and their bassist Craig Logan went with Tom Watkins, who had managed the Pet Shop Boys.

The other member of the Heart Management team was called Chic Murphy and he was the man with the money. Chic was an

Arthur Daley type, like he'd just stepped off the set of a *Kray Twins* movie. He was a tall, white-haired Cockney geezer in his late fifties who was constantly puffing on ciggies. He loved to tell us how he'd managed "one of the Three Degrees – the good one!" but we had no idea if that was true. He was a bit shady. I don't know if it was the tattoos on his ears, but we decided not to ask too many questions about Chic's background.

I'd been asked to learn "Signed, Sealed, Delivered (I'm Yours)" by Stevie Wonder – like I needed to learn that!

"You sounded like Elvis," Geri told me afterwards. I guess I was still getting over my tonsillitis!

Chic, Chris, and Bob were enthusiastic and wanted us to spend some time working together. "From Sunday, we'll put you up in a guesthouse in Surrey for the week. See how you get on."

I was so confused. *"Hang on, am I in the band?"* I thought to myself. We fired questions at them: What about our jobs? Was it paid? What would happen at the end of the week?

Chris, Bob, and Chic had a plan for us. They had witnessed the success of boy bands like Take That, East 17, New Kids on the Block, Wham! and Duran Duran and wondered about the potential for a girl group. At that time British and American R&B girl bands like Eternal, TLC and En Vogue were doing really well, but there hadn't been a pop girl band to break through since The Bangles, Bananarama and The Go-Go's in the eighties.

Chris and Bob (very perceptively) saw a gap in the market and decided to fill it. It was time for a pop girl band to rival Take That.

• • •

We turned up at the guesthouse that following Sunday bursting with excitement. The house was full of insurance salesmen, and we were all sharing a tiny room. Glamorous it was not, but we didn't care. Seeing the girls again brought back that funny feeling I'd had when I saw the ad. I just knew something was going to come from this band. I wasn't sure what, but I knew it was going to take me somewhere.

That week was a real bonding one for us. We were total strangers, yet we wanted the same thing: to succeed. We had the same dream too: to be part of the world's biggest ever pop band and we spent hours talking about what that might look like.

Chris, Bob and Chic kept us down to earth though. We were all in the band – for now – but we weren't given a contract or any money. They were running the show: this was their band and we had to follow the rules. They had already chucked out two girls, maybe one of us would be next.

We spent a week in the nearby council-run Trinity Studios learning a mid-tempo ballad called "Take Me Away", where we tried (and failed!) to get our voices to blend with the help of vocal coach Pepi Lemer, a small, very glamorous, designer-clad "luvvie" who had worked in jazz, musical theatre and panto. Bob and Chris had told Pepi she had a few weeks to get us ready for a showcase. "I need months, not weeks, dahlings," she apparently told them when she first heard us. We were so far off being ready, but Pepi was a determined character. She was incredibly patient with us and would do anything to help us find our harmonies, wherever they may have been hiding.

At the end of that week, we performed what we had. After we'd finished, there was some discussion over the fact that we hadn't chosen a lead singer. We had kept the vocals totally equal. "It's just how we've done it," Mel B shrugged, staring Chris, Bob and Chic down. They begrudgingly gave in and that was the first step of us bonding as a group. It was just a small thing, but it was the beginning of us starting to steer things the way *we* wanted, not how the music industry men around us wanted us to be.

Chic, the financial backer of dubious background, had an empty house in Maidenhead that we could all live in, he told us. The plan was that us five girls would live together in Maidenhead and see how things developed over the next few months. Whether it was to be weeks or months was unclear, but we had a bit of time to get ourselves sorted before moving into 38 Boyn Hill Road.

We spent hours on the phone to each other before we moved into Boyn Hill Road, imagining what it was going to be like in a pop group, what we thought of Chris, Bob, and each other. We were buzzing.

We all felt the same thing: that this was the start of something special.

• • •

The fun started in the summer of 1994 at our new home on a quiet, lower-to-middle class Maidenhead estate. It was a fifties or sixties semi-detached red brick, with white wood slats under the window and a red door that opened onto a porch. There wasn't much in the local area apart from a pub and a shop.

The carpets were blue, the curtains were pink and there was a lot of second-hand wooden furniture. It was far from a palace, but it was big, and it had loads of light. We ran excitedly around the house, looking in all the rooms and sizing them up as our future bedrooms. It looked like most of us would be sharing as there were only three bedrooms. "I'm the oldest so I get this one," shouted Geri, dumping her stuff onto the single bed in the tiny box room that would be hers and hers alone.

At the back of the house there was a room with two single beds, which became Michelle and Victoria's room. There was a little family bathroom and then the front bedroom. It had pink walls, a red carpet, and a double bed with a single bed next to it.

There was a pause as we clocked the two beds and Mel B looked at me. "You have it, I'm fine," I shrugged, keen to please her.

When I think about little moments like this, I can see that I created a rod for my own back. I never stood up for myself and said, "Oh, can I have this, please", "I'd really prefer not to do that". I just let everyone run around me and had whatever was left. That's not to blame anyone but me – I'm responsible. Besides, I'd had a single bed my whole life to this point. But for an easy life, I decided I'd make do.

For a joke, Geri brought us a red lightbulb, which earned our room the nickname of "the sex room". I put up a sign on the door that read, "Don't come in, I'm snogging Robbie". Cringe! Alongside a Take That poster and a multitude of Mel B's makeup and creams (I think my beauty products consisted solely of a cleanser and some deodorant) there wasn't space for anything else in that little room. We plastered the fridge with pictures of Robbie, Jason Orange, George Michael, Ryan Giggs, Keanu Reeves, and stuck up a massive *Reservoir Dogs* film poster in the kitchen.

Although we were initially quite shy around each other, we got to know each other very quickly. Mel B took dead long baths everyday, singing Mary J. Blige songs at the top of her lungs. She never locked the door, nor did Geri, so I very quickly had to get used to a lot of nakedness in that house! Within weeks though we were all leaving the door open, wandering in and out for chats as someone was doing a wee. Or worse! Even Victoria, clearly more uncomfortable with this liberated set-up, got used to it. We were all girls in it together.

I was the tidy one and would go around cleaning up after the others. Geri was the designated driver because I couldn't drive, Mel B didn't own a car and I don't *think* Michelle drove. Victoria did have a new Renault Clio (always the posh one) and I sometimes got in with her, but Geri's battered Fiat Uno is the Spicemobile I remember travelling in the most.

Our lives for the next few months consisted of that house and the rehearsal studios in Woking, around 30 miles away from our house in Boyn Hill Road. Trinity Studios was a large building, with a sprawling hall where they had Bingo nights and smaller rooms where we rehearsed. It was a bit old and faded, and permanently cold, even in the summer.

We would arrive at Trinity for 10 am five days a week and, apart from the two days a week when Pepi would be on hand for vocal coaching, Chris and Bob left us to it. They wanted us to put the work in of our own accord; this wasn't school, and they weren't teachers. The harder we worked, the better "Touch" would be. Yes, Touch, that was our first name. We were never 100% on it but it was a start. Touch, as in the London slang, "What a touch", meaning something great was happening. You see where we were going, but it was never going to last, was it?!

Chris and Bob very much ran the show though. We won the battle of not having a lead singer, but they wanted us to all dress the same, like all girl and boy bands did back then. Given we were five very different people, we weren't too keen on this. None of us particularly loved the songs either. "We're Gonna Make It Happen" was catchy enough, as was "Take Me Away", but they weren't songs that spoke to us. But we didn't think we had much choice. We got our heads down and tried to make it perfect.

There was no choreographer on hand, so Mel B and I led the way. We'd both had a lot of experience and were confident with dance. It wasn't always easy teaching the other girls the moves, but we worked really hard, Geri most of all. She was the only one of us that hadn't done drama or dance school or been trained in the Arts. I must give it to Geri though; she was very determined and had no problem with working hard. While we all stopped for a break Geri would carry on, patiently working on the routines. I would often stay with her, going over the moves again and again until she got it. The band had to be perfect, and I was prepared to do anything, and help anyone, to achieve that. We were all excited and totally driven.

All of us, except one.

We were having an afternoon break one day, which we usually spent having a drink, maybe a snack and going over what we'd done that day. "Where's Michelle?" said Mel B, looking around, in vain, for the fifth member of Touch. We peeked our heads outside and, lo and behold, there was Michelle, outside sunbathing – again.

Michelle, it turned out, loved her vitamin D. We'd be learning a routine and she'd be outside sunning herself. "She's just not committed, it's not good enough," Geri would mutter. Michelle had a place at university that September, which she was still deciding whether to take. She also had a Saturday job at Harrods and came from a wealthy family. We started to get the impression that she didn't want it as badly as we did.

Mel B had a long talk with her and, to be fair, she did get a bit better after that, but her cards were marked. We had a couple of weeks off at one point, and it was during that time that Chic, Bob, and Chris called her and told her she wouldn't be going back to Boyn Hill Road. Michelle was out of Touch. It was brutal.

You could feel sorry for Michelle that she missed out on this opportunity, but I think she's fine about it. She's said since it just wasn't for her. Michelle was too different from the rest of us, her mind was elsewhere. She wasn't convinced that Touch would take off and seemed keener on taking the place at uni. She lacked the passion and energy that Geri, Victoria, Mel B, and I had.

It didn't occur to us or to Chris and Bob to keep Touch as a four-piece. We knew we needed a fifth girl, and the search was on.

We scouted the streets of Maidenhead and met a couple of girls (including another one called Melanie, which was an automatic no). Then Pepi announced one day: "There's a girl I know. She studied at Sylvia Young stage school. Blonde. Great vocals. Let's see about her, shall we?"

CHAPTER FIVE

Nowhere To Run

The moment that Emma Bunton came along was the moment that we became the powerhouse that went on to rule the world. Her arrival changed everything.

We were all excited to meet Emma. We turned up to meet this stranger at Maidenhead train station, and there she was, with her mum, Pauline. She was so cute, this little blonde 17-year-old with big, blue, innocent eyes. She was wearing, no lie, a babydoll dress, knee-high socks, and platform shoes.

She looked so young, even though we were only a couple of years older than her.

It sounds ridiculous but from that moment the dynamic changed. It was magical. Although we were still called Touch, that was the day that the Spice Girls were born. That's when we felt like a real band. We may have been put together via an advert in *The Stage*, but with Emma's arrival, we started to find our own voices.

Emma had a bit more about her than Michelle, in the sense she was really driven and knew, like us, what she wanted. She just felt like one of us and we were certain we'd found the last piece in the jigsaw puzzle. We had a sense of completion. We felt, and in fact were, invincible. It wasn't a question of *if* we were going to make it, but *when*.

We were all signing on, and eventually we managed to persuade Chris and Bob to give us a bit of cash, the grand sum of £60 a week each. Considering we lived rent-free, this wasn't too bad. But we were always broke. Chic had put in a payphone, but we quickly figured out a way to cheat it. We just unplugged the payphone and put a normal landline in! Luckily, we moved out before Chic noticed. He must have had a massive bill at some point.

We had a lot of adventures in Geri's battered old Uno. During that half-hour drive from our house to Trinity, we took our lives into our hands each time Geri got behind the wheel. You see, Geri spent very little time looking out of the windscreen. She'd be turning around to talk to us or looking through the rear-view, waving her hands about, putting her lippy on. That was Geri: everything was always at a million miles an hour, she seemed to have thousands of thoughts running around her head at any one time.

We loved going to Windsor at the weekends (once again taking our lives into our hands as Geri bombed along the M4). Often, Victoria would go home on a Friday night to see her boyfriend at the time, and Emma would head back to her mum in Finchley too. But Geri, Mel B and I would drive over to Windsor on a Saturday where, for the very first time I had "posh" ice cream; Häagen-Dazs had a store there and I ordered my inaugural Cookies & Cream. What a revelation!

We didn't go out much – Maidenhead wasn't quite the epicentre of clubland back then – but sometimes on a Wednesday night we'd head to the town's finest club, The Avenue, for student night. We'd tell the door people that we were in a pop group called Touch and that we were going to be massive, and they'd let us in for free.

We swanned around, thinking we were the bee's knees. I'm sure people thought we were mad but collectively we had the confidence to pull it off. When the five of us were together, we felt unstoppable.

• • •

A few months in, the honeymoon period started to wear off slightly. Naturally, we were initially on our best behaviour, but slowly people's personalities started to emerge. As they always do. We were five girls in our very early twenties – in fact, Emma was still a teen. We had been randomly put together and we all had our own ideas and thoughts about the band. We were also in each other's pockets twenty-four-seven. Inevitably, this led to some tensions.

Geri quickly emerged as wanting to be the leader of the group. She struggled with the performance side of things much more than the rest of us (Emma was a trained performer too). Perhaps to make up for that, Geri took on the role of pseudo-manager: she had ideas on how we should dress, how we should sound and who we should be. Mel B had strong ideas as well, and they didn't always align with Geri's. Neither of them was afraid to express how they felt, and tempers flared.

Geri's ideas also clashed with Chris and Bob's, but to be fair, she was often right. Even though she was only a year or two older than the rest of us, I always had the sense that Geri was on borrowed time. She didn't have a moment to waste, there was an urgency that meant she'd bump heads with people, but this is what ultimately propelled the group forward to success. Not to say our success rested on Geri, but with her in an unofficial management role, and with the rest of us physically and vocally able to bring to life what we envisioned, we were invincible.

There were other issues too, such as homesickness. Emma had never lived away from home, and really missed her mum, whereas Geri, me and Mel B were used to being away from families and doing our own thing. Living in such close quarters didn't help. We'd get tired and frustrated with each other, but obviously, five people living and working together is going to be a bumpy ride.

Some of the girls were very confident and weren't afraid to make their opinions heard (Mel B and Geri) and the rest of us were relatively quiet and happy to go with the flow (Emma, Victoria, and I). Mel B and Geri could be very bossy and often Mel B would get frustrated with Geri doing a move or harmony wrong. From the beginning, I assumed the role of peacemaker, trying to calm things down and getting them to see each other's perspectives. Emma would often be the voice of reason too. Victoria was good at cutting through the tension with some perfectly timed droll remark.

I grew up with three brothers and I was used to scrapping with the boys in the playground, so I wasn't a total walkover. I had my limits, whether that was Stuart in the playground, or that girl from school talking about my mum. I would let things go for a while, but once I was pushed over the edge, I'd have to say my piece.

It wasn't ever anything major back then; we'd have silly rows over the cleaning or who'd run up the leccy bill or because someone had taken clothing or food without asking. That sort of stuff.

I'm not a go-getter or a networker like some of the other girls, but I was really happy onstage and in the studio. Give me a microphone and I'll happily take the lead. Emma was also confident in her abilities and was the backbone of the band in many ways. She was the baby, but she also held us together. She's a lot tougher than you think. Victoria was another good calming force and always had a good sense for business. I always wished she was more confident as a performer – she's so much better than she thinks or allows people to believe.

Geri and Mel B, from day one, were both very, very determined to succeed. As we all were, but those two had that extra bit of steel inside of them. Their personalities ensured that this band would be a success. Whatever it took.

We needed these different aspects of each other. That's what the band was about, it's why we were a success. It was a miracle of alchemy and chance and opportunity; it would be something future pop impresarios would go on to try to replicate, but the magic with us was that it was just there. Somehow, it simply existed, and it did, pretty much, from day one.

Although we were all so driven and knew, without question, that we could and would succeed, maybe we didn't acknowledge each other's insecurities and how that sometimes impacted our behaviours towards each other.

It's always easy in hindsight to know what you would have done differently, but I think if we'd been more aware of that at the time, we could have saved ourselves a lot of pain later. Power struggles, passive (and sometimes aggressive!) behaviours crept in which became unhealthy, for all of as individually and as a band.

· · ·

Chic Murphy's home was south of Maidenhead in a town called Bray, on the River Thames. To me, a working-class girl from the North West, it was the poshest house I'd ever been to. It was detached and set back off the street with loads of bedrooms, bidets in the ensuite (neither of which I'd ever seen in my life) and a swimming pool in the garden that backed onto the Thames. We loved going to Chic's place to use his pool and sunbathe. It was a luxury that none of us (bar maybe Victoria) were used to.

He invited us over one hot sunny Sunday. I laid down my towel on a sun lounger and soaked up the rays. After weeks of intensive rehearsals and being locked in the studio and that claustrophobic (and often messy!) house, it felt good to take a break. I half-listened as the girls talked to Chic about who had done dance classes and gymnastics at school and if we could incorporate any of that into our choreography. "I can do a round-off back-flip," I said, jumping up to show them how it was done.

I landed on both feet and lifted my arms up, triumphantly. Just as I shouted, "Taa-dah," Chic started coughing. "I'm surprised you can fucking do backflips with thighs like that," he said, stubbing out another ciggie.

I stood frozen in place, the smile slipping from my face. I felt sick. I turned to the other girls, who were looking anywhere but me. I was mortified. My whole face burned, the embarrassment spreading around my body. I tried to blink back the tears that were starting to sting my eyes. Forcing a smile back onto my face, I sat back on the lounger. No one said a word.

Victoria later told me that Chic had pulled her aside and said something similar about her weight. "Look at you in that bikini. You need to lose a few pounds, love."

That night, I lay awake as Mel B slept peacefully across from me. My mind was racing: *I dance all the time, I'm active, I'm a size 10, maybe a 12. Am I not seeing things the way they truly are? Am I overweight?*

If I was overweight, could that stop me from being a pop star? Each night after rehearsals we'd sit around and imagine what it would be like when we made it: playing on *Top of the Pops*, getting on the cover of *Smash Hits*, travelling the world, and performing our songs to millions of fans.

If I really wanted to make this thing work, then I had to do everything I could to make it happen.

I'd never had to worry about my weight before. I did gain a little in my late teens living away from home, when there was none of Mum's home-cooked meals. And of course, discovering the pub didn't help! But I was always so active, I didn't worry too much about it – every now and then I'd just cut down a bit and eat smaller portions. I maybe wouldn't go to the chippy on the way home from a night out.

Chic's words spun my head around. I've always loved my food and I have a pretty big appetite, but was I greedy? Was I "fat"?

None of us had the healthiest of diets at that time but mostly because we were skint, and people weren't as knowledgeable then about nutrition as they seem to be today. No avo on sourdough for us, it was all Super Noodles, instant mash and jacket potato and beans. Geri was the most food conscious at that time. She knew which foods were protein or carbs and, in the early nineties, fat of any kind was the enemy. Geri was slim and careful about what she ate, but I didn't think much of it. It wouldn't have occurred to me then she might have issues with food.

We didn't realise it at the time, but that first year in Boyn Hill Road, Geri was really struggling with bulimia and body dysmorphia. Over the Christmas of 1994, she confided in Mel B that it had gotten particularly bad, and she had taken herself to hospital to address her eating. We'd been given a few weeks off, and that's when she checked herself into Watford General Hospital.

The rest of us had no idea what was happening. Geri did ring me before I came back from Widnes, where I'd been home for the holiday. "Oh, just so you know I've put on a bit of weight over Christmas." And I said, "Yeah, of course, we all have, don't be soft, it's Christmas."

When I first saw her after the break, I was shocked because her appearance had changed so dramatically in such a short space of time. They'd encouraged her to form healthy eating habits while in hospital, so she was finally getting the nutrition her body needed.

At the time, to my mind, we were five girls who were having the most amazing time trying to make our dreams come true. But of course, we all arrived in Maidenhead with our own histories, issues, struggles and traumas. When we got together, it wasn't long after the first anniversary of Geri's dad's death. She had been so close to him and to have lost him at the age of 21 was, of course, going to bring up a lot of sadness and struggle for her.

The thing with Geri is that she's very ambitious and driven. She was always so energetic and outspoken but actually at the time – and I don't think I would have had the emotional maturity to realise this – she was very vulnerable. She's only older than us by a couple of years, but she felt very much our "elder"; she'd worked in Turkey as a presenter, she was studying English Lit at university at the time, she'd had her own place with a boyfriend, so we looked up to her. She fell into that role of being a leader because of her personality but also because she was more experienced in life. Yet she was a sensitive soul, despite her confident exterior, and like others of us in the band, really struggled with thinking about her weight in a healthy way.

Many of us were going through similar things at that time, not least became of the wider cultural messages we were receiving about the aesthetic of thinness. Let's face it, pop stars at the time were all slim, if not skinny. All of them. Actors and models too. I know that we as a band further promoted this image. We didn't know any different.

The idea of "heroin chic" came through in the nineties with models like Gia Carangi and Kate Moss. As sick as it sounds the desired aesthetic was to look like a heroin addict, i.e. to be rail-thin, bags under the eyes, pale and androgynous, in opposition to what had come before: wholesome women like Cindy Crawford and Elle Macpherson. At the same time, this extreme "heroin chic" look was reflected in Calvin Klein ad campaigns and films like *The Basketball Diaries* and *Trainspotting*.

Thank goodness that's changed today, and we celebrate curvier bodies now, because skinniness is about making yourself smaller, in every sense. It's funny that the diet industry is aimed so much at women, isn't it? How we're essentially encouraged to be smaller, not only physically.

But back then, magazine covers, ad campaigns and movies told us all differently and that absolutely influenced me. I didn't aspire to be skinny, but I was conscious of being in any way "overweight".

This was before the days of body diversity, in fact before any kind of diversity onscreen, when you only saw one image of what a woman should look like. And how she should be. We would read magazines, which told us, repeatedly, that our goal in life was to be thin, get a man, get married and have kids. Women's magazines were obsessed with what women needed to weigh, wear, think and look if we wanted to bag a guy. The key aesthetic was to be slim. Any magazine, billboard, TV show or film would tell you that. It was the time when high-street gyms became popular, and there was a proliferation of things like the Cambridge diet and the Cabbage Soup diet. We didn't know then that being thin didn't equal being healthy.

When I look at pictures of us now, it's heart-breaking because we were all so small, yet we were made to feel otherwise. Geri was just tiny. Yet the people around us, Chic, the industry, the media made us feel as though we had to be as small as possible. I'd never really thought about weight until this point. If anything, I'd wanted to build myself up, especially after the fight on The Bongs. But Chic's words about my thighs came at a time – and in a way – that shook me.

The next day was Monday and I had barely slept. Hearing movement downstairs, I got up and went downstairs, bleary-eyed, to the kitchen. It was 7 am. "I'm going for a run," whispered Geri, sticking her head around the door, "do you want to come?"

With Chic's words still burning my ears, I made a snap decision. "Yeah, give me two minutes, I'll put on some shorts," I told her, rushing off to change out of my pyjamas.

Following the run, I was buzzing. After months of not really doing any exercise, besides light choreography during rehearsals, I felt like myself again. I had more energy, I felt great.

By 10 am we were back at rehearsals. Chic's words were still there but I was aching a little from the run and I felt like my body was already getting stronger. I thought about my thighs that Chic had mocked. They might be "chunky" now, I thought, but you wait. At 1 pm, we all headed over to the nearby Sainsbury's caff as we did every day. "Jacket potato, butter and beans," I said automatically, as Geri ordered: "Jacket with beans, no butter."

"Actually," I said quickly, "just beans, no butter for me too." If the other girls noticed, they didn't say anything.

It was Geri who also introduced me to the gym. Despite having spent pretty much my whole life being active in some way or other, I'd never been to one. Well, I'd been to Popmobilty (which is like aerobics combined with dance) with my friend Ali and her mum Hazel at the Queens Hall in Widnes, but gyms were mostly for boxers and body builders back then – not anyone and everyone like it is today. It's amazing how gym culture has boomed over the last 20 years, because in the mid-nineties there weren't that many about.

We joined a basic one not far from Boyn Hill Road and Geri showed me the ropes.

When we left the gym, I had more energy, I felt good, just like when I went for the run.

No one is to blame, I'm responsible for my own self, though there were perhaps factors around me that led me down that path towards an eating disorder. Whether it was the messages I was receiving via the media, Chic's words, taking note of what the other girls were eating and how they looked or deciding to exercise a few times a week, I was on the path to a mindset that would ultimately be terribly destructive to me physically, emotionally and mentally.

I didn't drastically change my eating at that point, but I started going to the gym and began to be more conscious of what I was eating. I cut back on crisps and started to think about the calories in each glass of wine. It wasn't a problem.

At least, not yet.

• • •

We'd been in the band for over six months, and we were all start-ing to feel dissatisfied with the Herberts. We were getting bored of rehearsing the same few songs all day, every day. Bob and Chris kept dangling the idea that an industry showcase would happen at some point. "Why not now?", we'd ask. "You're not ready," we'd be told over and over. We started to feel constrained by the rehearsals and the songs they were making us sing.

We'd have a lot more fun at home, where we'd sing the music we were into. I'd put on a Take That video, and we'd have a laugh learning the routines. Geri and I idolised Madonna and had our own little fan club. Mel B would be blasting out Mary J. Blige, Snoop Dogg and Zhané's "Hey Mr. D.J." and we were all big TLC fans, they were one of the bands that me and the girls really looked up to. We loved their music, their women-first attitude, and their striking visuals. I'd watch "Creep" and "Waterfalls" on the telly in the gym with Geri. "Waterfalls" is a brilliant social commentary. It had a deeper meaning, and this struck a chord with us because we knew we wanted our songs to have some purpose too, and not just be love songs, or songs about being into boys who were treating us like crap. The four tracks we were given by Bob and Chris were drippy love songs focused on us girls trying to persuade some guy to get with us. The songs didn't reflect the women that we were.

Geri had an old Casio keyboard and we started to try to write our own songs. They were dead rough, but it was a start. I think the first song we wrote together was called "One of Those Days". Although the daily Trinity sessions were our official rehearsals, we started to find our feet as friends and as band-mates back home over those nine or so months that we lived in Boyn Hill Road.

Chris, Bob and Chic had also been saying for months that they were going to get us a contract, but no paperwork ever materialised. They kept dodging the issue, even though Geri was constantly on their case about it. Apparently, Chic was keen to keep us feeling insecure and therefore kept us working for it. But it only made us more frustrated and surer of our worth. They rarely complimented us or told us where we were improving, that we were getting there. I think it was that old-school mentality of "tough love", of keeping us on our toes.

I got the sense they didn't want us to become too big for our boots or get too many ideas above our station. Although Chris, Bob, and Chic could tell that we couldn't be controlled, they still wanted to keep a tight rein on us. They were in charge, not us.

I'm not sure that was, ultimately, the best tactic for us five.

We started talking about having more say. "*If* we made music and we wrote our own lyrics we'd want it to sound like this," we'd tell each other.

We started to form our identity as a band and within the band and began to think about how *we* wanted to sound and look, not how Chris, Bob, and Chic wanted us to be.

We weren't happy with the name Touch. Luckily, Geri had come up with a great alternative while me and her were in the gym. "Spice," she yelled at me enthusiastically across the gym floor during an aerobics class as a pounding techno remix of Kylie's "Confide in Me" played. I looked back at her, puzzled. "Five letters, there's five of us, we're five different flavours…" We went back home and told the others. Everyone loved it. At this point, we were simply known as "Spice" – the Girls was yet to come.

We let Bob and Chris know our new name and we also expressed our frustration that we *still* hadn't met anyone or done anything when we were so certain that we were ready.

They finally caved in and agreed to pay for a showcase that November at Nomis, the West London studio where we'd first met back in April. We would be performing four or five tracks in front of people from the industry – record label execs, songwriters and producers.

There was a lot of talk about how we should dress. Chic was keen that we all wore variations of the same thing because that's what girl groups did back then. He had given us a bit of cash to spend on costumes, and we were under strict orders to come up with a uniform look. Mel B and Geri went down to Camden Market and bought five adidas t-shirts that we all styled in our own way. The other girls wore jeans, and I wore trackie bottoms. Mel B had her Kangol on and Emma wore a white beret. The look was coordinated, but we made sure there were individual flourishes.

These were small steps, but these idiosyncrasies clearly pointed to a group of women who did not want to conform. We were becoming increasingly reluctant to be told what to do, say, wear or sing.

. . .

I think there was an energy radiating from us that day of the showcase. The songs may not have entirely represented who we were, but we knew we had something. We might not have been vocalists on a par with Whitney Houston. We may not have been able to dance like Michael Jackson. We didn't play numerous instruments like Prince. But we had that *thing*, that special something. That, dare I say, "X Factor". In the same way I'd had a feeling about the advert, I felt the same about the showcase. I didn't know quite what would come of it, but I knew something would.

The day was split into several sessions, and after each one we'd schmooze with the various publishers and writers hoping that they'd buy into both our performance and our personalities. "We think there's a massive gap for a band like us," Geri said as we spoke to the (mostly older white men) about our vision for the band.

Towards the end of the day, Mel B burst into the room on the back of a big, tall man. "This is Biff," she told us as this startled bloke looked around the room, albeit with a big grin on his face. "He's made songs for East 17, so I told him we'd give him a private showcase." Mel B had walked past Biff in a studio, told him he had "a bum like a black woman", asked him what he did and promptly jumped on his back so he could "come and meet me mates".

That's how we met Richard "Biff" Stannard, a songwriter and producer who became so central not only to the Spice Girls, but to my own career. And we never would have met him at that point if Mel B hadn't been so... Mel B! Biff later compared the experience of being around us like a car being jump started. Exhilarating... but exhausting.

Alongside Sheffield-based songwriter Eliot Kennedy, who had worked with Take That, Biff was the biggest writer we had in that day, and we clicked immediately. After we'd performed, he went off to phone writer and producer Matt Rowe, his friend and creative collaborator with whom he'd written and produced East 17's "Around the World".

Another important person we met that day was Marc Fox, who had been in the eighties band Haircut 100 and by then was a music publisher at BMG. Geri somehow sensed Marc was important, and very cannily managed to get his business card while Chris and Bob weren't looking.

The showcases went well, there was a real buzz. We could all feel it. We'd never done anything like this before, but you could sense the excitement in the room. People seemed to get what we were doing even though the music itself was a long way off being anything near good.

Unsurprisingly, Chris, Bob, and Chic suddenly and miraculously decided they did want us to sign a contract after all. Of course, none of us had any legal knowledge, though luckily, we were able to turn to Victoria and her dad, Tony, who had once been in a band. Tony told us, in no uncertain terms, not to sign. They were looking to take a big percentage of our earnings. It didn't feel right.

We were also fed up with being told we should dress the same. Although we had half-heartedly tried for the showcase, we were all too different from each other for that to work. Imagine me in a babydoll dress, I'd look like a dick! Geri in a trackie? I don't think so! One day at rehearsals we looked at ourselves in the mirror and it clicked: we should just be ourselves. Emma had her babydoll dresses, I was always in a tracksuit, Geri would be in some quirky get-up from a charity shop, Mel B was a bit cooler with Kangols and jeans, and Victoria (though she might now be known for her little black Gucci dress), well, it was more Karen Millen dresses at that point. The fact we were all so different was great. Just because pop bands hadn't done that before didn't mean we couldn't try.

It wasn't a conscious thought really, but it turned out to be a part of what people loved so much about the Spice Girls: that we were individuals, and everyone could relate to at least one of us in the band.

Christmas came and went, and it was after we'd been back in Boyn Hill Road a few weeks that we started to talk about our options. Did we want to sign this contract, or did we want to go our own way? We were finally in the studio with some great writers – including Matt and Biff – and we'd been promised time with Eliot Kennedy, who we were dead keen to work with because he'd worked with Take That.

By the time May arrived, we had a couple of new songs under our belt and were feeling super confident. We still hadn't signed the contracts though, and Chic was getting impatient.

Between us, we started tentatively thinking about leaving Heart. We *felt* like we had something special, but if we dumped Chris and Bob, would we get laughed at, or turned away? What if the writers and producers we were working with had a relationship with management and wouldn't work with us?

Maybe we should see what our options were before we made the decision.

It turned out Geri had already spoken with Marc Fox. Marc's interest in us was focused on his role as a publisher and us as a new band. He'd told Geri he had writers on his roster that could help us create the songs that we clearly needed to get to the next level. After a couple of phone calls, she arranged to meet him in his office at BMG Publishing in West London.

Mel B and I drove up to Putney with Geri in the increasingly unreliable Uno. For some reason I've long since forgotten, the plan was for Geri to go up alone while Mel B and I waited in the car outside.

She put on some makeup, zhuzhed up her hair, adjusted her boobs and prepared to use her "feminine wiles" as we did back then.

Geri was gone for ages; in fact, she took so long that Mel B started getting agitated. "Where is she? I really need a wee," she moaned as I looked at her. Oh no! We picked around the rubbish in Geri's car and quickly came up with an old Coke bottle. "That'll do," she grinned, before grabbing another one. "Just in case." Typical Spice Girls. Rather than finding a loo or somewhere to squat, she had to do it in a bottle, which is actually very hard to do. If anyone can wee in a bottle (or two) it's Melanie B!

Geri eventually came out, giving us a big thumbs up. Marc was going to help us. He wanted to see all of us the following week.

It was never discussed what we would do at the meeting but we went into that building like a thousand bulls in a thousand china shops.

Ordinarily, Marc's secretary would let him know his next appointment had arrived in a very orderly fashion, but in our case the main reception downstairs got there first, caught up in the mayhem of our arrival. "Marc, there's a bunch of girls down here saying they've got a meeting with you."

"Send 'em up", we heard him say.

Marc remembered us arriving as some sort of stealth assassins, albeit assassins stinking of hairspray and ciggies: Mel B and Victoria charmed the pants off the boys sat in the main room; Emma sweet-talked his secretary; I offered to help the assistant make the tea; and Geri jumped all over Marc like a puppy. We stormed into those offices and sent everything and everyone flying. But honestly, we never discussed this beforehand. It was just the way we were. We were five very different personalities yet together we were a real force to be reckoned with. We seemed to innately know which roles to take, and we embodied them without even thinking about it.

I don't think record labels, certainly not the more sterile, formal atmosphere of a publishing company had seen anything like this before. Before long, we had the demo tape playing, and I'm backflipping, Mel B's jumping on a sofa and Marc's got the whole of BMG Publishing outside his office, noses to the window, thinking, *Who the hell are this shower?!*

BMG Records were also in the building, and it soon filtered around that this new band were causing havoc on the fifth floor. All this despite the fact our demo tape included only a few admittedly terrible songs that none of us liked, and that we knew weren't right for us. Somehow though, we intuited that we had to sell us first, and the rest would come later. We realised that we had to distract people from hearing the actual music by dazzling them with *us*. We were selling Spice at this point; the music would follow.

Because he'd been in a band, and now worked on the other side of the industry, Marc was full of brilliant advice. He didn't encourage us to leave Bob and Chris exactly, but he pointed out that bad management would kill our career. If we left the Herberts, we had to make sure we worked with someone who would build us up and enhance what we had.

He also explained to us how publishing worked, which is one of the most important parts of the industry, although it's not considered as "sexy" as the record label side.

Getting a record deal is often the focus for a lot of artists, but it's publishing that's important because it's there that you get paid for what you write. A record label pays you to record an album, and it'll promote it and distribute it for you, and so on, but publishing will make sure you get paid every time your song is covered or sampled by another performer, when it's played in Zara or when it's used on an advert, TV show or a film. It's important you write your songs otherwise the only money you get is from record sales, and you won't be getting much off each one after the label, lawyers, management and the other four band members have taken their cut. Especially now in the age of streaming where you get around half a penny per stream.

Writing your own music for financial sustainability isn't the only reason it's important, Marc told us. "Otherwise, you're going to be given any old crap from old, middle-class, white men who will treat you as vessels to sell their interpretation of what it is to be a young woman. It's not about making money, it's about being authentic because if you have that, people will believe in you, and they'll buy into you. Never, ever, sell yourselves short." He urged us to: "Think about the phrases you say to each other, the stories you tell, the ideas that you have. A good writer will be able to help you craft and shape these ideas into, hopefully, hit records." He gave us some great advice.

We asked Marc if he'd take us around the music industry and introduce us to managers and record labels. "Girls, the room is brighter with you in it. I'd love to help you if I can."

• • •

With all this percolating, we spoke to Matt and Biff, who we were growing ever closer to thanks to some early writing sessions at their studio in the Strongroom in East London.

We felt free with Matt and Biff, they seemed to instinctively understand what we wanted to do – pop music – while Chris and Bob had kept trying to push us towards a more R&B sound. We told them we weren't happy with Heart, and we were thinking about leaving them, and Matt and Biff said they'd *maybe* heard similar complaints from other bands. "What should we do?" we asked them.

Geri told them that Marc had mentioned a guy called Simon Fuller, and did they know him, which made Matt and Biff's eyebrows shoot up. "If you want this, you've got to have the best team around you, because you can have the most amazing artists and if they haven't got the right team, they're not going to get anywhere," said Biff. "You've got to go for it. Simon Fuller is a big deal."

They said if we did leave Heart, they'd stick with us.

We got home that night and talked over our options. I think it was Victoria who finally said out loud what we were all thinking:

"We need to ditch Chris and Bob."

"You're right. We can do this ourselves," said Geri.

"We're ready. Let's not wait anymore," said Mel B.

We all looked at each other and laughed. It was the beginning of what I've always thought of as our *Scooby-Doo* approach to life: the five of us agreeing on a mad plan and, despite not knowing what the outcome might be or what the odds were, we decided to risk it all anyway. Whenever we had these huge, life-changing decisions to make, it was always the same. Someone would say what the rest of us were thinking, we'd all look at each other like "*Shall we?*" and then there would be lots of screaming. At that point, we were completely all for one, one for all. We were in it together.

We had Marc on our side, and we had Biff and Matt, now all we needed were the demo tapes we'd made. Though we weren't that happy with the quality of the songs, without them we had nothing to play for people. Geri came up with an elaborate plan. We didn't think the tapes would be at Heart's office, out in Lightwater, Surrey. We knew we needed to head to Trinity, where the engineer, Tim, was (in our heads) guarding the tapes with his life.

Mel B and Emma went to Lightwater to distract Chris and Bob, while Geri, Victoria and me went to Trinity, furtive as anything, no doubt looking dead suspicious. I stayed in the control room, keeping an eye out, while Victoria and Geri made their way towards Tim in the adjoining studio.

As Victoria pushed her boobs out and pretended to be deeply interested in whatever Tim was saying, Geri snuck in and got the tapes. At a loss of where to put them, she stuffed them in her knickers. Or maybe it was her bra. Either way, I don't know why she didn't just put them in her bag! Once I saw that Geri had the tapes, I tipped Victoria the wink and we all sidled out separately.

We left Trinity, for the last time, and ran to the car park, where Geri jumped into the Uno and me and Victoria got into her car. I was the tidiest out of all of us, so Victoria knew her beloved Clio was safe with me in it. "Meet me on the roundabout," said Geri, referring to the halfway point between Trinity and Chris and Bob's office, before disappearing in a cloud of Fiat fumes.

When we got to the roundabout a few minutes later, Geri was literally parked *on* the roundabout. Like, parked on top of it. The car *itself* was on the roundabout. Very Geri!

We had one more job to do. We needed to clear out of Boyn Hill Road, so we very grandly decided we'd do a "moonlight flit", albeit at 10 in the morning. We picked up Emma and Mel B, drove back home and dashed around the house, hearts racing and laughing our heads off as we gathered up our clothes, Pot Noodles and posters.

We shut the door, never to return to that house, to Trinity, or to Chris and Bob.

We piled into the battered Fiat Uno and drove off into the sunset. Bye Chic, bye Chris, bye Bob. We five wanted to do things our way and on our own terms.

We were on our own and we were completely fine with that.

CHAPTER SIX

Fearless

We didn't know it yet, but we'd already written two number one singles – and we were about to write a third.

Our sessions with Matt and Biff had proven to be very fruitful. We had come up with this quite mad, quirky song that we were calling "Wannabe", and we'd also started to work on a ballad called "2 Become 1".

Things were going great with Matt and Biff, we felt so comfortable with them, and so creative. But we were in a bit of a dilemma. Before we'd done our flit, Chris and Bob had arranged for us to work with Eliot Kennedy. The session was due to be that week, but we didn't have a contact for him and, well, obviously we couldn't ask Chris or Bob. Matt and Biff didn't know how to get to him either. We really wanted to work with Eliot.

All we knew was that he lived in Sheffield.

So, once again, in true *Scooby-Doo* style, Geri and Mel B hatched a plan to meet him.

Without telling anyone, they set off up the M1 in the old Uno on this crazy adventure, with one mission in mind – to find Eliot and persuade him to work with the Spice Girls.

They somehow knew that he occasionally recorded at a studio called FON, so after five hours of driving, they rocked up there. "Do you know Eliot Kennedy? We're, uh, supposed to be working with him today." "Well, yeah, he works here sometimes but he's probably at home," the receptionist told them. It turned out Eliot lived in a small town south of Sheffield called Worksop. Mel B blagged an address out of the studio, and they set off once more to try and find his house. Mel B rang the three of us along the way, from Geri's massive brick of a Motorola that she'd bought a few months before to match Victoria's: "We're near his house, we're gonna knock on the door!" They also rang Matt and Biff, telling them, "We're up North, we're in the car trying to find Eliot!"

They finally turned up at midnight and found a very affable Eliot, who seemed to think it was perfectly normal that two young wannabe singers were on his doorstep in the middle of the night. "We've left Chris and Bob. Will you still work with us?" Incredibly, he agreed.

Say what you want about the Spice Girls, but we were ambitious, driven and prepared to go all out to make our dream come true.

Me, Emma and Victoria went up the next day, and Mel B, Geri and Eliot came to pick us up. We had nowhere to stay, so Mel B and Emma stayed at Mel B's mum's in Leeds, which was about an hour's drive away. Eliot let the rest of us stay in his three-bed house, which was incredibly generous. I think he ended up on the sofa while we took over the bedrooms. He's a very low-key guy and we'd spend most nights on the sofa in our pyjamas with him, watching *Star Trek*. He likened our arrival to "a hurricane" in a recent newspaper interview.

I was buzzing being in Eliot's home studio, the exact same place Take That had been just a year or so ago, recording "Everything Changes".

The first song we wrote with Eliot was the *Spice* album track "Love Thing". We tried another couple of ideas but the big one that came from those sessions up North was "Say You'll Be There". He'd had the idea for the song and played us some chords and messed around on the piano a bit as we sat on the floor, listening. As Eliot remembers it, we heard the melody, whipped out our notebooks and got writing. It took us an hour to write that one. There's a version somewhere in existence with a Mel B rap on it. It's another song that, really, is about friendship. It was us saying to each other, "*Whatever happens, I've got you, we're in this together*". After being force-fed boring songs about blokes, during those sessions with Eliot we discovered a real freedom in writing about what interested us – friendship.

We stayed in Sheffield for a few days before returning to London, where Matt and Biff had booked us in for some more sessions.

We made a lot of *Spice* at their studio in the Strongroom on Curtain Road in Shoreditch. Nowadays, Shoreditch is a party hotspot, but back then there was very little going on. There were no shops, really, or bars. There were very few streetlights or people just out and about, especially at night. It was a bit of a ghost town.

But there was a lot of creativity going on underneath the sketchy surface. You had Goldie doing drum "n" bass night, Metalheadz at the Blue Note on Hoxton Square, and Turnmills was down the road, with its huge house and techno nights. Upstairs at the Strongroom, The Prodigy was recording what would become *The Fat of the Land*, we had Spiritualized on one side of us recording *Ladies and Gentlemen, We Are Floating in Space* while Orbital were on the other side, working on *In Sides*. On the floor above, Alexander McQueen, one of the best British designers of all time, and who Biff had grown up with in Bethnal Green, was creating his fourth show, the controversial Fall 1995 *The Highland Rape* collection, which would ultimately lead to his very prestigious appointment as head of Givenchy.

In the middle of all that, there was us, the Spice Girls, with Biff Stannard and Matt Rowe writing three-minute pop bangers like "Wannabe"! We were right in the heart of the burgeoning "Cool Britannia", as it was later known.

We just didn't realise it at the time.

We didn't really know who anyone was, so we'd chat to these random blokes, not clocking that it was Phil from Orbital or whoever. I think we annoyed people sometimes because we'd be in the courtyard rehearsing choreography, completely oblivious to the fact that, like, Liam Howlett was sitting in his car trying to get out.

We spent each session writing for three or four hours and the rest of the time we were hanging out, having fun, talking about our lives. Geri would constantly ask Matt and Biff questions like "Who's a good publisher?" and, "Actually, what is a publisher?" arming herself with knowledge about the music industry.

I have wonderful memories of being in that tiny little studio with Biff and Matt – there was lots of messing about and laughing. It was coming up to Christmas towards the end of that year, 1995, and it was Matt's birthday, so Mel B and Geri decided to get him an extra-special present. Can you guess what it was?

So the stripper arrived, dressed as a sailor, all oiled up, with his little boombox. He was actually very sweet and polite but then the next thing we knew he couldn't find his cassette and so Geri said, "I'll put the radio on and whatever comes on, you have to dance to it," and, because it was Christmas time, the first song that played was Cliff Richard's "Mistletoe and Wine". It was so awkward! He kept trying to get us to touch his arse and then it all got a bit icky when he bent over, popped a roll of paper right *up his bum*, and said, "Which one is Biff?"

We all pointed to Matt, and Matt had to pull the message out!

Bear in mind this is literally 2 pm in the afternoon and we were all stone-cold sober.

The seven of us sat there, open-mouthed, totally dazed as the stripper popped his clothes back on and, normal as anything, said, "So what you guys recording? Oh, you're in a band? Oh, that's great, well, good luck with it all..."

So, we worked hard but, you know, fun was had!

And that was important. When it comes to songwriting, or at least certainly back then, you would spend a lot of time getting to know producers and writers. They'd ask you about your experiences, what you'd been through, your personal life and so on. Some of the way music is written now, as I said before, is much more conveyor belt, lots of people in separate rooms just trying to make a hit. But people want different things now, which I totally get.

I think part of the magic of *Spice* was that we got to know the people we were working with, and they got to know us. I feel with music, you should be making something that reflects you and who you are, what you've been through. Like Marc, Biff gave us some great advice. He said, "You don't want to be copying anyone, you want people to be copying you." It's a Lennon and McCartney thing, isn't it? You want to *be* The Beatles, not compared to The Beatles.

I wonder now how on earth we knew how to write a song, given none of us had studied music or had a clue about song composition. We had no idea about a middle eight or how many lines should be in a verse, or where the chorus should be. We just exploded with ideas and possibly that was part of the magic. We broke the rules because we didn't know the rules, so we were able to create this collection of songs that not only sounded great but also had something to say. Matt, Biff, Eliot, and Absolute (a production duo we also worked with) were able to bottle this chaotic creativity for us. I think it's something I'd encourage people to do now; you might not be classically trained or have the "right" education but don't let that hold you back from creating. Pick up that camera, that microphone, that paintbrush and see what comes out – you never know what might happen.

I know we made pop music, but we were quite punk (in spirit, if not sound!) in terms of how we created the album; we weren't just making it up, but also… we were kind of just making it up!

It was through talking to Matt and Biff that we started to really think about what we wanted our message to be. We were inspired by TLC, Stevie Wonder and Prince, who each had something to say in their music. And so, we asked ourselves: what did we have to say?

At the time, there weren't really any British pop stars (men or women) speaking directly to us. In 1994 and 1995, the dominant sound was pop, but the most respected genre was indie. Nirvana had just introduced the world to grunge, and Britpop was born thanks to Oasis, Pulp, Suede, and Blur. We had Hole, Garbage, Bikini Kill, and Elastica representing the women but struggling to get the same recognition. Take That had loads of fans, but they weren't respected like their guitar-wielding counterparts, even though they should have been.

In 1994, Wet Wet Wet were number one for *15 weeks* in the UK Charts with "Love Is All Around"; the second most popular song that year was Whigfield's "Saturday Night", followed by East 17's "Stay Another Day" (not produced by Matt and Biff, but you can see why we were so keen to work with the people who were working with the East End foursome). In 1995, there were a grand total of 10 women featured in the top 50 most popular songs of the year, many of whom were North American balladeers like Celine and Mariah or were members in otherwise male-dominated bands, like Mary Joe who fronted Sweden's Rednex and Alex Natale, the DJ in Italo House quartet Alex Party. The UK was represented solely by Tracey Thorn from the indie/electronic duo Everything But The Girl.

We inherently knew that we had something to say that wasn't being said, in a way that we wanted to say it. We weren't the only people thinking about Girl Power and feminism, there were a lot of great female bands around at that time too, with the Riot Grrrl movement in America led by Bikini Kill and Sleater-Kinney.

Over on this side of the Atlantic, we had the British duo, Shampoo, who released the song "Trouble" during the summer of 1994. They were a lot edgier than we were though – less pop, more punk. In a weird coincidence, the week before we went to number one with "Wannabe" in July 1996, Shampoo went to number 25 with a song called "Girl Power". I don't know why we weren't both able to exist at the same time, but shortly after that single, their sales went into decline.

We didn't want to be punk, indie or R&B – we wanted to be pop. But *good* pop. We naturally gravitated to lyrics that were about friendship, sexual freedom and empowering each other to be confident in who we were. We knew if we made songs that we wanted to hear, then perhaps other people would want to listen to them too. We were chasing the energy and ethos of indie but presented in pop packaging.

I know *Spice* isn't a PhD in Feminism, but we were saying what so many other young people felt. We instinctively wrote songs we wanted to hear because we didn't feel like anyone else was doing that, at the time. There were few, if any, in the pop space talking about friendship in the way we were, that it was the most important thing and should be cherished. Sod bad partners, it was our friends that mattered most. Why would we want to date stupid controlling men when we could be having a far better time with our mates? For some people, friends were family. Chosen family. This idea of inclusivity wasn't forced – we didn't think "*Oh, we should be like this so people will like us.*" It came out naturally.

We simply wrote about what was important to us. With "Wannabe", for instance, we thought about the times when we had boyfriends that none of our friends liked, and how hard that is in any group. We were chatting about it and Biff said, "That must be tough, going out with one of you lot and the other four hate you." And that's where "If you wannabe my lover, you gotta get with my friends" came from.

"Wannabe" flew out of us in half an hour. There was something going on in the room that day. Matt and Biff had already come up with the backing track – Biff later told me he'd been trying to channel "Summer Nights" from *Grease* – and we all sat on the floor and started scribbling. Someone at some point shouted "Zig-a-zig-ah", and Biff said, "Yep, let's get that in."

Everyone always wants to know what Zig-a-zig-ah means. There are lots of crazy theories still flying around online about its origins, but the truth is that it came from us lot messing about and making up words and silly phrases. I can't remember *exactly* how Zig-a-zig-ah came about but in the song it means sex. I hope I've not broken some secret Spice Girl code! I remember sitting on a bed somewhere writing out our little dictionary of ridiculousness in the back of a book.

I need to find that book...!

Matt and Biff let us roam free. You could see Emma and Mel B's minds ticking away as they listened back to the loop. They decided the song needed a rap. Mel B grinned and started scribbling on her notepad. *"So, here's a story from A to Z, you wanna get with me you better listen carefully...."* That's how the rap in "Wannabe" came about.

Mel B often took songs to a different place. If you think about that emphatic laugh and "Yooooooo" of hers (well, Biff insists it's her, I'm still convinced it's Geri!) right at the top of the song, it's brilliant. It made us immediately identifiable from the first few seconds. People would have the radio on and as soon as they heard that "Yooooooo" they'd know it was us. Not to mention we managed to create a chorus that refused to leave your brain. In fact, in 2014, "Wannabe" was officially declared the catchiest hit single of all time by Manchester's Museum of Science and Industry.

It may have driven people mad at some points, but what an introduction to a new band that was.

It took us ages to find the chorus for "Mama". Mel B had come up with the idea for us to write a song dedicated to our mums. At that point she had been arguing with her mum, they were really going through it. I think she wanted to remind herself how important her mum was, how important they were, and still are, to all of us. Everyone went off to different corners of the studio to write their own verses and then we came back together. We finally finished the chorus together, just playing around on the piano. At first, we were like, *"Is this too cheesy, have we gone too far?"*, but Matt and Biff added heavier drums and brought in a gospel choir and, well, a hit was born.

Nowadays, it's not only the creative approach to songwriting that's changed, the recording is really different these days too.

Back at the Strongroom, we were recording onto physical tape and that was expensive. These were the days before autotune and computer programmes like Logic. When you hit a flat note, it wasn't just a case of pushing a button to make it sound right. The engineer would have to rewind the tape to the exact point and then "punch in" as you re-did the note, to overwrite the mistake you made. You might have to do one word 30 times. Worst-case scenario, you'd accidentally tape over a whole line or a whole verse, and then you'd have to redo *that*. It could, and did, take hours. A band could rack up thousands of pounds and hours if they didn't have their shit together.

It took us a week just to record the vocals for "2 Become 1". Now you can do two songs in a day, easily. We all had to figure out mic-control and ad-libs and punching in. It was an intense learning period for us all.

There were a lot of snarky comments about some of the band's singing voices, but when it comes to vocals, take one of us away and we're not the same band. I was always there for the ad-libs and the high notes, Emma had that innocent pop voice, Mel B delivered the soulful tones, Victoria had a great lower tone which became almost like the bass, and Geri was Geri! We wouldn't be the Spice Girls without that one. We just wouldn't. It might take her longer, but she was so dedicated and determined that she would do what it took to nail the vocal.

. . .

Marc thought we would benefit from working with some other producers, just to see what came out. He sent us off to meet Paul Wilson and Andy Watkins, also known as the production outfit Absolute. They quickly became known to us all as the Absolute Boys.

We set off in Geri's Fiat to work with these guys who lived in deepest, darkest South West London. We drove past lots of roundabouts and factories until finally we reached a little footbridge, which took us into an industrial complex full of bunkers and boatyards. It was called Taggs Island and it was surrounded by water, and, according to Mel B's memory, there was a brothel there too. I never saw anything, but nothing would surprise me about that place.

Things didn't go smoothly at first. Paul and Andy were much more soulful, R&B style producers, a little Acid Jazz if anything. And there was us five loud, gobby wannabe pop stars. Our music didn't align at all, and I don't think they knew what to do with us. But we talked them into doing something up-tempo, something fun and "Who Do You Think You Are" popped out, inspired by... the music industry!

As the music started to come together, we knew we needed a manager, and so we started meeting people. Some of those meetings were disastrous. They'd sit us down, being all big and important and just drone on at us about what they thought we should be and how we should sound. These industry types would advise us not to get our hopes up: "You know, girl bands don't really sell, right? Girls want to buy music by boys they fancy?" Oh, really? Because we all love TLC, SWV, Eternal and Bananarama and they seemed to sell quite well, mate.

We wrote "Who Do You Think You Are" as a response to all these men trying to order us about. The more people told us what we should and shouldn't do, the more it solidified who we were and what we wanted to be.

You're telling *us* what young girls want? We *are* young women, we might have a bit more insight than you! We didn't want anyone telling us what wasn't possible; where were the people telling us what we could achieve? By that point, "Never lose your soul… never lose control," was firmly ingrained in us.

We also made the album tracks "Last Time Lover", "Something Kinda Funny'" and "Naked" with Paul and Andy, and we returned to them a year or so later to make "Too Much" and "Stop" for our second album, *Spiceworld*. They also produced our Eliot Kennedy tunes, "Say You'll Be There" and "Love Thing".

It was with Paul and Andy that I became the resident Spice Girl ad-libber. Once we had recorded the song, the boys got me to record an ad-lib track. It's quite a technical thing, but I'll try my best to explain it… *clears throat*.

Just sing any old shit!

That's it, that's the explanation!

It became a bit of a Sporty thing because I love recording ad-lib tracks. You bounce around the melody adding new ideas, breaths, "oohs", "ahhs" and high bits. It's so spontaneous and creative. You have to lose your self-consciousness and go for it (and trust me, no one wants to hear the outtakes), but if you feel free, you never know when the magic is going to happen.

Not every track we wrote made the final cut. In 2021, we did a reissue of *Spice* for the 25th anniversary, which included some of our previously unreleased demos. The very first song we all wrote together was called "Feed Your Love" but that was a bit too... raunchy... even for us! There were other tracks too that didn't make the anniversary release. We had a song called "Serial Killer" that I sang and another one called "Overnight" that was about a sex worker doing what she had to do to survive. Emma came up with "Likely Stories (C U Next Tuesday)" about a particularly horrible man, which never made the cut. It sounded very much like a future Lily Allen.

None of those tracks were quite right for us at the time, but they were all early expressions of our version of feminism. We wanted to write songs from the perspective of women, specifically working-class women.

Not that the press seemed to understand that. Much of the early coverage centred on us being this marketed, factory-made, pop band, which just wasn't the case. A *Rolling Stone* review of *Spice* compared us to the Village People and insisted we had been brought together by a "manager with a marketing concept".

We had been found by Heart, but we dumped them because we had our own concept; we didn't want theirs.

The week after "Wannabe" went to number one, *The Guardian* published a piece about how we were "the latest manufactured group to go from nowhere to number one" who had been put together "about ten days ago" and likened us to the Stock Aitken Waterman band Big Fun, a "faceless boy-trio who had some feeble hitlets around 1989". I should also say that Caroline Sullivan, the journalist who wrote *The Guardian* piece, wrote another feature in 2016 in which she said she had been wrong!

But that was the rhetoric across the media then.

Of course, the Herberts had put us together, but we very quickly established we weren't puppets. We decided not to have a lead singer, we chose what to wear and we sacked (well, ran away from) our managers so we could be the band we wanted to be. We were across everything, from artwork to songwriting, production and choreography. All of it. Manufactured, we were not.

And songwriting was a very collaborative process for us. Geri and I worked together a lot; we were real doers. Geri has a million ideas a minute. In those early days at Boyn Hill Road, she went to night school to study English Literature. She was, and is, a writer. She'd come with an idea but wasn't always sure how to make it work rhythmically or musically, which is where Emma and I would come in. Melodically, myself and Emma were confident at thinking about top-lines and choruses.

Mel B would always inject something cool or quirky. Victoria was musical; she knew instinctively how to write songs, but I know she has spoken on various occasions about how she felt she lacked the confidence we all seemed to have. On the upside, Victoria found her creative confidence with fashion and beauty. We are all extremely proud of what she has gone on to achieve.

Between us, whether we wrote just a bit of the song or a lot of it, we added that Spice Girls magic. A melody, a harmony, a rap. There was never any frustration that one of us wasn't doing enough, it was always a team effort. That was, I think, the beauty of that dynamic and those songs.

Things would tumble out of all of us five girls and whoever we were in the studio with. We always had the bigger picture in mind. We'd be writing, for example, "Stop" and someone would start making up Motown-style choreography for it, and one of us would say, "We should have a sixties theme in the video." It would be a cascade of random ideas and thoughts, some of which would end up in the bin but some of which we'd go on to refine.

And of course, we had Biff and Matt, the Absolute Boys and Eliot.

Matt and Biff worked in a unique way. Matt came from a more traditional songwriting background; he played piano and so he would come up with melodies and beautiful lyrics as we shouted out our thoughts. He did a lot of engineering too; he was a technical whizz but also very creative. He wrote two of my very favourite songs, "Viva Forever" and "2 Become 1".

Biff is the guy for ideas, concepts and melodies. He'd say, "I'm thinking along the lines of 'Summer Loving' but not that," and Matt would nod and start playing something. He's a very visual person so he'd be thinking about artwork and videos and chore-ography too. He's also a mentor figure; he took us under his wing and guided our ideas and gave insightful advice, professionally but also personally.

Biff has worked with me across my solo career, including on my most recent album, *Melanie C*. Among other tracks, Biff and I wrote "Who I Am" together, which of course inspired the title of this book. Biff married his wonderful husband Pat in June 2011. I was so happy to be there and felt so honoured when their first dance was to "2 become 1". What a moment!

Matt and Biff, Eliot, and the Absolute Boys, they are Spice Boys through and through.

• • •

We knew we had some amazing music, now we just had to find ourselves a manager.

Because, thanks to Marc Fox, we were now spending so much time in London meeting people in the industry, Geri, Mel B and I decided to get a place together on Cyprus Road in Finchley Central near Emma, who was back at her mum's in North Finchley. Victoria was up the road with her parents in Goffs Oak, so she'd drive down and meet the rest of us at Emma's.

The Cyprus Road place was a fun flat, for the most part. We had a plaque made that read "Spice HQ". We weren't there for long, thank goodness, because it was a dump – it was a bit like *The Young Ones*. The carpets were filthy and the furniture, such as it was, was old and crap. At one point, Mel B decided to "do up" the toilet with loads of porn pictures, which was... nice.

I had my own room with two single beds, and if you went through the back bedroom that I was in, you could climb through the sash window and onto the roof that was above the flat below. We'd go out there to sunbathe (not when we were busy, of course – no one was trying to do a Michelle!).

We took a lot of meetings. We'd congregate first at Emma's mum's flat, where she'd pack us off with rounds of toast wrapped in foil to keep them warm and then head into town, or West London, to meet various managers or record label people. We approached this part of the band like a military operation. Marc Fox was amazing and set us up with so many people. We'd make sure to do our homework and find out a bit about them before we barged our way into their offices. Of course, we didn't just walk in nice and polite and hand over our demo. Oh no.

In the same way we'd transported the BMG offices into a stage, we would steamroll into these offices and "Spice" up whoever we met. We'd press play on our portable stereo, jump on tables, and perform "Say You'll Be There". We met managers and label heads in their offices, at restaurants and even once at a racecourse. We actually rollerbladed into offices and I did literally do a backflip on a boardroom table.

We naturally found our groove when it came to the meetings, replicating what we'd done at BMG. Mel B would steam in all guns blazing with Geri at her side talking the hind legs off a donkey. I'd go in after them, tidying, picking up chairs and apologising. Victoria would be eyeing up the money being offered while Emma smoothed it all over by being completely sweet and loveable. The dynamic and the personalities we naturally had meant that we complemented each other. Some had strengths where others didn't, and I don't mean "strong and confident" necessarily, because you did need Emma to smile and smooth things over, or me to be peacekeeper and tidy up the mess and Victoria to crack a funny joke to relieve the tension. Between us, we had all the bases covered.

Sometimes we'd turn up to a meeting bickering about God knows what, the door would open and Boom! We were all smiles, sugar and Spice and all things nice! "Hello! We're Spice," we'd press play on the tape and off we went.

There was a lot of razzle dazzle with us, but before we left any meeting, we would perform an a capella of "Wannabe" because we needed people to know that we could sing. It was our way to remind these hotshots that they might want us, but did we want them?

And *then* we'd disappear in a cloud of chaos.

Once we had a sneaky look through one prospective manager's address book, while he'd gone out to make tea. "Oh my God, he's got Seal's number," said Geri as Mel B hurriedly copied it down.

Can you believe we rang Seal later that day from a payphone? He didn't answer (thank goodness!), but we left him a voicemail of us all barking like seals. Total idiots. We did admit this to Seal (and apologised profusely) when we met him a couple of years later at a party in LA. He was very gracious.

The "Wannabe" video is completely inspired by those days of going around labels and meeting managers. We upset the balance; we challenged the norm. We'd turn up in an office somewhere, tear the place up and leave, everybody's ties and hairs blowing in the wind. We were a tornado.

We met some ropey types along the way, and we'd have to take it in turns to call them and say, "Thanks, but no thanks," and "It's not you, it's us." Some of the bigwigs didn't take too kindly to being turned down by five women but we very quickly got a feel for people; we seemed to be able to sense those who were trying to blag us or others that simply saw the opportunity to make a quick bit of cash.

We knew there was a manager out there, we just had to find them.

• • •

There weren't many managers and execs that met Spice and said, "No, thanks", but there was one notable rejection.

We met Simon Cowell in the office of his label, RCA. He was actually on the floor below Marc because RCA had been bought by BMG a few years previously, so they were in the same building. We did our usual bit, ending on a triumphant backflip and a "taa-dah"! At the time, Simon was known for working with novelty acts like Zig and Zag and Robson & Jerome. This was years before *Pop Idol*, let alone *X Factor*, so to us, he was just another industry guy who we needed to impress. I'm sure he was a huge fan of pop stars trying to write their own songs or artists with opinions of their own. Clearly, we were not about to be a match made in heaven.

Pretty much as soon as we started talking, it was game over.

"It's a no from me, girls," he said in that droll, deadpan voice of his, adding, "I don't think you've got what it takes." We didn't feel too bad – Simon also turned down Take That. He had said, "I'd sign them without the fat one." So that tells you about the culture of the industry then. He did say, later, that not signing the Spice Girls was the biggest mistake he'd made. Well, he said that he'd tried to sign us, but that we turned him down, but that's not how we remember it. Regardless, you can't knock the success he has had. I guess we just weren't for him.

It was during some of these meetings that we started being told that girl groups just weren't viable. It's still being said today. Even Little Mix who, like the Spice Girls, proved the naysayers wrong, were told girl bands don't work, blah, blah, blah. Women still have to fight for their place, even in pop music. But don't get me started on that... yet!

Simon wasn't the only prominent person, well, man, to turn down the Spice Girls. Very early on, we set our sights on *TFI Friday*, hosted by Chris Evans, arguably the most influential pop culture show on British television at that time. This was a couple of months before we released "Wannabe", but people in the industry were getting to know us. We ended up in a meeting with Suzi Aplin, one of the show's producers and Chris's girlfriend at the time.

We met her at Chris's offices in Egton House, just by Broadcasting House. Chris had his radio production offices on one floor and down in a dark, dank basement was the home of the *TFI Friday* production office. We, as ever, bounded in, guns blazing. We did our usual bit of singing and dancing in a chaos of Buffalo boots and Nike trainers and as we did, Chris, who was in one of the offices on the side, spotted us.

"Why don't you go back to *Live & Kicking*?" he shouted at us through the glass – i.e. you're a crap pop band.

It was the nineties, the peak of Britpop, and I guess Chris didn't quite understand what we were doing. Of course, he had to eat those words later; we went on to be the only band to have a whole show dedicated to us. On 1st May 1998, we did a *TFI Spice Girls* special, where we performed some songs and Chris interviewed us one by one. He let us have what we want on the rider, so of course, we asked for our ever-reliable Spice Girls special, bottles of Lambrusco. Delicious…!

Despite dismissing us when he first saw us, Chris ended up publicly apologising to us on that show. I've gone on to work with him many times over the years.

Our next appointment was with another Simon. This one was called Simon Fuller, and he owned 19 Entertainment, so-called because he had a big hit in 1985 as an A&R (artists and repetoire) guy with the Paul Hardcastle song "19". That launched Simon into working in management. His mentor was Chris Morrison, who managed Blur and Elastica, and they shared office space down near Battersea Power Station in a place called Ransome's Dock.

I think Marc always had it in mind that we'd end up with Simon because he had worked with some of Simon's artists at BMG. There was an additional link via the Absolute Boys because Pete Evans, who ran Native Management, managed Absolute. Simon Fuller was about to, or had recently, offered Absolute a publishing deal, and at some point, Paul and Andy told him about this new girl group they were working with. The Absolute Boys played Simon a demo of "Something Kinda Funny" and Simon said he would like to meet us.

What was interesting about this was until now we'd been asking to meet people. Simon Fuller was, possibly, the first person to contact us and ask for a meeting.

Once again Marc Fox agreed to come with us.

I was really into Blur and Elastica so I was already impressed by Simon's connection to Chris. That and him (Simon) managing one of my childhood idols, Annie Lennox. I remember the day we walked into that office in May 1995 quite clearly. It was all open plan and we had to walk all the way down to the back, past Chris's section, to Simon's office.

He kept us waiting, which was definitely planned, knowing Simon as I do now. He wanted to make sure we knew he was the one in control, not us.

I remember, vividly, that he had turn-ups on his Armani jeans and I thought, *"I'm not sure about them."* He was very gently spoken and nodded along politely as we did our "Spice" thing.

We had written a lot of the album by this point, certainly "Wannabe", "Say You'll Be There", "Mama" and "2 Become 1", so Simon knew what he was getting musically. The meeting was to establish if we would get on well together. He asked us lots of questions and listened to us very attentively as we proclaimed we wanted to be the biggest band in the world and that we wanted to be authentic, we needed to be real. He didn't try to feed us bullshit. He told us he thought we could make it, with or without him, and that he would help us get to where we wanted to be, if we decided to work with him.

Simon managed both Annie and Cathy Dennis, two women from the UK who had both had considerable success in America. Things were looking good.

Although I wasn't sure about his jeans, we all instinctively knew that Simon was the manager for us. We decided he was our man.

· · ·

Now we just needed a record deal. Simon got people fired up very quickly. Every record label and publishing company in the country wanted us.

We were hot property and there's nothing record label bosses like more than proving who has got the biggest... chequebook. A bidding war began, which was great for us because it meant as the numbers kept climbing higher and higher, the keener the labels were to prove the size of their... chequebooks!

Marc got us meetings with RCA and EMI, and I think he was expecting that Simon, who worked closely with the president of RCA at the time, would encourage us to sign with them.

In fact, it was at this point that Marc fades from the Spice Girls story. I believe Simon had different ideas to Marc about the label he thought fitted us best, and when Simon whisked us away from RCA, Marc was told, essentially, his services were no longer required.

For us girls on the rollercoaster, we didn't really stop to question it too deeply. But we knew that he was working with Natalie Imbruglia, who had just put out "Torn", and we were really happy for him.

Marc was the first person who I believe really understood who we were as a band and went out of his way to help us. He, Matt and Biff even spoke about managing us themselves at one point, but they decided to stick with what they knew best. Marc also knew, and was proven (mostly) right, that Simon Fuller would do right by us.

It's a harsh game, the music industry, and people do get shuffled about and sidelined. Although we lost touch with him back then, Marc was an important part of our story, and I will always be grateful for all he did for us.

Meanwhile, Simon was busy positioning things so that a bidding war broke out between London Records and Virgin Records. London had East 17, who Biff and Matt had worked with, as well as New Order and the Happy Mondays. They were very young and very cool.

We all liked Virgin's roster, which included The Verve, Annie Lennox and Massive Attack, and they were about to sign Daft Punk. They seemed to understand who we were and what we wanted to achieve. Yes, we were a girl band and yes, we kept hearing that "girl bands didn't sell" but we were completely convinced otherwise. Not one of us five doubted for a second that we had what it took. Virgin seemed to share that vision.

I think we always knew we wanted to go with Virgin, run by Paul Conroy and Ray Cooper with Ashley Newton as head of A&R, but that was the game – to play Virgin and London off against each other to get the better deal. We decided to have some fun with it. "If you really believe in us, show us," we told Virgin. We enjoyed keeping them guessing – and we loved the first-class treatment even more, as they sent us posh cars and wined and dined us over the following weeks. They even flew us out to America to meet the bigwigs there. This was *before* they signed us.

On 13th July 1995, we figured we'd kept them waiting long enough but thought we'd give Virgin one final heart attack before we agreed to sign on the dotted line.

We were due to meet with them at 4 or 5 pm to sign the deal, but we decided to keep them waiting, and told them we had another very important meeting before theirs.

The clock was ticking, when suddenly, a limo turned up to Virgin's offices on Kensal Road in West London. Relieved, they opened the doors to find five blow-up dolls we'd brought from Ann Summers with wigs stuck on their heads. Five lookalikes, but no Spice!

We kept them sweating a bit longer before finally showing up to sign on the dotted line. We were whisked up to the rooftop, where we celebrated with champagne. Somehow the dolls ended up in the nearby canal, and we waved them goodbye as they bobbed along the murky grey waters.

Simon announced he was taking us for dinner at the swanky Kensington Place, and we five hailed a black cab. By the time we arrived, the taxi was a wreck; there was lipstick, champagne and flowers all over it. Somehow, Victoria's knickers ended up being chucked out of the window... I think Fuller, as we took to calling him, had to give the very disgruntled cabbie 50 quid when we fell out of the cab. Terrible behaviour. We steamed into this incredibly posh restaurant, stinking of booze and ciggies, and crashed onto the table. The other diners were not amused. By this point, Victoria was so drunk she pretty much fell asleep face down in her dinner. She was still knickerless!

After dinner, we five went back to Cyprus Road to carry on the party, though we had to put poor Victoria straight to bed.

I have vague memories of a massive flower fight as I played Blur's "Girls and Boys" on repeat.

We were absolutely buzzing. We were yet to release a song, but we felt like rock stars that night.

. . .

A couple of weeks before signing our record deal, in the ultimate move to win us over (which worked, let's face it), Virgin flew us to Los Angeles to meet the team from Virgin America.

We were flown first class to LAX and picked up by a massive stretch limo, complete with a telly and everything. The chauffeur drove us to our incredibly posh hotel, the Four Seasons in Beverly Hills. It was the beginning of a long-lasting affair with the five-star hotel. An affair that continues to this day.

We quickly discovered that LA is full of famous people; we'd get into a lift with Elton John or see Eric Clapton by the pool. This one time, Elton was staying in the Four Seasons, and when Elton's in town, he has the whole floor and security is super tight. The lift would only take you to certain floors, and so on. A little bit tipsy (okay, drunk!), we decided we'd go and say hello and somehow snuck up to his floor. Mel B and Geri started banging on the door, shouting at Elton to come out of his room. One of them (I'll not name names) suddenly needed the loo and for some reason, decided to take a pee in the plant pot outside his room. Luckily, Elton never appeared, and they got away with it.

I should have probably said earlier, prepare yourself for a few wee stories...!

On another occasion Geri and Mel B blagged their way into Courtney Love's hotel room by pretending to be friends with

Amanda de Cadenet and managed to hang out with Courtney for a bit. She didn't seem to mind that these two randoms had gotten into her suite. That's the thing about Americans – they love British people. As soon as they heard our accents, a lot of doors magically opened.

We fitted in seamlessly to the LA lifestyle, despite it being a million miles away from where we were from.

None of us were used to such luxury. We were working-class girls who came from nothing. Geri's mum was a cleaner, Mel B grew up in a council house, I'd spent time in council accommodation, Emma's mum was in a council flat even after the band kicked off. Even Victoria, whose dad had done well, was hardly devastatingly rich. But we never felt intimidated. Not once. Not even in the very beginning did we think, *"Oh, we don't have the right shoes/bag/clothes/accents/whatever"*.

We'd walk into these gigantic posh hotels, swanky restaurants or meetings in huge offices with vast views of Los Angeles and totally be ourselves. We didn't for a second feel that we didn't belong there: we had as much right to be in these fancy places as anyone else.

Being a Spice Girl gave me the confidence and courage to speak to anyone, whether they were a bigshot Hollywood player, royalty or a pop icon. No one, regardless of who they are or what they do, should ever feel like they're not good enough. You can walk into Gucci and have a look at a bag. Sod anyone that says you shouldn't be there.

I hate thinking that people feel they don't belong somewhere. If I'm with friends and they're nervous about going to a certain place for dinner because they don't know what cutlery to use... who cares what knife or fork it is! You can go where you want, don't let anyone stop you. Don't let anyone intimidate you. Don't let anyone make you feel like you don't belong. Don't ever let anyone make you feel like you're not good enough.

The other thing the girls taught me is to ask questions. If you don't understand something, ask. If you don't know what a word means, ask. You're not stupid if you don't know something; you're stupid if you don't find out what it means, because you've missed an opportunity to learn something.

With the backing of the girls, I had the confidence not only to say, but to *know* I belonged everywhere and anywhere.

I feel very grateful to the other girls for giving me that ability to speak to people, to all people, and to ask questions. I'm not afraid to talk to somebody whether they're more or less intelligent, more or less wealthy, more or less experienced, and so on. I feel like I can hold my own in any environment and that's very much down to the girls.

It was as we were taken around to meet people like Ken and Nancy Berry, who ran Virgin in the US, that Simon noticed we kept being referred to as "those Spice girls". "What do you think," he asked us, "Spice Girls? It's what everyone calls you anyway." There was an American rapper called Spice and so we needed to do something with our name – Spice Girls made perfect sense.

Towards the end of our trip, Simon took us out for dinner. He was great at teaching us about food and drink. I don't think any of us had been to a sushi restaurant before 1996, when Simon and his company credit card came calling. This one night, we'd had a lovely dinner with some amazing wine, and we'd ended things back at the Four Seasons bar. For some reason, someone ordered a port. As you do.

We must have arranged to meet in one of our rooms because we were all in our dressing gowns, crowded on someone's bed. Anyway, the next thing, some mad fight broke out about something. Who knows what, probably nothing. A fist did fly that may well have been mine and I think it caught poor Geri, as well as its intended target. Suddenly Mel B stopped, dead dramatic, and started puking up. "Oh! My! God! Look what you've done, I'm bleeding," she screamed, drunkenly holding up her fluffy Four Seasons dressing gown. "You've made me bleed!" There was red all down her dressing gown. I froze. Oops!

"That's not blood, you idiot, that's booze," said Geri. It was the port, nothing to do with me. Luckily.

There was always one drama or another with the five of us. There was rarely a dull moment and much of the time it was fun and games and all girls together. Things blew up between us, but they blew over quickly too.

Quite soon though, that began to change, and silly little arguments started to become a bit more serious. As the pressure piled on, we all started to feel it.

Some of us more than others.

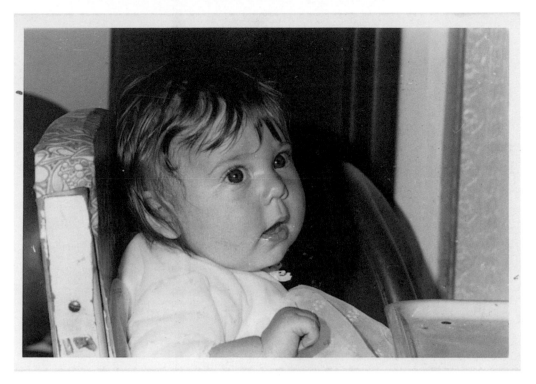

Hungry in a high chair. Me at 6 months at my Uncle Victor's wedding in 1974.

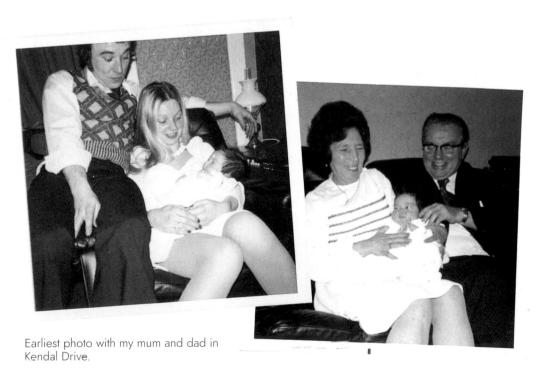

Earliest photo with my mum and dad in Kendal Drive.

Proud grandparents Nannie Kay and Grandad Billy.

Silver Jubilee, 1977.

Beaming with my mum and dad sometime in '75. Nice tank top, Dad!

I always loved this pic of me and my mum in Greece. I was once a natural blonde!

Staying hydrated in the Summer heat, rocking my first bucket hat.

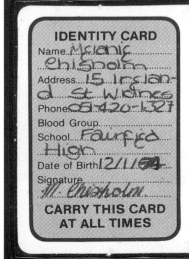

IDENTITY CARD

Name Melanie Chisholm

Address 15 Ireland St Widnes

Phone 051 420-1327

Blood Group

School Fairfield High

Date of Birth 12/1/74

Signature *M. Chisholm*

CARRY THIS CARD AT ALL TIMES

Old school photos. From a jumper knitted by Nanna Alice to my high school identity card. Looks like I cut my own fringe in the last one!

Me and our kid dicking around.

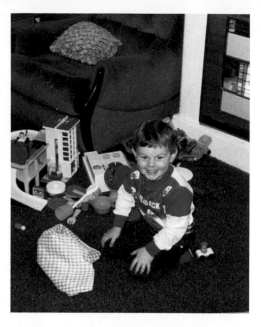

Ah, how cute is he here? Paul was always obsessed with cars, from Fisher Price to touring cars.

Our little living room in Ireland Street. Yes, that is my trophy on the fireplace!

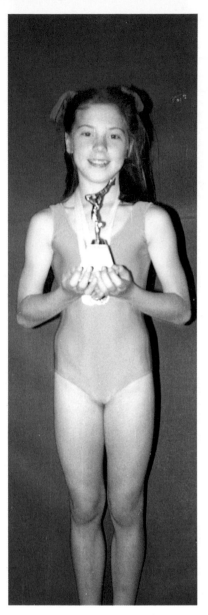

Fairfield Juniors Gymnastics Champion.

In my favourite Liverpool trackie, celebrating our trio win with my besties Steph and Ali.

More gymnastics success at Fairfield Juniors. How baggy is that leotard?

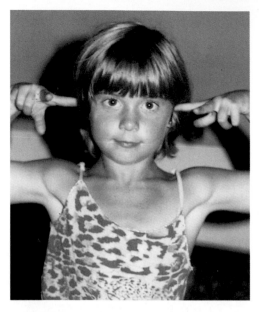

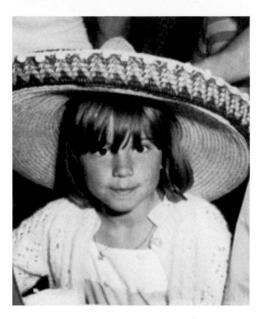

The infamous leopard-print top that cost my dad a week's wages on holiday in France

More happy holidays, this time in Spain.

The endless Christmas party at Auntie Lynne's, with my cousin Neil.

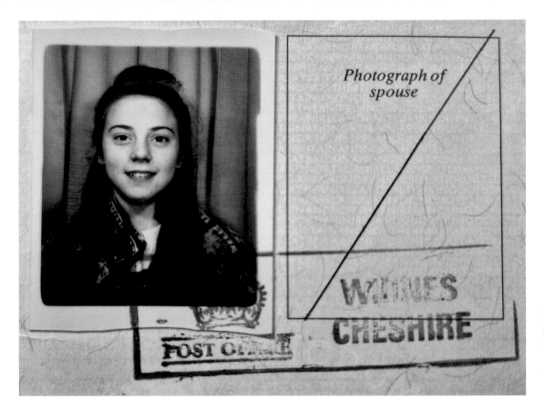

My early passport. What a look!

Visiting Dad and Carole for a long Spanish holiday.

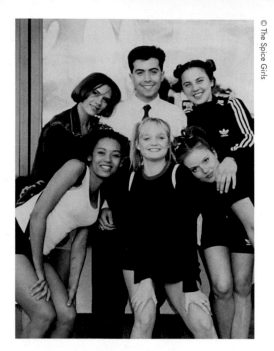

A really early picture of us girls on our first trip to LA. Plus random waiter!

The calm before the storm: Taken on a holiday to Maui with the girls before 'Wannabe' was released.

Tattoo Mania, Sunset Blvd., pre-Celtic cross and before I discovered heavy weights!

Us in the studio, 1998.

The happiest of times with our favourites Matt and Biff!

One of our first promo trips, singing karaoke in Tokyo.

© The Spice Girls

A day at the races.

© The Spice Girls

Our first radio roadshow. 'Wannabe' wasn't even released and everyone knew all the words!

Switching on the Oxford Steet Christmas lights in 1996.

Promo shoot; I did have more than one trackie!

Top: Taking the US by storm. It was mind-blowing being on Oprah!

Left: *Saturday Night Live* with Rob Lowe.

Meeting HRH The Queen for the first time.

A magical day in South Africa.

BRITs '97.

BRITs '98.

CHAPTER SEVEN

Never Give Up On The Good Times

The album was nearly done, and we were all itching to perform again. Although we weren't due to release our first single for another few months, we were told that once we did, we'd be doing a lot of personal appearances at radio roadshows not to mention, hopefully, telly performances too. We'd not been on stage together since the showcase at Nomis, over a year ago. We were out of practice!

So we decided to do a showcase for our parents and families. It would put us in front of an audience to see what they thought, and it would also be a great chance for all the mums and dads to meet each other.

On Friday 19th January 1996, we rented a room at the Moat House hotel in Elstree and got everyone to come to dinner, after which we did a makeshift performance for them. While most of our parents had so far been supportive, I'm sure they'd all been a bit worried about what was going on. We'd joined some band two years ago, moved in with strangers, then fired our managers and found ourselves a new one. Were we just wasting our lives on a band that might not come to anything?

Any doubt was quickly erased when they heard songs like "Wannabe" and "Say You'll Be There", performed by the five of us at peak energy. We had a huge amount of self-belief, we had some great songs, we had five very distinct personalities and, more than that, we had this undeniable chemistry. Our parents immediately got it. Den said he had the same feeling watching us as he had when he watched a new band called The Beatles in some back-room bar in Liverpool decades before.

Mum was impressed too. From what she can remember. Mel B took it upon herself to get Mum absolutely leathered. Every time she looked away, Mel B was there, filling her glass back up with rum and coke!

It was the beginning of a lovely friendship between all the parents and our siblings. I often say that Mum and Den talk to Tony and Jackie Adams more often than Victoria and I speak. Over the next few years, we'd often travel en masse together, bringing our close families and friends to shows and awards ceremonies (and the premiere of our movie). The parents built their own friendships out of it, and this huge extended family formed, almost overnight.

Things were really coming together. We had over 30 songs to choose from for our album, and now we had a manager and a record deal, which meant finally we might see some money.

After we'd signed to Virgin, Simon handed us each a cheque. "Well done, girls", he said, "you deserve this." Someone squealed. I looked at the cheque. There were a lot of zeros! Four of them. Ten grand! I'd never seen anything like that amount of money before.

The first thing I did with that paycheck… I went straight to JD Sports on Oxford Street and bought the trainers I'd had my eyes on for weeks. Nike Air Max.

The first thing we did as a band was to tie up the loose ends with Heart, by paying Chris and Bob compensation for what they'd put into Touch. I think we gave them around 60,000 pounds in the end. We could afford it.

Cheques began streaming in for large sums of cash. Huge amounts, at times. Cheques! They sound so old-fashioned now.

As wonderful as it was to feel the financial weight lifted from our shoulders, coming from very little and ending up wealthy in my twenties complicated things. It complicated my relationships with people, it complicated the way I felt about money, how I spent it, how I felt about spending it. Becoming financially successful brings a lot of guilt with it. Especially when you've come from nothing and you're getting cheques for a day's work that might be someone's annual salary.

There were times during the Spice Girls that I'd ring Mum for a chat, and she'd tell me Den had had a bad day on the cabs. "When he finally did get a fare, they bloody did a runner. He's made a fiver, Melanie." I would feel embarrassed thinking about how much I had in my bank account and how little my own family often had.

I think for all of us Spice Girls, who pretty much came from working-class families, suddenly being given a ton of cash as young women brought with it a lot of mixed emotions. I spent a long time feeling guilty about the money, and not feeling worthy of having earned it.

The dynamics within families get turned upside down too. As we get older, it's often said that the parents become the children and vice versa, but we had this a lot earlier than most people do. With all the financial changes that came with being in this huge band, you almost become the head of the family, as you're now able to financially support a lot of people. It puts you in this strange position that is not only uncomfortable for you, but your family too.

I don't know if it makes your relatives feel like they can't look after you, but I think it takes something away from them. In my twenties, I became self-sufficient, and so I technically didn't need anyone's help. However, being able to take care of yourself financially and emotionally are two very different things. I think it's hard for everyone to figure out what happens when things change so dynamically.

When I became famous, my parents, friends and wider family were all fine with what they had. They didn't have much, but they also didn't want for anything much. But here I was suddenly able to provide new homes, holidays, and cars. The guilt drives you to splash out on everyone, but the cash doesn't necessarily keep rolling in like that forever and it's hard to do an about-turn on generosity, especially when you look at your bank account and think, "*Oh, it's only a few hundred quid*". Or "*Buying this person a flat will literally change their lives*".

I also had a feeling of unworthiness: who am I to have all this cash? Am I really that special? Do I deserve this success?

While I've worked hard and been lucky and successful and I've earned a lot of money over the years, I've never been motivated by money. I gave a lot away because I wanted to sort everyone out but also because I almost didn't want it. I've never wanted to be seen as doing something for the money and have always been ashamed of the thought of that.

It's taken me until quite recently to realise that if you work hard, you earn money, and that's okay. I am also acutely aware that many people work incredibly hard and don't earn a lot of money. In fact, those people often work the hardest for less. The world is so unfair. So, I've felt uncomfortable sometimes with the money I've made which, at times, was for performing a couple of songs, or being in an advert for a packet of crisps. Of course, I'm grateful and I appreciate all I have, but I've struggled to find peace with it. There's a huge amount of disparity in the world and I recognise that.

There's been a price to pay with the money I've made. I think it's important that people know that, especially young people looking at Instagram and TikTok stars thinking, "*Those guys have it all: looks, fame and money*". If I'd thought there was anything simple about becoming wealthy (or famous), I was wrong. Sometimes there's no amount you can earn that can make up for some of the difficulties you face. You can buy stuff and do things that can make things a hell of a lot easier, but no amount of cash can take away sadness, anxiety or pain.

Money can do a lot of things, but it can't do that.

• • •

We were now officially a band, our own band, with a record ready to promote. We started doing more television and radio and print interviews. As with before, we would often hear, "You guys are great, but you know girl bands don't sell, right? It's teenage girls that go crazy for boy bands, they buy the records, that's the market. It just doesn't work."

We'd heard it all before. "Fuck that. We need to be a girl band for girls. We need to show that we can do this too, and we're doing it for all the girls out there."

It's around that time that Geri, I think it was, started using the phrase "Girl Power". It was a slogan that emerged in 1991 from the Riot grrrl band Bikini Kill, who did a zine called *Bikini Kill #2: Girl Power*. Shampoo had their single, "Girl Power" which I think is where Geri first saw the term. So, it was very much in existence already. It was then Geri who shouted it during an early television interview and it stuck. It became a part of us.

We began to do a few more interviews, and it was during lunch in West London with Peter Loraine, then editor of *Top of the Pops* magazine, that our nicknames were first dreamt up. *Top of the Pops* loved giving pop stars silly names: Madonna was known as "Madge"; there was Britney "Broccoli" Spears and Natalie "Umbrella Stand" Imbruglia while Bros bassist Craig Logan became known as "Ken" because... who knows?!

Peter said it would be a good idea to each have nicknames and we all loved the idea. He went back to the office and he and the team came up with "Posh Spice" first and, as he tells it, the rest of the names flowed out as easily. We'd done a couple of shoots with them by then, so they'd got the measure of us. They mocked up a spice rack with each of us as a different spice. It felt ridiculous at the time. Little did we know the impact that would go on to have.

In the same way that we decided to embrace our individual style, the names also just happened to become a big part of our success. There wasn't anything cynical in it. There were no chats with a marketing team, no one held a focus group. It was just a joke for a magazine that ended up brilliantly defining us to each other and our fans.

Sporty, Scary, Baby, Posh and Ginger were ready to take on the world.

And take on the world we did. One song at a time.

• • •

The biggest night in the British music industry calendar is the annual BRIT Awards. When we were living in Boyn Hill Road, one of the things we'd daydream the most about was being at the BRITs. Playing at the BRITs. Winning a BRIT! That was always our goal. The BRITs were a big deal to us.

So, when Virgin invited us as their guests that year, we were excited. Even though it was still early days – we didn't have a single scheduled for release, let alone out at this point – the label continued to pull out all the stops to impress us. Yet while we were still "nobodies", there was a little buzz about us within the industry, so we knew we wanted to make an entrance. Which, to be fair, we did. At least in our minds!

The BRITs 1996 took place at Earls Court, the famous Art Deco-style exhibition centre in West London. Back then, the BRITs were wild. Each table would be groaning under the weight of alcohol, although certainly not food. Think average wedding grub that's cold, as they try to feed hundreds of people in a draughty cavern of a venue. It didn't do much to soak up the vast quantities of free booze (let alone the other substances that were also in plentiful supply if that was your cup of tea). There was always an expectant energy there that anything could – and did – happen. The BRITs back then were a lot more rock "n" roll than they are today.

So it was the 19th February, and we were all cold and miserable as we froze our socks off alongside the thousands of people queuing to get in. We shuffled inside, where over a hundred tables were laden with thick white cloths, perfectly polished silverware, and ample bottles of booze. As soon as us five entered, there was a slight shift in the air. Some of those in the room had been at our showcase, some had tried to sign us, while others had heard about this new girl band from Virgin called the Spice Girls.

I was in trackie bottoms and trainers, Geri was in neon green, and Emma wore a babydoll dress. With Victoria in full glam and Mel B looking as cool as ever, we stood out a mile. Full of confidence, we strode purposefully through the crowds of rubberneckers, liggers, blaggers, suits and pop stars to take our seats. Most people didn't have a clue who we were, but we felt invincible!

We spotted our table (near the front) at the same moment as we heard someone say, "Oh, it's the Spicy girls." I realised Jason Orange, Gary Barlow, Howard Donald and Mark Owen were all grinning at us. We waved back, a tiny bit starstruck. We had spent hours at Boyn Hill Road watching their videos, studying their interviews and learning their choreography. Take That were a big inspiration to us. We loved girl bands like TLC and Eternal but because we were so much more pop, Take That really appealed to us – though we did want to be a bit cooler than them!

That was the only exchange, but something passed between us. Robbie had left the band a few months before, and a short time later the rest of the boys decided to take an extended break. We felt the metaphorical baton being handed to us that night and we grabbed it with both hands, ready to take it on to new heights.

We took our seats next to Lenny Kravitz and Vanessa Paradis, at that point the world's coolest couple. We were also seated with Ken and Nancy Berry, the head of EMI/Virgin and The Brotherhood, a rap band who had also just signed to Virgin. Drinks were poured, small talk was made, and then the lights dimmed, and a voice boomed out: "Ladies and gentlemen, please take your seats, tonight's show is about to begin…"

It was a BRITs to remember. The show was hosted by Chris Evans (who we silently booed!) and Michael Jackson was rumoured to be performing. Oasis beat Pulp, Take That,

Radiohead and Blur to win the award for Best Video, which the swaggering Gallagher brothers accepted from INXS lead singer Michael Hutchence, who would be found dead in a Sydney hotel room just 18 months later. "I've got nowt to say except I'm extremely rich and you lot aren't," proclaimed Noel, pointing the statue at the audience at the front. "Has-beens," he continued, waving the award this time in Hutchence's direction, "shouldn't be presenting awards to gonna-be's." When winning another award later, this time presented by our table mate Lenny Kravitz, Liam very charmingly pretended to shove the BRIT up his bum before turning to the crowd and shouting, "Come and have a go if you think you're hard enough."

Of course, those very same words would be repeated on that very stage a year later, but you'll have to keep reading if you want to find out who said them…!

Towards the end of the ceremony, Jarvis Cocker made another piece of BRITs history. The rumours were true, Michael Jackson was indeed there to perform "Earth Song". Wearing his signature white gloves, wind machine on full blast and surrounded by kids, I was captivated by the sight of the world's biggest pop star performing in front of me. In true dramatic Jackson style, a crane hoisted him high up above the audience. Suddenly there was a kerfuffle and Jarvis scrambled onstage, where he proceeded to do that infamous dance which included waving his bum at the audience and the television cameras. He's said recently that he was really unwell at the time and hates talking about it now, understandably.

Michael, oblivious, was lowered back to the stage, where he took off his shirt and trousers (his actual trousers) to stand, all in white like Jesus on the cross, as the little kids took it in turns to hug him. We all looked at each other. "Bonkers," said Geri.

It was almost too much to take in. By this point we'd all necked a lot of booze and had been busy spotting the likes of Tony Blair, Cyndi Lauper, Damon Albarn and Elton John. The show finally came to an end. With the cameras turned off, people started to mill about, and we joined our labelmate Annie Lennox at her table. Having listened to her music throughout my youth, I hung onto every word she said. She'd won Best British Female and as we took turns to hold her BRIT, she bestowed some wisdom upon us all in that famous Scottish drawl. "Keep your heads down and focus on the music," she told us. "There's a lot of bastards in this industry. Be careful, watch out for them."

They were wise words and not dissimilar to what I tell pop stars today, as well as reminding them to find a moment to take it all in. Because it all just flies past. It's gone before you even realise it was there.

The BRITs '96 was a line in the sand. It was the last point where things were still just about normal, yet we all *knew* that we were on the edge of something special. We had complete confidence that something huge was about to happen, although we had no idea how big, how exciting, or how terrifying it would be. We were signed to Virgin, we had a bit of cash in our pockets, and some amazing songs under our belt. That year at the BRITs we all started to imagine how next year, or the year after might look. Maybe we'd be on that stage next time, who knew?

With this buzz and excitement came pressure. We all felt it, I'm sure. We would always be there for one another; if there were any issues with boys, shifty industry types or anyone, we'd close in and protect each other. We had always been (and remain) very protective of each other. But I had felt things start to shift as we became more aware that we had something very precious. This band had the potential to be huge and none of us were allowed to fuck that up. So, rules very slowly started to appear, but the problem was that the rules, as they were being created, shifted slightly person to person. I had started to feel ever so slightly monitored, by some in the band and by management. And nowhere more so than at the BRITs that night.

We stumbled back to find our car that was waiting for us somewhere outside of Earls Court. What happened next is, to be honest, quite sketchy because I was a bit drunk. Mel B mentions it in her first autobiography, *Catch A Fire*, so I can only presume this is how it went down. There was some argument over me taking my hair out of my ponytail, which for some reason annoyed the girls in case we got photographed. I don't remember our style being completely cemented at that point – as in me in a pony, Victoria's bob, Emma in bunches etc – or that anyone was interested in photographing us that night, but regardless, it upset the girls. Though she never normally joined in, even Victoria got involved, telling me I had to tie my hair up. Under my breath I muttered, "Oh fuck off," as we went through the main doors and into the brisk winter air. Our cars were waiting for us, and Mel B, Geri and I got in and began the journey back to Watford, where Mel B and I were living at that point.

No big deal, I didn't think anything more of it.

I don't remember falling asleep that night. It was one of those *when your head hits the pillow you're out cold* moments, and I woke up early the next day a bit hungover. Desperate for a glass of water, I headed to the kitchen and realised Mel B and Geri were already up. I could hear them talking in the living room.

As I stood at the living-room door, I knew something was going on.

Mel B had a face like thunder and Geri was looking equally stern. "What's wrong, what's happened?" I asked, wondering if we'd had bad news.

"We need to talk to you, Melanie," said Geri pompously, shuffling about on the sofa to make herself look taller. "We need to talk about last night and what happened, especially between you and Victoria."

"Me and Victoria? What you on about? What happened?"

"To be honest, I'm disgusted with the way you spoke to her," said Mel B, as Geri nodded along in agreement. I looked from one to the other, waiting for them to break into laughter and say they were only messing.

They didn't.

"Honestly, I don't even know what you're talking about," I insisted, racking my brains through the fog of last night's booze.

"The way you spoke to her was just disgusting. I can't even look at you right now," one of them, I can't remember who, continued. I was shocked. "We're appalled with what you did. And how you spoke to her." I blinked back tears. "Is this because I told her to fuck off? Is that literally it?" I asked, flabbergasted – it had been a flicker in the night, a tiny second that I had to dredge back up from the furthest recesses of my mind. "The way you spoke to Victoria, it's just not on," said Mel B. "We're supposed to be a band, a family, a sisterhood."

Alongside Chic's fat-shaming a year earlier, I don't know if there's ever been anything before, or since, that has shocked me more. The way the other girls spoke to me (how we all spoke to each other, really, when we'd had a couple of drinks and were being a bit rowdy) was a million times worse than what I'd said under my breath, drunk, to Victoria. They continued to tell me off as I tried to take in the words, confused about what the real problem was.

Maybe my behaviour was worse than I'd remembered but surely, I'd have had some recollection?

I tuned back in when they told me I could expect a call from Simon any minute.

"This can't happen again, Melanie," Simon told me as I fought back more tears on the phone a few minutes later. "If it does, you'll be out. This band must be built on trust and respect and if you're not delivering that, it puts the whole group at risk. Do you understand?"

• • •

An awful lot changed that day. For one, I was devastated because I saw that this dream I'd had since I was a kid could be taken from me in the blink of an eye. For something I'd done.

For something, in fact, I barely remembered doing.

From that moment I became hyper-aware that there must be no outbursts, no arguments, no fighting back. The girl who stood up to the bullies at school, that girl started to fade into the background, she disappeared into thin air following that night at the BRITs.

Remember, two other girls had already been ditched, let alone Michelle who was, to all intents and purposes part of the band, or so we thought. I didn't take these threats idly.

I might have been the quietest of the girls, but I would stand up for myself when push came to shove. And I was confident when it came to performing. I knew I was one of the strongest dancers and singers – I felt totally comfortable and at ease in the studio and onstage. Maybe some of the others didn't like that. Perhaps there was an element of keeping me in my place.

It was subtle at first but soon I was being told what to say, or rather what not to say. Better yet, Melanie, I was told, maybe don't speak at all. On top of that, Simon Fuller's management style appeared to be divide and rule. He seemed to communicate different rules to different people. And it began to widen the cracks that were starting to appear. A circle of isolation formed around me, and a coldness spread inside me.

I started to consciously make myself smaller. *"Fly under the radar. Avoid detection."* I thought, *"If I don't speak, I won't get in trouble. If I don't get in trouble, I won't risk losing the thing that means the most to me: the band. Don't fight, don't argue, don't stand up or stand out."*

My confidence began to be stripped away, and it happened so quickly.

It was as though I'd reverted to that kid whose parents divorced and whose life got turned upside down. Don't make a fuss, stay small, keep quiet, keep everyone happy. The difference, this time, was it was happening in my place of sanctuary. To dance, to perform was my escape from the anxieties around me as a kid. Now my safety net was in danger of being taken from me.

This small yet devastating event crystallised within me this need for control. I was about to lose the thing that meant the most to me. I wouldn't jeopardise this ever again. I was seized by a gripping, overwhelming need to rule everything in my power: my weight, what I said, what I drank, how I behaved. I quickly learned to stay quiet and not rock the boat. I became very hard on myself.

The BRITs '96 is such a pivotal moment in my personal psyche, my emotional journey, my wellbeing, because from that moment I couldn't let go. I had to control, I had to be controlled. I couldn't mess anything up.

From then on, nothing short of perfection would do. It took me years to understand it and recognise it, but it was almost immediately after the BRITs '96 that my mental wellness started to subside. My previous passing interest in eating more healthily and exercising quickly began to spiral into something else.

I turned into a robot. A robot who would stop at nothing to deliver excellence and embody perfection. A robot who no longer expressed emotions, thoughts or ideas. I just went along with it, all of it, pretty much, and focused solely on making myself the best dancer, singer, performer and pop star that I could possibly be. I returned to that 11-year-old girl obsessively practising choreography in my mum's living room, shutting out everyone and everything in my determination to succeed.

If the girls were going to be hard on me, then I'd be harder on myself than they could ever dream of.

I would be the best I could possibly be in every way.

It would nearly kill me.

CHAPTER EIGHT

Spice Up Your Life

It had been two years since I'd first met Melanie Brown, Victoria Adams, Geri Halliwell and Emma Bunton, but, finally, the Spice Girls debut single was ready to drop.

The problem was, what should the first single be?

Here's where our first major disagreement with Simon and the label began.

We knew, without a shadow of a doubt, that we needed to lead with "Wannabe". Simon Fuller, however – and Virgin agreed with him – thought it should be "Love Thing" or "Say You'll Be There". They felt that those tracks were a smoother, easier introduction to the band, save the big guns until later and so on.

I think they also thought "Wannabe" was too much, too weird. But just as we'd known about our name, our image, our music, everything, us five knew, without doubt, that "Wannabe" had to be the first single. "Yooooooo"… It was so unlike anything else out there; we knew it would make a massive statement. Not only was it catchy, but it summed up everything we wanted to say:

that we were mates, that friendship comes before everything, even boys. Especially boys!

"Wannabe" couldn't follow anything, it had to be our introduction to the world.

Fortunately, our contract stipulated that we had creative control and so we prepared to do battle. Geri had a meeting with Simon Fuller. I don't know where the rest of us were, but she called us all one by one from the office, asking what we wanted to do. She told Fuller we agreed on it. "It's not negotiable, Simon, 'Wannabe' has to be the first single."

Maybe if the single had flopped, we would have been dropped. Who knows? But our insistence on debuting with "Wannabe" was a gamble that paid off. We paired it with the B-side "Bumper to Bumper", produced by the Absolute Boys and co-written with the-then pop star Cathy Dennis, who went on to co-write Britney's "Toxic", Kylie's "Can't Get You Out Of My Head" and Katy Perry's "I Kissed A Girl".

We were supposed to shoot the video at a posh hotel in Barcelona, but we couldn't get permission for some reason. So instead, it was shot in what was then the Midland Grand Hotel, next door to St Pancras station. This was still years before the regeneration of King's Cross, so there were a few dodgy characters hanging about as we arrived to begin shooting around midnight on a freezing April night. The building itself was empty and pretty much falling down by this point but the crew worked their magic with some drapes and strategic lighting, so it looked almost palatial.

The staircase we danced on is still there and there's a little plaque on the wall outside the hotel too. Fans go to take pictures of the plaque and on the stairs, which I love.

The hotel now is lovely, but back then it was so derelict that we couldn't use any of the rooms, other than where we shot, so they set up trailers on the ramp outside so we could get our hair and makeup done. We were thrilled to be given a wardrobe budget; I got straight in there with some adidas trackie bottoms and a halterneck top, Geri was in a 20-quid sequinned playsuit from Oxfam and towering heels (that she kept falling off), but Mel B really lucked out, blowing the budget with a tiny lime green Calvin Klein vest and some great Jean Paul Gaultier trousers.

Because we were doing it in one take, we had to do a load of rehearsals to get it right. Let's not forget I had, for some reason, been given the task of doing a backflip on a table laden with candles and flowers and table settings! That was quite challenging. And when I say challenging, I mean terrifying. I did it though. All those years of gymnastics didn't half pay off.

There were also lots of extras that we interacted with, so we rehearsed it dozens of times before they started to shoot. We had one guy following us around with a huge Steadicam strapped to him. He must have been knackered by the end.

"Wannabe" was quite ground-breaking at the time; not many pop bands had done a one-take video, though we were in good company alongside Janet Jackson's "That's The Way Love Goes" and Madonna's "Love Don't Live Here Anymore". (To be honest, we ended up piecing together two takes, but you can't tell!)

In a horrible turn of events, the director of the video, Johan Camitz, was run over and killed four years later in Soho in New York. The driver of the car had been shot while parked in his car outside a nightclub and, while attempting to flee, he lost control of the vehicle. Both he and Johan died.

Johan was a talented person; he'd started out as a sculptor and then directed lots of high-profile ad campaigns, before making "Wannabe". He was just 38 when he died; I'm sure he would have gone on to do many more incredible things.

He certainly did an amazing job with "Wannabe". Johan captured our spirit and our chaos (and in some cases, our nipples!) perfectly. It was cold that night! We got an edit back, and, again, Virgin weren't happy and wanted us to reshoot it. The Asian markets were refusing to play it because of Mel B's nipples, and they thought we needed something slicker for the American market. It was too shoddy, they thought.

I'm sure you've worked out by now what we had to say to that.

It had cost £130k and besides that, we loved the video. It perfectly captured what had happened over the past year or two; us barging our way into the music industry and causing a right mess. And we were just getting started.

Shoot it again? I don't think so.

· · ·

Back in the nineties, there was a music cable show called The Box. People would text in to play their favourite videos. Pretty much as soon as "Wannabe" went onto The Box, it flew. It was selected so frequently that it reached the top of the viewers' chart within two hours of going on air and stayed at number one for 13 weeks. It was finally replaced by our next video, "Say You'll Be There". The stats were mad. At its peak, up to 15% of the quarter of a million weekly telephone requests to The Box were for "Wannabe", and it was aired up to 70 times a week, becoming the most requested track in the channel's history.

We made our first appearance on live TV on Cilla Black's show, *Surprise! Surprise!* in May 1996. All our mums and dads set their VHS's that day. After it aired, I went to the Harlequin Shopping Centre in Watford, where Geri's mum was a cleaner, thinking, *"God, I'm probably gonna get mobbed."* No one recognised me. Not one single person! That took the wind out my sails, let me tell you.

The next big telly we did when we were a bit more known was on GMTV. We filmed at London Studios on the South Bank, which is sadly no more. It was such an iconic location. Every big show was filmed there: *CD:UK, SMTV Live, Loose Women, Blind Date, Graham Norton, Ant and Dec's Saturday Night Takeaway...* I've got lots of great memories of that building. We stood there that first time, freezing by the River Thames at some mad time of the morning because they'd decided we should perform outside rather than in the studio. Thanks for that! My main memory is that I accidentally called the show *TVAM.* Oops!

If you watch it now, you might notice that Mel B keeps her head down and that's because the day before filming her, Geri and me snuck down to Kensington Market to get bits and bobs pierced! I'd already had my nose done and was going to have my belly button pierced but watching Geri have hers done put me right off. Mel B had her tongue pierced but hadn't told her mum, so was conscious she'd give it away if she said a word on the telly!

TV loved us though radio, initially, wasn't having it. Radio 1 refused to play the record, and of course we'd had Chris Evans telling us to get back to kids' TV. The radio plugger at Virgin was having a terrible time.

Luckily, they couldn't resist us forever, and slowly, slowly, even Radio 1 came round. We spent most of June '96 running around the country, meeting and schmoozing with as many stations as we could. Back then, radio could make you or break you. It had as much power as a Spotify playlist today. Mum and Dad came to see us play our first radio roadshow, for Rock FM at Avenham Park in Preston. "How does everyone know your song?" Dad wondered, amazed by all these people singing along to "Wannabe" word-for-word.

The single itself came out on 8th July 1996. We had had a phone call while shopping on Carnaby Street to say that we were number six in the midweeks, which meant we should at least earn a top ten that Sunday. A top ten! We were chuffed to bits. That following Sunday, we were at Geri's stepsister's house when we heard it had actually gone in at number three. We couldn't believe it.

Back in those days, a new band would often release their debut single and album in Japan first as a testing ground, which we had done. Things were already kicking off for us over there, so the week after "Wannabe" came out, we were booked to do a bunch of promo stuff in Tokyo.

It was as we landed in Japan that we found out we'd gone to number one in the UK, so our first performance on *Top of the Pops* was after we'd stepped off a 16-hour flight. I don't think any of us had gotten much sleep. We drove to a hotel for a quick change and a breather. I called Mum and Dad to let them know. "When are you gonna get a proper job?" said Dad, before laughing. "Well done, love, I'm so pleased for you." I stuck on my Liverpool FC top and shorts and off we went to a nearby temple that had been chosen as the backdrop for our performance, which was beamed back to the UK, to be shown on BBC1 later that week.

It was all a dream really, made more surreal because we were halfway around the world and completely jetlagged when it happened.

I have no memory whatsoever of doing that first performance on *Top of the Pops*. Imagine, the thing I'd dreamt about doing for years, and it completely passed by in a blur of shock and exhaustion. I'd watched Kate Bush, Madonna, Queen, all my heroes on that show and thought, *"One day, that'll be me."* There are so many things about success that you don't factor in; that it takes so much work to get there that you can tend to forget the big, important moments.

Of course, it was massively exciting but also so hard to take in because we weren't in England with our family and friends listening to the countdown live on Radio 1. When something's kicking off at home, but you're in another part of the world, it doesn't feel as intense, it doesn't feel that real. We were so busy working crazy hours that we didn't have time for it to sink in.

It felt like we were in Japan for a long time, and it probably was a good couple of weeks. I absolutely love it over there and they were some of our most fun trips. But we were dying to get home and perform on *TOTP* at the show's actual studios. But that wasn't to be just yet. "Wannabe" stayed at number one for a second week and another crew was sent out to film us, this time at a beautiful Japanese garden in Tokyo. Luckily, we stayed at number one for a *third* week and made it home to perform in the studio.

Dream accomplished! It stayed at number one for seven weeks, so we needn't have worried, but we were all dead chuffed to get to perform it at the home of *TOTP* itself, like we'd seen so many of our heroes do over the years and talked about doing ourselves for hours on end at Boyn Hill Road.

We quickly realised, once we landed back in London, that it was madness. We all started to get recognised in the street, and kids would scream and follow us for an autograph. It wasn't fever-pitch at this point, but, almost overnight, we had a fanbase.

Our schedule, which was already packed, became three, four times busier. With the single being at number one for so long, well, we were officially a hit. And the press frenzy around us, which started then, didn't let up.

Since the release of "Wannabe", it seems like at least one of us is written about, mentioned, or referenced in some way, in the press every single day, to this day. Or if not every day, then most. Even after all these years.

In fact, I did a Google News search, just today, to see what had been written about us this past week (I'm writing this in March 2022). I counted 11 stories just in the first two pages of results; seven of them were about Victoria, one was about me wearing a pair of leggings (literally), a couple were about whether we're reuniting at Glastonbury in 2023, and one was about viewers of the TV series *Naked Attraction* being "traumatised" watching semi-clad contestants dancing about to one of our songs (fair enough).

It's mad though when I think about it. It's been nearly 30 years since we first released "Wannabe" and we are still talked about all the time.

Lovely (for the most part these days), but mad.

· · ·

I'll always remember the first day I met Melanie Brown. I thought she was the coolest person I'd ever seen. And it was really comforting for me to be around a fellow Northener, one of my own, especially when you're down South surrounded by Southeners.

Mel B, Geri and I spent a lot of time together in Boyn Hill Road, with Emma and Victoria going home most weekends. Then, the three of us moved into Cyprus Road while we did rounds of meetings.

I think Geri found it hard though, because of the intensity of her friendship with Mel B. As I've said (and as they've both said, many times), they were either thick as thieves or at war. They'd go on holiday together, hang out at weekends, and were often completely inseparable – to the point where me, Emma and Victoria couldn't get a look in. Until there was a monumental fallout, and then things got tricky because we didn't want to appear to be taking sides or "ganging up". Woe betide the person who took the wrong side.

It's the same within a lot of friendship groups and family dynamics; each person has a very different relationship with the other people in the group and how you might be with one person, you might not be with another. It can create brilliant, close relationships but also, when the balance is disrupted, the knock-on effect impacts everyone.

With us, there was a bit of vying for position, even in those early days. Nothing too much, but the seeds were starting to be sown. Geri would often take it upon herself to make decisions (or try to) on the band's behalf, always with the best intentions at heart, but Mel B didn't like that. She would get annoyed if she felt Geri wasn't being entirely open or truthful about what she was up to. True to her "Scary" nickname, Mel B could be very plain speaking and that can be hard to deal with.

As I've said, Geri also found the performance side difficult. In fact, she and I had a close relationship because I was the most willing to help her with choreography and vocals. Mel B would get frustrated with Geri because she wasn't always very patient (which you can see in an unofficial online documentary called *Raw Spice*) when Geri got things wrong.

It had its upsides, in some ways, I suppose. Mel B and Geri drove the band forward relentlessly. They would stop at nothing to make the group a success. But it did make for an intense atmosphere at times. After a couple of months, Geri found it all too much living with us two and decided to go and live with her stepsister.

She headed back towards Watford, and we followed her there because Geri's stepdad had a place in Watford, just across the road from Ana, Geri's mum, on Jubilee Road. Me and Mel B took over the lease in the spring of 1996, just the two of us.

The house was fine but decorated quite plainly. After an eventful trip to Costo, where the windscreen on Mel B's beautiful new car was smashed by a wayward barrier (never a dull moment!), she decided to add her magic touch to the house and within days, we had stars on the ceiling, a leopard-skin dining room, and a bright blue bathroom. She painted every wall in the living room a different colour – white, green, blue *and* red and plonked a lime green Argos sofa in there.

I didn't have a bed frame, but I somehow acquired a mattress, so that's what I slept on for the first few months (I was still sleeping on a mattress on the floor when "Wannabe" went to number one).

The first few weeks were okay. We would be out doing meetings or recording bits of the album in the week and then we pretty much did our own thing at weekends. I was, by this point, spending a lot of my spare time in the gym. But things were slightly strained between the two of us, especially after the tensions following the BRITs, which had happened just a few weeks before.

A few days after we moved in together, Mel B stopped speaking to me, almost entirely. "Do you want a cuppa?" I'd ask her, popping my head around her bedroom door. She would just stare at me.

My need to please people, to keep the peace, went into overdrive and I found myself trying harder and harder to win back her friendship, start a conversation, just a "yes" would have done at this point. The more I tried, the further away it drove her.

One Saturday I went to the local shop to pick up some bits. "Mel," I called when I got back, "I've got you some flowers." There was no answer, but I could hear the telly was on and I walked, timidly, into the living room. She barely turned her head. "What have you got me those for? I don't want them." The flowers all but drooped in my hand as I backed out the door and went quietly to my bedroom.

It wasn't just me; Mel B was also very low in spirits in general. She was going through relationship problems, and I guess we were all feeling the pressure of the band. We still had rehearsals and studio time to get to, but as soon as we got home, she'd go to her room. I could hear her crying over the noise of her music, or I'd walk past the door, and she'd just be lying there, staring at the ceiling.

"What's wrong, why are you so sad?" I asked her. "It's a beautiful day outside, you've got so much to get up for," I said, as gently as I could. "I'm fine," she insisted, quietly. "I'm just tired, that's all."

In the years to come, Mel B would apologise to me over and over for her behaviour towards me, particularly during those early years. She talked about our time in Watford together in her own book, and spoke a little about how, after we moved out of Watford, she often found it hard to connect with me. But I'd learnt my lesson by then: keep quiet, keep the peace, keep your head down.

We were in Vegas in 2007, during our reunion tour when Mel B came up to my room and gave me a very heartfelt apology. I think she realised that she'd been tough on me. I really appreciated that, and we've been much closer over recent years.

As things kicked off with the band though, I knew one thing: I wanted my own place. I got a copy of Loot (the classified ad mag which makes me feel as nostalgic as writing the Yellow Pages!) and found a small, one-bed flat in Finchley, on the same road as Emma and her mum. It wasn't particularly swanky, but I loved it. My own space, peace and tidiness.

• • •

After the release of "Wannabe" we spent the next few weeks in a whirlwind of press, promo and performances all over the UK, Europe and Asia. Before we knew it, we were flying back to LA to shoot the video for "Say You'll Be There" in the Mojave Desert. The single came out on 14th October 1996 and became our second number one a week later.

We weren't the only ones stunned by our success. I think Virgin were as shocked as we were. They were an experienced team who had had their share of successful bands, but no one had seen anything like this. We had taken off like a rocket, catching everyone by surprise. You can imagine, in addition to plotting single and album releases, artwork, promo and so on, they had to work out getting five young women flown all over the world to do dozens of interviews a day. There were performances to consider, travel plans, hair and makeup, what we would be wearing, where we'd stay. Can you imagine the to-do lists! Our shoes alone took up 10 suitcases. But we were all on the rollercoaster – us, Simon and 19, and the label – and there was no getting off now.

We were, of course, aware that things were going well, but there was one event that took place in London in November 1996 that really drove that home.

Until now, we'd done a bunch of radio roadshows and television performances with screaming fans, but we would be sharing the bill with other artists. We could see we had fans, but we were never sure who was there to see everyone on the bill, and who was just there for us.

Turning on the Oxford Street Christmas lights would be the first time people were coming to see us, no one else, just the Spice Girls.

Turning on the lights is a big deal. Since 1981, everyone from Bob Geldof to Cliff Richard to the cast of *Corrie* had undertaken the task. It was, and continues to be, a recognition of a person's (or group's) popularity that they're asked to undertake this prestigious act. Victoria would go with her family every year as a kid. Now she was the one hitting that button.

Virgin had hired out a few rooms in the Berkshire Hotel for us to get ready. It was just by Bond Street station, a few doors down from the HMV outside of which we would be switching on the lights that evening. We ended up crowded into one room, as we usually did back then (the separate cars and hotel rooms on different floors were still to come at this point), while our team, Jennie Roberts (hair) and Karin Darnell (makeup), helped to get us ready.

We'd had the sense that there were a lot of people as we drove in, but it wasn't until me and Emma stood at the corner window looking down that we saw how many people had shown up. There were *thousands* and thousands of fans flooding onto Oxford Street. People were lining the roads and we could hear them singing "Wannabe" and "Say You'll Be There" at the tops of their lungs. It was absolutely electrifying.

"That's all for us," I said to Emma as we watched, speechless.

I was crying me eyes out, to be honest. I felt so moved, to think of where we'd come from and to see all these people here for us. "It's quite scary really," said Emma in disbelief. "Our songs are playing all over Oxford Street."

That was the moment we realised that we'd done it. Really done it. It's amazing to get number ones, and travel the world, but to see fans, to see people who were buying the music, meant so much. We knew we were popular, but seeing all those people gathered there, to see *us*, really brought it home.

Our security guard, Jerry Judge, told us the cars were ready to drive us around and, on a signal from the police (it was like something out of a movie!), we rushed out of the hotel lobby, into the cars and then around to the HMV. There were thousands and thousands of kids screaming, shouting our names, holding up banners and placards. What a moment! How many times had we been told girl bands didn't sell? It was moments like this that affirmed our instincts and proved that we had been right, after all.

Mel B grabbed my hand, and we went to the front of the barriers to shake hands and take pictures. Geri picked up a little boy, threw him over her shoulder and walked around with him. Dr Fox from Capital Radio was hosting the evening alongside the then Lord Mayor of London, Sir Roger Cork, and we made our way over to the stand, where we climbed up onto a cherry-picker so the crowds could see us better.

It was overwhelming. The noise of the people, the noise of us as well, as we shouted into the microphone, eager to communicate with our fans. Dr Fox tried to talk to us, as did the Lord Mayor, but we were too buzzing. We just shouted at them, over each other, and at the crowd. It was chaos. It was amazing to see the range of our fans; it was kids in push-chairs, teens, young people our age, parents, grandparents. It was completely overwhelming.

Somehow, we did the big countdown, pressed the button and POW! on came the lights as tens of thousands of people cheered us on.

It was all over very quickly. None of us wanted to leave but we had to. The police and Jerry made sure of that. We were whisked back to the hotel before heading to the OXO Tower for the album launch party hosted by Virgin, which culminated in a very expensive fireworks display over the Thames. The idea of it being our party is funny because it was one of many parties thrown "for us" that wasn't about us. We didn't have our mates or family there; it was all record label personnel and people they wanted to impress, like DJs and journalists. We were expected to turn up, smile, take pictures, sign stuff and then be wheeled off out of a back door and on to the next engagement.

Funny old business, the music industry.

. . .

The band ended the year on a massive high. "Wannabe" went to number one in 22 nations (eventually rising to 37) and selling 15 million copies. "Say You'll Be There" sold another three million globally, and we got our third number one, and our first Christmas number one, with "2 Become 1". A couple of weeks before that, our debut album *Spice* hit the top of the charts, outselling the entire top five by four to one and selling nearly two million copies in just seven weeks. We had 10,000 thousand people a week joining the fan club, leading the press to compare the madness to Beatlemania.

Spicemania was born.

Over the last six months, we'd been catapulted from total unknowns to a best-selling band with three number one singles and a number one album. We were everywhere.

The press couldn't get enough of us. We sold papers. Lots and lots of papers. Whether it was gossip on who we were dating, former lovers and friends selling their stories, or the topless pictures of Geri from years before that came out, they must have thought we were the gift that kept on giving.

The media loved to set women against each other, and with the Spice Girls, they had the perfect opportunity. The tabloids would often run "polls" of which Spice Girl was the most popular, who was the hottest, who was the best. It was horrible because when there's a "most", there's a "least". We all got it, some of us were considered "prettier" or "more popular", but it is so hard to read things like that over and over. It's so damaging. Or it certainly was for me.

We would be followed everywhere, and Simon made us doubly paranoid about anyone seeing any of us doing anything, ever. We'd be convinced photographers were lurking in the bushes, and that our phones were tapped. It turned out we weren't wrong about either of those things.

For every positive there's a negative, isn't there? It hadn't occurred to me all those years ago in Widnes, watching Live Aid and imagining myself on that stage, that there was a price to pay with fame. All I ever wanted to do was perform; the stage was the ultimate place of comfort to me. But I hadn't considered everything that surrounds performance, and fame, especially if you do become one of the very few to become really, hugely successful.

As a kid, the idea of becoming a "celebrity" seemed nothing but fun: signing autographs, chatting about yourself on the telly, walking on red carpets. I had no idea that fame can highlight all your insecurities, that it can exacerbate even the smallest issues with, for instance, eating, drinking, drugs (pharmaceutical as well as recreational), and so on. Reading about myself, in often a very negative light, quite quickly took its toll on my mental wellbeing.

I was already conscious of my body weight; since Chic's comments and then the incident at the BRITs my focus became almost exclusively about control, which was being driven by an increasingly negative internal voice. That voice wouldn't cut me the slightest bit of slack. No matter how busy we were, how long the days, how physically hard I'd worked, my eating remained restrictive, and became even more so. If I had a flight at 8 am, I'd get up at 5, just so I could get some time in at the gym.

I don't think I had body dysmorphia as such at this point – I'd look at the hundreds, thousands of pictures being printed of me and see that I was slim – but I was terrified of putting on any weight, or looking anything other than what I considered, at that time, my best.

I started to become obsessed with what was being said about me, what people thought about me, how I looked in photos. I was already at the edge of an eating disorder, and constantly being written about and photographed fed right into that. The more pictures I saw of myself, the more determined I was to stay "fit and healthy". But I was becoming incredibly thin.

This was also during a time when certain parts of the media could be harsh about people in the public eye. Both Geri and

Victoria were made to weigh themselves, live on air. They were put on scales in front of an audience on a television show broadcast live on Channel 4. It's on YouTube to this day. A year or so after that appearance, Victoria was asked during another TV interview if she had an eating disorder. "Are you anorexic?" Michael Parkinson wondered when she appeared on his show, "How do you know that [you're not]?", he continued before asking her what she ate every day. It's a brutal interview, he's quite intrusive.

Magazines would highlight cellulite on women's thighs, rolls of fat on their stomach or sweat stains under the arms and call it "the circle of shame". They would cheerfully berate those who put on weight but then reprimand those who'd lost too much weight. You literally could not win. Women's bodies were the source of constant scrutiny and scorn, and it was completely accepted. This didn't only affect those being talked about, it sent out such damaging messages to the women reading this rubbish too. It was such a harmful time.

Along with everything else around me, I wasn't immune to this culture either. I was obsessive about what I ate and how I looked and what was being said about me. On a typical day, I'd wake up and cycle to David Lloyd gym, where I'd usually be one of the first there as they opened. First stop, straight to the newspaper stand for the *Daily Star*, the *Daily Mirror* and once a week, the *News of the World*, to see what was being written about us. About me. Then a two-hour workout, cycle home and stick Teletext on (ask your mum to explain if you don't know what this is!), scouring for any mentions there.

What a way to start your day.

In many ways it was lose/lose. Even if there were nice things printed, you'd only focus on the negative. If there was nothing in there, there would be relief, swiftly followed by the realisation that one of the other girls was splashed across four pages.

It began to breed a few issues within the band. Initially, Mel B and Geri were written about the most, but then Victoria met a new guy and, boom, a new tabloid sensation was born. Take any five young people and pit them against each other in what amounts to a popularity contest, and it's going to cause problems. It just is.

It was incredibly unhealthy to use the tabloid press as a barometer of your worth. But we were so young, and so new to it all, that we fell for it hook, line and sinker.

• • •

The first two months of 1997 were as mad and manic as 1996 had been. Having had such incredible success in the UK, Europe, Japan and elsewhere, we turned our attention to the United States. Everyone knew how hard it was to crack America. Some of the biggest and best bands in the world hadn't managed to do it. But we didn't want to let that hold us back. We knew how difficult it could be, but we were very driven, and we believed in ourselves, individually, and as a band. Our belief never faltered; it was as though we *knew* we would do it. We felt unstoppable.

If any of us ever did waver, the other four were there to boost that confidence we needed to achieve these huge goals.

America was the ultimate prize, but we knew we could do it.

What's mad is that we did. Whether alchemy, the stars aligning or sheer good luck, America fell in love with the Spice Girls. And fell in love hard.

As we flew first class from Canada to New York in late January, "Wannabe" was busy becoming the highest debut single of any track ever in the Hot 100 Billboard chart (US, UK or otherwise). We had gone in at number 11, selling 700,000 copies before challenging Toni Braxton's classic ballad "Unbreak My Heart" for the top spot. "Wannabe" went on to knock Braxton off and go to number one. By this point we had had four UK number one singles, a number one album and now a number one single in America. "Wannabe" alone had reached number one in 32 countries around the globe (later reaching 37 countries). In May of that year, *Spice* topped the Billboard album charts, the first album by an all-female group to do so since the Go-Go's in 1982!

So great was our success that *The Times* reported that we would be substantially contributing to the growth of the UK economy. In 1997/1998, the music industry was worth £3.3 billion a year to the country (in 2018, pre-pandemic and pre-Brexit, it was up to £5.2 billion). Thanks to revenue we were generating globally, we were adding a significant amount of cash to that pot. By the time we came home, the press were saying that we were to Tony Blair what The Beatles had been to Harold Wilson.

We were a success story not only for Virgin Records and the music industry, but for the country itself.

There was a lot riding on us, and the schedule was brutal. We weren't in the US long, but it was a full-on trip. Mel B and Geri had got the flu in Canada and as we flew into JFK airport, Victoria came down with it too. We were all run down but there was no stopping the machine. This was our big moment. That trip was a whirlwind week of non-stop promo in New York, Miami and Los Angeles, shaking hands with record label people, dinners with MTV, and meet and greets, including a party bus with radio station Z100, which took us and some fans around New York. In true Spice Girls style, Geri somehow ended up driving the bus for a couple of blocks. We had journalists with us too: someone from

The Face magazine flew out and a tabloid journalist joined us at one point.

The US trip ended up being cut slightly short so we could get home to appear on the National Lottery, which back then had an audience of over 15 million. We also launched Comic Relief's Red Nose Day and announced that "Who Do You Think You Are" would be the official single for that year, with "Mama" as the Double A-side (back in the days when people still pressed singles). We donated all proceeds of that Double A-side to Comic Relief.

For Comic Relief, we did an alternate video for "Who Do You Think You Are" featuring some of our favourite women dressed up as us. The Sugar Lumps consisted of the legendary Lulu playing Baby and comedians Dawn French and Jennifer Saunders as Posh and Ginger, Llewella Gideon as Scary and the brilliant Kathy Burke playing me.

We'd grown up watching Comic Relief and idolising these women and everybody involved with the charity, which was set up by comedian Lenny Henry and screenwriter Richard Curtis. To be playing a big part in the fundraising that year was such an honour and, as I'm sure you can imagine, ridiculous fun. There was a whole sketch where the five of them spoofed us and then they joined us for the video, which was just chaos of us teaching them the moves and generally having a right laugh.

Dawn and Jennifer have continued to be in our lives. Dawn came to the first night of our *Spiceworld* tour at The Point in Dublin in 1998 and brought the icon that is Alison "Only You"/"Is This Love" Moyet with her. I was later on the judging panel with Dawn on *Superstar* in 2012, Andrew Lloyd Webber's ITV show to find Jesus for his arena tour of *Jesus Christ Superstar* in which I later played Mary Magdalene. And in 2011, Jennifer wrote *Viva Forever*, our ill-fated musical… more on that later.

For all of us girls, 1997 to 1998 is a blur. We didn't stop to take it all in because we just didn't have time. Between January and February '97, we flew to 10 different countries, that I can remember. We were in Departures so often that even the customs officers couldn't believe how much we travelled.

I've still got a diary from 1997, a little brown leather book and it's crazy to see what the schedule was like. In between shooting the video for "Who Do You Think You Are", we flew to Germany, then Belgium, came back to London to record a Pepsi advert at Abbey Road Studios, (me and Geri managed to squeeze in getting kicked off stage at a Blur gig at the Astoria that same night), launched the new McLaren car at Ally Pally with Jamiroquai, popped across the Atlantic to New Orleans for a photoshoot, returned home to do more vocals at Abbey Road, before playing Sanremo in Italy (where we met Lionel Richie for the first time) and then finally (this is day twelve) went to Dublin for the IRMA awards where we appeared alongside Boyzone, Peter Andre and Alisha's Attic.

That schedule was typical of those two years between 1996 and the end of 1998. There was no stopping, very few breaks, and very little sleep.

We had one day off between Dublin and our BRITs rehearsals, where we would be performing on Monday 24th February.

Simon Fuller asked me and Victoria if we wanted to join him and Ashley Newton at Chelsea, who were playing Man United on the 22nd. I was well up for it, as was, weirdly, Victoria who as far as I know had no interest in footie, outside of fancying a couple of players, like we all did. It turns out Simon Fuller, ever the canny marketeer, had "plans" for Posh and those plans included football's newest star, a young player called David Beckham.

Victoria came to mine in Finchley on Saturday, and we headed down to Stamford Bridge. I'd only been in the Kop (the famous home stand at Anfield) end before, right behind the goal, but now we were "the Spice Girls" so we had a great view practically on the pitch at the halfway line. The match was a draw, but we got to see two great goals – one from Gianfranco Zola and one from David Beckham, who had scored from the halfway line against Wimbledon a few months earlier. It's still considered one of the greatest goals of all time.

We went to the players' lounge after the game where we were accosted by a very drunk Simon Le Bon from Duran Duran. I sidled off to escape him, as Simon Fuller rescued Victoria. A few minutes later, I turned around to see Victoria talking to the man with the number seven shirt: David Beckham himself.

A couple of weeks later we had the chance to go to Old Trafford to see the team play on their home turf. I called Victoria. "Fancy it? We'll have to fly up and back the same day because we've flying to Florida on the Monday." Already smitten, I reckon, Victoria immediately agreed. Off we went from Heathrow on the short flight, before landing to have lunch with the chairman of Man United. At halftime, we were invited onto the pitch to do the charity tombola and read out the halftime scores (which I had to help Victoria with because she had no clue what she was reading!).

I had, of course, made no secret of the team I supported, and there is a long-held rivalry between Liverpool and Manchester, mostly to do with the footie but also... well, just because the two towns are so close to each other, perhaps. I love Manchester, and all my Manchester mates. But when it comes to it, football and Liverpool always comes first.

We got to go in the tunnel and out onto the pitch, which was amazing. Having spent years at Anfield watching the game from the stands, to be on the pitch was a real buzz.

I soon came crashing down to earth though when the Man U fans clocked me. The whole stadium, and I mean, the *whole* stadium, started shouting, "You Scouse bastard! You Scouse bastard!" I was really entertained by that and did my best Liam Gallagher moment flicking the Vs all round. It was like, "Fuck you lot, I'm on the pitch!"

David and Victoria got together quickly after that second meeting and, well, we all know the rest of that story. As soon as they swapped numbers, they were inseparable. Victoria would drive up to Manchester, where he was playing and training, and he'd drive down to London, so who knows when they slept because they went to the ends of the earth to be together. They were madly in love. It got serious so fast and it's just wonderful that they're still together with their four beautiful children.

I think it makes sense that a lot of pop stars and footballers ended up together. We were all working class kids who came from nothing who suddenly found themselves very rich and very famous. And the pairing of pop stars and footie players only raised everyone's profile. When David came through, footballers were catapulted into a whole new league, with huge paychecks and constant coverage in the tabloids, this time on the front page, rather than the back page.

Before it all came out though, a couple of weeks after they got together, I got a late night phone call at nearly midnight, and I was in bed. "Melanie, it's me," said Victoria, "You know you said we could come to yours if we needed to?" Victoria hadn't told her Mum about David at this point, and Simon had told them to do whatever it took to avoid being papped, so they'd found themselves without anywhere to hang out. About half an hour later, they turned up at my place in Finchley.

"Come in, come in," I said, grinning my head off as David took in the walls. Pride of place in the hallway, above the landline, were my Liverpool FC posters. I'd looked at them before they arrived and thought, "Hmm interesting!" And no, I didn't take them down. As if.

David and Victoria stayed a couple of hours and I remember Victoria dragging me into the bathroom to ask me what I thought of her new bloke.

David quickly became one of the girls. Don't forget, "If you wanna be my lover, you gotta get with my friends", and lucky for him he was allowed into the inner circle. We liked him because he was quiet and he didn't get involved, he didn't interfere. He was always very sweet and he was very shy back then. He supported Victoria, and us, and he also had his own very successful career to focus on.

"Posh and Becks" became, arguably, the most famous pairing in the world, certainly during that time. And it only helped us as a band. The Beckhams coupling added to Spicemania, bringing the band even more attention than we already had. When I saw them together after those first couple of dates, I had no idea just how influential they would become as a couple.

No one, surely, could have predicted that.

Nor could we have anticipated the recognition we were about to be given by the BRITs. We'd found out just before Christmas 1996 that we'd been nominated for five awards – Best Single, Best

Newcomer, Best Group and two Best Videos for "Wannabe" and "Say You'll Be There".

Not only that but that we'd be performing at the show.

And when they said performing at the show, they meant opening the show.

This was it. This was our big moment to prove that we weren't some manufactured pop act. It was time to show this music industry what we were made of.

CHAPTER NINE

The Moment You Believe

If last year we had been *wannabes* (pun intended), we really were the stars of the 17th BRIT Awards in 1997. In 1996 we were guests – in 1997 we were the opening act, performing alongside The Manic Street Preachers, Prince, The Fugees, The Bee Gees and Diana Ross.

The band was up for five awards, and we were opening the show with a performance of "Who Do You Think You Are", with a bit of "Wannabe" thrown in for good measure. We returned from a whirlwind month of promo and press exhaustion, after endless rounds of interviews and flights, and with just one day to prepare for what might be our biggest night yet.

We already had the moves sorted for the videos, but the choreographer Priscilla Samuels was enlisted to pull things together and try to give us a bit more structure in the chaos. We needed to put an actual *performance* together for the BRITs.

Last year we'd gone in the front entrance, but this time it was straight through the back as our cars whisked us into the loading bay of Earls Court. From there, we were taken through to the dressing rooms to get ready.

Our hair and makeup team on the night were the brilliant Jennie and Karin. It's incredible that we only had one hair and makeup artist between the five of us. It took an eternity to get us all ready. Of course, all of us girls had different looks and needs, but somehow I usually drew the short straw of getting in the chair first, which meant they'd all get to sleep a bit longer! "You're Sporty, you're up early," one of the girls would say. Although, to be honest, I think I always offered. Anything for an easy life...

We worked with Jennie and Karin for years, and sometimes still do. The "glam squad", as it's often referred to these days, are people you end up spending most of your time with. Not only are they helping transform you into your pop persona ("What? I woke up like this!") but they were the keepers of many secrets, shoulders to cry on and full-on therapists on many occasions. What hair and makeup people could tell you about the folks they work with...! They really do see it all.

Once we were dressed and made up, it was onto the red carpet for the press run, and photo ops. A lot of the questions were focused on "Spicemania" and our success in America, with everyone wanting to know how we felt. We were all speechless (even Geri, for once), to be honest.

The backstage area was filled with famous faces like the Manic Street Preachers, Noel Gallagher, Naomi Campbell and The Fugees. "Would you like a photograph with Elton?" someone asked, and that's how we met Elton John for the first time. Elton had a bespoke dressing room, which was a small cabin surrounded by AstroTurf and a white picket fence.

Reading all these names it all sounds very glamorous but, seriously, while being backstage at these events is incredibly exciting and fun, it's never really that glamorous. The dressing rooms were either prefabs or sectioned-off "rooms", often with no ceiling. I bet being next door to us lot when you were preparing to go on was fun! They'd obviously pushed the boat out for Elton with his AstroTurf and picket fence. Maybe they thought he might fancy doing a few keepy uppys before going on stage?!

We bumped into the icon that is Diana Ross outside her dressing room. She spoke to us briefly, congratulating us on our success in America. More pictures were taken. It felt strange meeting some of the biggest stars of the music world and them wanting to have a photograph with us as much as we did with them. People seemed as happy to pose with us as we were with them, which felt so mad.

Geri spotted someone from one of the labels who had turned us down a couple of years back. She grabbed me and we swaggered over to him. "Hello, remember us? You turned us down," she grinned, going full Julia Roberts *Pretty Woman*. "Big mistake!" We turned on our heels and ran off giggling as the hapless bloke stood there opening and closing his mouth like a goldfish.

There were people everywhere, it was manic, and it was all I could do to find a quiet space in my mind to run over the choreography. I had completely buried the events of last year's BRITs. It would be years, in fact, before I even recalled that awful night, during my *Desert Island Discs* interview with Lauren Laverne in 2020. But in 1997, subconsciously or otherwise, I had a lot to prove. To myself, to the band, to the world. I was determined this would be perfect. It had to be perfect. There were thousands in the audience, with over 12 million later watching on telly in the UK and 30 million worldwide.

We returned to the dressing room to wait nervously before the show got underway. Someone chucked on the stereo, and we spent all our nervous energy jumping up and down to Republica's uplifting anthem "Ready to Go" on repeat.

Geri had bought us all little candles shaped like statues. "Even if we don't win, let's have the best night," she said as a floor manager knocked on the door. It was time to go and once more we were led along countless corridors to the arena, where a live audience and numerous cameras were ready to watch us perform.

I'll never forget the five of us standing on the stage, our backs to the audience, holding hands, waiting to hear the host Ben Elton say, "It's... THE SPICE GIRLS", before the cannons went off, the lights went up and we were all systems go. Of course, we mimed (not our choice) but the performance went brilliantly.

The photographers in the press pit were, as ever, angling their cameras up the skirts of those of us that were wearing them. It's unbelievable to me that it was so accepted and acceptable at that time and that it's only *recently* become a criminal offence to take a photo up someone's skirt.

On 12th February 2019, the Voyeurism (Offences) (No.2) Bill, known as the "Upskirting Bill" received Royal Assent in England and Wales (Scotland had already changed its legislation on voyeurism to make it a specific offence in 2010). So, from 12th April 2019, upskirting became a criminal offence in England and Wales, which is punishable by up to two years in prison. This is over here, though. Hailey Bieber has discussed being upskirted leaving a restaurant in LA as recently as 2021. The paps are still at it, whether it's illegal or not.

The level of intrusion from the paparazzi, both physically and emotionally, was intolerable at times. It didn't matter what you were going through – you might have lost someone close to you, you might have just had some bad news, you might be in a rush somewhere – the paps didn't care. Thank goodness I never saw it on the level of someone like Princess Diana, but even still, it was relentless. The press used to have access at airports, so you'd step off a 24-hour flight from Australia to lightbulbs flashing in your face. You'd be trying to leave a venue, the safety of your fans utmost in your mind, as the paps would push and shove to put the camera as close to the car as possible to get a picture of... someone sitting in a car? They would do anything to get a shot of a male celebrity angry, and a woman either naked or appearing to be drunk. And they'd employ every trick in the book to get those pictures; riling a man up about his partner or mum and taking pictures of people where inevitably their eyes are half-shut. Oh, look at so-and-so "tired and emotional" again.

Back then, we'd puzzle how on earth they knew where we would be, and when. We'd look suspiciously at friends, family or people working with us. Did you tip them off? Did *you*? We even thought maybe our phones were tapped, but surely, we're just being paranoid.

As we were to find out in the wake of the News International phone-hacking scandal, it turns out we weren't being paranoid at all. I can't say too much about my case because it's ongoing, but it's been extremely illuminating to discover the depths that certain journalists would go to for that "scoop".

So, the BRITs was loads of fun but we had one eye on those pervs trying to take a picture of our private parts.

We put quite a bit of thought into what we were wearing that night. I decided on fabulous Antonio Berardi trousers and a cropped gold, brown and blue strappy Dolce & Gabbana tank top and signature Nike Air Max. Emma was in a full sequined purple halter-neck babydoll dress, Mel B in a skin-tight leopard print all in one, with Victoria in a white skirt and matching bikini top and killer heels. We had gone all out.

Of course, Geri stole the show in *that* Union Jack dress which, let's be honest, was a stroke of genius. It was a simple, black Gucci dress (no more vintage for Geri by this point!) and her sister sewed a Union Jack tea towel over it. She added the CND (or as Mum says "ban the bomb") to the back because she was worried the flag alone might look a bit too nationalistic.

We were already being credited for buoying the economy with our global sales. Geri wearing that dress connected her, connected us to New Britain, New Labour, a time of prosperity and hope. Tony Blair was very savvy too; he could see that by allying himself with us, and others like Oasis, that it would bolster his votes with young people.

On the lead up to the 1997 General Election, some smart alec asked Blair and the-then Prime Minister John Major to name each member of the Spice Girls. Major named two; Blair got me, Victoria and Geri! He also proclaimed that one of his favourite songs of 1996 was "Say You'll Be There". Funny that, though, because just a year before he wasn't so interested in the Spice Girls. Something else happened that night at the BRITs in 1996 – Geri saw the future Prime Minister and approached him at his table. "Mr Blair, I'm Geri and I'm in a girl band. We're going to be huge. We're about to make our first video. Would you be interested in appearing in it?" He declined!

But with an election coming up in May 1997, he'd had second thoughts. His closeness to us worked in both our favours. It propelled us beyond pop stars into global superstardom, faces of the country, a cultural phenomenon. There even became such a thing as "The Spice Vote", which genuinely bewildered us all. To think we could have any impact on a general election was totally mind-boggling.

. . .

The crowd went mad as we finished our performance and all five of us felt on top of the world. After months, *years*, of hard work, we had reached the pinnacle of success, and what a moment it was.

We came flying off the stage after our BRITs performance, laughing, hugging and crying. But the night was far from over. We headed back to the dressing room to get changed before being taken to our table in the auditorium to find out if we'd won anything.

And we had! We took home two awards that night. The first was voted for by The Box, the TV channel that had really supported "Wannabe". The award was presented by the comedian Frank Skinner. "Now they tell me it's polite to actually kiss the winners when you hand over the award, so I know who I'm hoping for," he said, as he opened the envelope. "And the winner of The Box Best Video Award is – thank you, God – the Spice Girls!"

I wish I could tell you how it felt, what was going on in my mind, but it's such a strange sensation. It's out-of-body, really. A heady mix of pure happiness and raging adrenaline. We jumped up, laughing and smiling, Geri's boobs nearly popping out of her figure-hugging red Jessica Rabbit dress, people reaching out to touch us and congratulate us. Geri grabbed my hand and we walked towards the stairs that led to the stage. Frank got his wish with a big smacker from us all, and we all took turns to say our thank you's. Just as we were finished, Geri lifted the trophy over her head as we shouted, "God bless Britain". Her nipple escaped again.

Alongside the Union Jack dress, that picture was on the front cover of every tabloid the next day. *Lovely BRITs*, said the *Daily Star*.

The second award we were up for was Best Single for "Wannabe", presented by Mrs Merton, the brilliantly talented comedienne Caroline Aherne, who sadly died of cancer in 2016, aged just 52 years old. Before announcing the winner, she made a joke about someone called Charlie: "Can you make yourself known, they're all asking for you backstage." The BRITs and its love of excess clearly hadn't diminished since the year before…!

The award was voted for by commercial radio listeners and though "Wannabe" had been a massive hit, nothing was guaranteed. While we had this huge success and the numbers to back it up, we were still very much the underdog in many ways, certainly in the eyes of some people in the music industry. As we well knew, pop music was popular at that time, but it wasn't respected. And it seemed like we were the most hated of all. Barely a week went by without some indie band or other offering their opinions of us. "I want them tarred and feathered. My wish is for the complete and utter destruction of the Spice Girls," exclaimed Shirley Manson of the band Garbage. Thom Yorke from Radiohead said we were "The Antichrist".

Liam Gallagher had also made headlines just a few days before the BRITs, with *The Sun* reporting he was snubbing the show because if he "bumped into the Spice Girls, I'd chin 'em." Why was everyone feeling so violent towards us? I think one reason we inspired such vitriol – and I'm sure people wouldn't want to admit this – is that they were jealous of our success. I'm a massive Garbage fan, but I'm sure Shirley hated the music we were doing, she might have hated the way we looked and possibly the way we portrayed women, I don't know. It's ironic when we could have done with women supporting women. I'm sure she feels differently today.

The Spice Girls weren't to everyone's taste, I get that, and we were irritating to certain people. They probably thought the music was annoying, and so our success was probably infuriating because they didn't think there was validity in it, because it wasn't to their taste. And pop music really wasn't cool at the time. Liam Gallagher wouldn't have looked very credible if he'd told everyone how much he loved the Spice Girls. Music was a lot more snobbish then; you were a fan of one genre, and one genre only and anything outside of that (especially pop) was the pits.

But it didn't matter what other musicians thought, it was the fans that counted. And it's thanks to them we did so well that night.

The category for Best Single featured some huge hits like "Lifted" by The Lighthouse Family, "A Design for Life" (The Manics), "Return of the Mack" (Mark Morrison), "Don't Look Back in Anger" (Oasis), "Firestarter" (The Prodigy), "Born Slippy" (Underworld), and "Fastlove" by my would-be husband George Michael, who was unable to attend that year because his mother was seriously ill.

We were competing with some massive songs but because this was a public vote, we had allowed ourselves to hope that maybe, just maybe, we could win this one too.

"We've seen the brazen hussies earlier. The little Spice Girls," said Mrs Merton, announcing our second win.

We leapt up and headed once more to the stage, holding hands as we went. Victoria, Emma, Mel B and Geri said their thank you's before I stepped up to say my piece.

"I just wanna say, Liam, come and have a go if you think you're hard enough," I yelled as the other girls all cheered me on. Offering out the lead singer of Oasis, little old quiet me, who would have thought? But I had to stick up for myself, for the Girls and for Liverpool against those Manc troublemakers. It was all tongue-in-cheek of course.

Noel came over to our table that night and apologised on behalf of his sibling. "Sorry about my brother – I'm sure he didn't mean it," he grinned.

We made up with Liam eventually, too. I used to see him quite often when I moved into my flat in North London. No one else has that silhouette – you can see him strutting around Hampstead from a mile off.

We met properly around 2000 when he was dating Nicole Appleton from All Saints. I'm good mates with her sister, Nat. I was over at Nat's house down the road from mine one day and the door went. She peeked out to see who it was. "It's Nic," she laughed, "Fucking hell, she's got Liam with her." I opened the door to find Liam standing there, mouth wide open. He grinned when he spotted me. "Come on then, Scouse," and took up a boxing stance.

We've got on alright since then, with both him and Noel. In fact, Noel tells a story about Liam turning up to an Oasis gig at Wembley around 2000, completely pissed after hanging out with a certain Spice Girl. I think we'd been in a pub in St John's Wood – me, him, Nic and Nat Appleton – before he went off to sound-check. He was so drunk onstage that night that he told Chris Moyles on Radio X in 2019 that he's not drunk onstage again since. Can I just say for the record that I was merely there, I'm not taking the blame for it!

I saw Liam again, later that summer, when "I Turn to You" went to Number One. It was my second solo hit and so I threw a bit of a celebration, a bit of a session, at a place that was then called House on the Hill in Hampstead. I was on top of the world and being proper lairy, dancing on tables and popping bottles of champagne. Liam was so embarrassed that he left! I thought if I've embarrassed Liam Gallagher, well, there's nowhere else left to go after that. We had a laugh with him after the 2012 Olympics too, when we all went back to George Michael's house in Highgate for one of his infamous parties. This might be a bold claim, but George was the number one party host, ever. And sorry guys, but what happens in Highgate...

At the BRITs in 1997, between Geri's boobs and my fighting talk, our two wins and a stellar performance, the night belonged to the Spice Girls. The record industry had told us time and time again that a girl band wouldn't work. Indie bands took the piss out of us, saying we were shit. Very few people believed we could make it and many people were peeved that we had. But the fans, the country, had voted. As the saying goes: Men lie, women lie... numbers don't.

For us, it wasn't only the tangible feeling of success, winning two awards and, we hoped, winning a few more people over – it was also triumphing against the odds. They said it couldn't be done, and yet, guess what? We'd done it.

After being in the US and starting to see success there, the BRITs that year were a real coming home moment for us. It was our BRITs, we opened the show, we won two awards, we felt like it was all about the Spice Girls. We felt such an appreciation from the British public too. It was such a special time.

We celebrated in style, leaving Earls Court for a party held in our honour, thrown by Virgin at Quo Vadis in Soho with guests including Richard Branson, Simon and Yasmin Le Bon, footballer

Robbie Fowler, Gary Barlow and Robbie Williams. Yes, he who I'd had a poster of on my wall for years.

According to the papers the next day, we left at 5 am before going back to our hotel but even though I wasn't drinking that night – not after last year's BRITs – I can't remember what time I got home.

By this point, I was incredibly slim. With all the travel, rehearsals, performances and flying across numerous time zones, it was a punishing time on our bodies, but I continued with my relentless low-calorie diet. The day after the BRITs, I was back to my routine – a 10-kilometre run, two-hour workouts, and very little fuel.

We were all being carried through on a high, really. We were constantly exhausted but continually full of adrenaline, nerves and tension. I felt like I couldn't have a life beyond the band. I felt dehumanized by my own restictions, and the ones put on me. I shouldn't have a boyfriend, I shouldn't speak too much in interviews, I shouldn't speak up too much at all.

This was also when more issues and problems started to seep through. I was certainly falling deeper into an eating disorder, and the other four had their own private battles too. Between us, tension and frustrations were bubbling. There were still the power struggles, still the feeling that some people could do what they wanted, whereas others couldn't.

On the face of it, things couldn't be better. We would go on to sell 19 million copies of *Spice* and win numerous awards, on top of the two BRITs. Every magazine, TV show and radio station around the globe wanted us. Every song we released was going to number one. Nothing we did could possibly go wrong.

We were living the dream. Everything we said we wanted to do, we were doing it, it was happening.

Emotionally though, I was sinking deeper into this state of being a robot. I wouldn't deviate from the things I had to do to achieve the things I wanted to do. I was pretty much sober, eating in a very restrictive way, and training like a demon in-between jumping on and off long-haul flights.

I was vulnerable. So, so vulnerable.

• • •

In between the relentless promo and the publicity, shooting the Comic Relief video, playing and winning at the BRITs, and travelling to and from America, we filmed the video for "Mama", written and produced by Matt and Biff. We already knew what the video would look like when we were writing the song. I mean, it was obvious! We were all so family-orientated that we knew we wanted our mums to be a big part of the visuals. The idea was that we would be performing in front of fans, and we'd all arrive at the stage by different means. Emma and Geri drove in in a convertible car, and I was somehow talked into sliding down from the ceiling from a rope. Although that bit was never used, so braving those heights ended up being a waste of time. Thanks for that, everyone!

We were happy that our mums would get to see a snapshot of our lives. Shooting a video sounds so glamorous but it can be tough and often very boring. In those days you'd arrive in the middle of the night and you're usually still there twenty-four hours later. It's exhausting, and I think all our mums were absolutely knackered by the end of it. In fact, "Mama" was a two-day shoot, which was a first for us. This was a time when record companies were booming, and budgets were huge. It's very different today, for most artists.

We took a break in shooting, and I used the opportunity to go to the loo. Our assistant, Camilla banged on the door. "Melanie, your Dad's on the phone, he says it's important," she said, passing the phone under the cubicle door. "Dad, I can't really talk, I'm shooting a video," I began before he cut me off. "Melanie," he started, "I've got something to tell you. You know you've always wanted a sister? Well, you've got one." I paused to take this in. "Oh. Is Carole pregnant again?" "No, she's nothing to do with Carole. She's from before. She's actually just a few years younger than you."

And that's how I found out I had a sister called Emma.

A few years after Mum and Dad broke up, he'd met a woman and had a brief relationship. It wasn't extra-marital, no one cheated, but for whatever reason it didn't work out. But it turned out that she was pregnant. When his daughter, Emma, was born, Dad went to see her, but Emma's Mum had met someone else, and Dad was told to stay away. Which he did.

In 1997, when I was told about her, Emma was a teenager, living in Llandudno in Wales. Emma's friends kept telling her how much she looked like me, which she thought was funny but didn't think too much of it. One day, though, Emma's mum was reading the paper and saw this man she once knew – he was the father of a Spice Girl, Melanie Chisholm. But she'd remembered me as being a blond (which I was as a kid) and they'd also used my Dad's name, William (Alan is his middle name), so she wasn't one hundred per cent sure it was the same person she'd known all those years ago.

For some reason, Emma's aunt decided to fax a tabloid and tell them that my Dad might have another child that I didn't know about, and by the time Emma came back from school, there was a reporter on the doorstep. Emma says now that their family was naïve, and hadn't really thought through the whole thing, so she basically ended up doing an interview with them, aged just fourteen years old.

The reporter called the next morning and said they'd found her Dad and would she like to meet him. Luckily, Dad managed to get hold of Emma's Nan first, and so they were able to meet initially, just the two of them, without the papers being there.

"The thing is, love," he continued as I struggled to take all this in, aware of the harassed looking crew trying to rush me back to set. "The papers have found out and they're saying that it's best if we work with them." I'm not sure how this happened, in retrospect, but the first time I met Emma it was in front of a tabloid reporter and photographer.

Dad and I drove up to Llandudno and we got there early so that the three of us had a little bit of time to ourselves before the cameras turned up. I think we were both very shy and felt a bit awkward. From Emma's perspective, she's not only meeting her sister for the first time, but this person happens to be a Spice Girl. It was so surreal for us all.

Once the photographer had taken their pictures on West Shore beach, we were able to get some more time alone, me, Emma, Dad, and Carole was there too. Our brothers, Liam and Declan were still tiny at this point, five and three years old or thereabouts, so Emma didn't meet them until a day or two later. We walked through the town to another beach, North Shore, and the pier and talked a little about our lives. Emma told me she'd been a bit bullied by kids at school, who said she was lying about being related to a Spice Girl. We saw this group of lads at one point, and she said, "That's some of them there." I immediately went over and said, "Alright lads", and I think that shut them up. I instinctively felt very protective of my new little sis, who of course was still a young teen at this time.

Was it the ideal way to meet a sibling you didn't know existed? No.

The story does have a happy ending, though. Emma is amazing. When we met each other, we realised we were quite alike. We both have pet allergies, and we like the same things; we're kindred spirits and we're both sensitive souls and people pleasers. She also used to get nosebleeds, and from the same nostril as me, which is so weird, as our Declan does too.

And we both look like Dad!

Emma is an incredible woman; I am in awe of her. She works her socks off in social services, where she manages refuges for both men and women who are victims of domestic violence. She has to deal with some harrowing situations.

She's got two boys, Finn and Tate, my gorgeous nephews, and and she's married to the most fabulous man, Gareth. She's a brilliant mum – sometimes to all of us lot too! Once we became parents, around the same sort of time, that really bonded us more. Nothing is ever a problem, and she always looks fabulous. Emma is the kind of person that makes everything feel alright. She lights up the room, my sister, I'm very proud of her and my life wouldn't quite be the same if we hadn't found each other. She's a wonderful addition to my (already complicated!) family.

CHAPTER TEN

Overload

From the early days of us meeting Simon Fuller, we'd talked about the possibility of doing a film, like Cliff Richard, Elvis and The Beatles had done back in the fifties and sixties. Again, call it intuition, call it naivety, but the idea that we shouldn't or couldn't do a film didn't cross our minds. At some point, one of us said, "Let's do a Spice Girls' version of *A Hard Day's Night*," and that's what we decided to do. Why would we not give it a go?

We were approached by a lot of studios. We flew out to Los Angeles to take a meeting with Disney to test the waters and we started to work on a script with Kim Fuller, Simon's brother. He'd written on popular shows like *Not the Nine O'Clock News* and *Spitting Image*, so he knew what he was doing. Whenever we got a chance, we'd go round to his house and tell him all the mad things that we'd been up to.

Before we had even started the movie, we went to Cannes Film Festival to announce it. We had a few details at that point: Alan Cumming had signed on to play a documentary maker who would be following us around, and Richard E. Grant would be playing our manager. The movie would be directed by Bob Spiers, who was known for *Absolutely Fabulous* and *The Comic Strip*. Between Bob and Kim, we were in good hands and the hype around it quickly built.

We caused a stir immediately by arriving in a helicopter, and then spent our time in the South of France sleeping on a yacht and being whizzed around in speedboats. It felt very movie-star-ish! We took over the Promenade de la Croisette in Cannes and whipped fans and the media into a frenzy, telling reporters that the film would be a parody! A comedy! A thriller! We stood on hotel balconies, brought traffic to a standstill, performed on the beach, and basically stole the show.

On our first night there we went to an opening party for Planet Hollywood hosted by Johnny Depp, and it was like a who's who of famous people: Naomi Campbell, Iggy Pop, Demi Moore, Liv Tyler, Kate Moss. It was like they'd gathered every single "cool" person in the world and invited them to the same party. I remember it was packed and we all felt a bit uncomfortable and left quickly. Getting there was intense too because people were going mad. We'd leave the yacht mooring or wherever we were being interviewed and we would be mobbed. People were chasing us, chasing the car, screaming, and going mad trying to touch us, or get pictures and autographs.

We first experienced real, hardcore fans in Japan. It's incredible when it happens, that "Spicemania", but in some ways it can become an inconvenience and dangerous too. It gets very frenzied, and people start running after you, which can be scary. Getting onto the tour bus after a show when there are fans trying to get an autograph and photographers trying to take pictures can be disorienting and quite frightening. I've taken a few blows to the face! There were times when it would become so intense that security inevitably lost their grip and that got scary. Not only for us, but the fans too. We'd be so worried that someone could get seriously injured or crushed.

There were many years when we couldn't really go out. Well, we could, but it would end up being disastrous. I'd go home at Christmas and go shopping with my mates, and someone would ask for an autograph. Of course, no problem. You'd look up and you'd suddenly get a crowd, and that was always a bit unnerving then, when it's you and your mates and there's no Jerry Judge to help you out if it goes awry.

I did a couple of events in Brazil and Mexico in 2017 and getting off the plane was like going back to the nineties. The love and passion for the Spice Girls is still there. You hit the tarmac, and you're immediately in chaos. I got mobbed.

Different countries had their own favourite Spice Girl, each of us had a territory that was more "ours". France was Mel B, I was Spain, for some reason – the Spanish loved Sporty! – even though Geri is part-Spanish. The Americans loved a bit of Ginger. Posh did well in Italy and I'd say Baby was number one in the UK.

Once we got back from Cannes, the pre-production for the film stepped up a gear and we were asked who else we'd like to have in the film. We'd always said, "Let's aim for the stars and see where you end up", so we drew up a dream list. So many people said yes. The cameos were incredible: Roger Moore, Elton John, Bob Hoskins, Bob Geldof, Jennifer Saunders, Stephen Fry, Hugh Laurie. The then-unknown Dominic West (before *The Wire*, *The Affair* and *The Crown*) played a photographer. It was amazing working with people like Alan and Richard because they were very experienced and talented actors. To be on set with them could have been intimidating but instead it was just loads of fun.

The fabulous Meat Loaf, who died while I was writing this book, played our exasperated tour bus driver, Dennis. He was a wonderful guy. When he died in January 2022, Mum reminded me of when we hung out with him at Courtney Love's birthday party in LA during the US leg of the 1998 world tour. It was a huge event with burlesque dancers, and Courtney's band Hole, who I loved, played live. It was full of Hollywood royalty, like Danny DeVito. We apologised to Seal for that unfortunate voicemail. Anthony Kiedis from the Red Hot Chili Peppers was invited, though we'd already met by this point. I'll return to Anthony later...! Winona Ryder, Drew Barrymore and Cameron Diaz came over to tell us they were big fans and would fight over which Spice Girl they would be when larking about on girly nights in. It was one celeb after another.

· · ·

It's amazing that we got a movie shot in six weeks because (i) that's very little time but (ii) this is the Spice Girls we're talking about. There was always someone messing about and dicking around.

It was intense and it was shambolic, and God knows how we made it, but we did. Those six weeks involved lots of filming, lots of recording and very little sleep. We hadn't seen our family and friends for ages, so Ali and Zoë came to visit me on set, as did my parents. After having not spent any time together for years, Mum and Dad were now totally fine at being in the same room. They came to everything, shows, award shows, parties. Dad would bring Carole, and Mum would have Den, and they all get on fine. Water under the bridge, as they say.

As well as the movie, the pressure was on for album two. We'd released *Spice* in November 1996, but the label and Simon wanted the follow-up out less than a year later, in autumn 1997, to come out alongside the film.

The plan was that the film would feature songs from the second album, which was a great idea because the movie would help sell the album and the album would help sell the movie.

There was one problem though.

We hadn't written any songs.

Writing *Spiceworld* was so completely different to writing *Spice*. A lot of that album was made before we were signed, when we had no manager, no label. There was no pressure, no expectations, and no opinions or involvement from anyone. It was us five girls drawing on our lives, our experiences, our thoughts and making music out of it. The whole process took a year.

This time we had four months, including mixing, mastering and pressing the record. And a movie to shoot.

We were also a bit more diva-ish at that point if I'm being very honest. We got shouted at quite often by Simon and 19 because we were all too busy ordering expensive clothes and cars, and so our focus wasn't what it had been on the first album.

In general, we became a bit harder to pin down. We would often roll up to Abbey Road studios or Whitfield Street studios still in costume and makeup, which Matt and Biff found frustrating. There would be fans outside shouting for us or singing our songs. Some of us might have a boyfriend in tow. It wasn't that conducive to creativity.

Just a year or so earlier, we'd spent months with Matt and Biff, crafting our debut to perfection, and here we were popping in for an hour or two in a full face of slap, our minds all over the place. We had this one session booked in with them at Whitfield Street to finish off some of the verses for "Spice Up Your Life". Matt and Biff were livid when we turned up with a film crew from MTV. I think we only had half an hour that day too: "Okay, lads, let's write a song in front of this random film crew, please. Oh, we've got about 30 minutes, cool?"

One day, at Abbey Road, Biff was feeling particularly frustrated. He'd had a run-in with one of the security guards who kept holding up his watch at him. He stopped the session. "Right, we need to take this back to album one. Let's get out of here." We left this big, grand studio and he found, down the back of some staircase, a relatively small vocal booth. It was probably the size of the biggest room at the Strongroom, but it had that cosiness, the more relaxed vibe that we needed.

We sat on the floor, and an hour later, we'd written "Viva Forever", which is, for all of us, one of our favourite Spice Girls tracks. Geri led the lyrics on that one, so it's got a real Spanish-vibe, sort of like our version of Madonna's "La Isla Bonita". We were talking about holiday romances and, as with so many other singles, it just poured out of us. It's bittersweet, that one, because it would be our last single with Geri.

Apart from that session, though, it was so unruly. We wrote a lot of the album while we filmed the movie. We had a mobile studio on the set where we did quite a lot of songs with the Absolute Boys. All our lovely producers would spend hours, sometimes days, sat around in trailers in various parts of London in the hope that one of us might pop in to make a song.

"I've got an idea – 'Too much of something... da-da da-da,'" Geri shouted through the door, dashing back out to go and be filmed pretending to play chess with Mel B. Andy and Paul would be left there going, *"Okay, how we do we build on that, then?"*

We finally finished "Too Much" a couple of weeks later while we were shooting a scene on the Thames. The fans had found out where we were and mobbed the set. One by one we'd be hustled in to see Andy and Paul to try and get our vocals down but there was pandemonium going on outside. It was like those videos of kids trying to eat an ice cream on a rollercoaster; that's what recording *Spiceworld* was like.

I remember one time we were squashed into a trailer with Matt and Biff on the piano singing, "La, la la, la-la la la-la-la", as the production runners were banging on the door, trying to get us back on set.

We wrote "Stop" in the mobile studio with the Absolute Boys. The beginnings of the song had once again derived from one of Geri's driveby sessions – "I've got this in my head – 'Stop right now, thank you very much'… what about that?" and she was off again.

That song was about how we were feeling about Simon, about how hard we were working and how much was going on. We just needed to stop, we just needed to catch our breath. We just needed to slow down.

After my first run-in with Simon back at the BRITs '96, I'd had quite mixed feelings towards him. And I wasn't the only one. We had had this huge, massive success with our first album and, rather than celebrate that and take time to recuperate and plan the next stage of our career, we went straight into the second album, with a film dumped on top for good measure.

We worked so hard during 1997. While everyone else would go for lunch or home after we'd wrapped, us girls would head to the Winnebago or the studio and try to find the inspiration to write songs. It was non-stop and I think a wiser person might have put in a break at this point.

And yet, what can I say? The creative energy was still very much there. It's often said you have your whole life to write your debut album but a few months to write your second. You put all your inspirations, all your good ideas, everything you've been through into that first record, and so the second one can tend to be a bit... limp. They call it the "second album syndrome" and "the sophomore slump".

Once you've gone stratospheric with a debut, the critics are ready to look for any signs of a tail off. Because we were so busy, possibly because we had this crazy energy running through the five of us, the songs poured out: "Spice Up Your Life", "Viva Forever" and "Too Much" gave us a further three UK number one singles, although our run was halted by "Stop" which couldn't, as hard as it tried, knock Run-D.M.C. Vs. Jason Nevins' "It's Like That" from the top spot.

The album managed to sell 14 million copies, so we didn't do too bad, all things considered. But it did sell less than the first. Who knows, if we had been given time out, we could have lost momentum. But also, maybe we would have made the same songs but had more time and energy to execute things better and take things even further. Maybe Geri wouldn't have left. Maybe I wouldn't have also ended up being desperate to escape too.

We'll never know.

You can't argue with this though: *Spice World: The Movie* was released in December 1997 and remains the highest-grossing film of all time by a musical group.

• • •

It took me years to be able to watch the film. I knew that going there would mean having to face a lot of things about myself that I probably wasn't ready for.

I finally watched it, for the first time since the premiere, in 2014, when Scarlet had a sleepover with her friends, and they asked to see it. I sat and watched it with them. I was surprised how fun it was, how high-pitched our voices were, and how Scouse I was. It got quite knocked at the time. In fact, we received six nominations at the Golden Raspberries, the parody awards that honour the year's worst in film. When it was announced we'd collectively won Worst Actress, our performance was described as "a five-member girl group with the talent of one bad actress between them". Not very nice, is it?!

Regardless of what the film critics thought, I am very proud of the film, but I knew that watching it again could have the potential to trigger a lot of emotions. Not all of them good.

I was possibly at my thinnest when we shot it in the summer of 1998. I was so small. At that time, I was still living in my rented flat in Finchley. Because I was there alone, I had more freedom to restrict my diet without anyone seeing what I was doing. I was so limited with what I ate, essentially fruit and vegetables, a small amount of protein and very little, or no, fat or complex carbs. And there was no one there to question me or challenge me and say, "Melanie, you need to eat properly."

I wonder now how I had time to excessively exercise when I look at my diary. We were shooting all day, every day. If we weren't on set, we were in the studio.

Despite all this, it remained vital to me that I was able to get to the gym, no matter what I had to do that day. I was, in all honesty, frightened to break that routine. I would tell myself that I was a robot and that I didn't have any choice, this was what I had to do. I'd get up, eat whatever I was eating, go to the gym and run for an hour, do ab exercises and get home in time for my pick-up at 8 am.

The gym was a place where I was safe. Everyone knew where I was, but they wouldn't bother me, they wouldn't call me. It was my safe space.

My "diet" and exercise started quite innocently and was based on being healthy and fit. But when it gets obsessive, then of course that becomes a problem. Here I was constantly on camera, continually having to think about how I looked, what I wore, how I stood. Whether shooting a film, or doing a video, a photoshoot, it was all so visual: *"This is how you're supposed to look to be in the position you're in,"* I'd tell myself. That was the mindset that I was in.

I had a lot of complicated feelings around my body and how I was treating it. I had a lot of shame in having an eating disorder and not being what I, as a Spice Girl, was supposed to represent: being your true self and being proud of who you are, whoever that was. In Spice World, everything is acceptable: shape, size, sexuality, identity, religion, race, everything.

But I was stuck in a trap of thinking that to deserve what I had, I had to be small. I had to fit the desired aesthetic.

People often ask me if being called Sporty Spice put me under pressure, but I don't think it has to do with that. It was very personal to me. It was how I felt I had to look and how I felt I looked best. I was never diagnosed with body dysmorphia but I don't think I could see the truth anymore when I looked in the mirror. I wasn't seeing reality. I thought I looked okay, but looking back, God, I looked so thin.

I didn't reach the point where it was explicitly apparent that I was ill. I never, thankfully, reached levels of dangerously thin where I had to be hospitalised. But many years later, family and friends confessed they had been so worried about me – they just didn't know how to help.

Throughout 1998 and 1999, I didn't really live; I existed. Experiences would happen to me; I would rarely be in a good enough emotional state to appreciate or enjoy them. I could only think about my weight, about not making mistakes, about keeping my mind and my body as small as possible.

I was a long way from recovery; in fact, my darkest days were still to come.

• • •

After the movie wrapped (during which time I'd also managed to fit in driving lessons *and* pass my test) and the album was almost finished, we were due to head to New York to shoot a video for "Spice Up Your Life" and to attend the MTV Video Music Awards, where we were nominated for two awards.

I got up on the morning of 31st August 1997, the day before we were due to leave for New York, and put on the telly. There, on Teletext, was the announcement that Princess Diana had been killed in a car crash in Paris. I was flabbergasted. Anyone that was old enough at that time doesn't need reminding of how shocked the whole country was.

We arrived at Heathrow on the Monday after she died just... speechless really. I remember us all looking at each other in disbelief. It was surreal.

We all wore black armbands when we collected our award, Best Dance Video for "Wannabe" (we, inexplicably, beat The Prodigy). "We'd like to dedicate this award to Princess Diana, who is a great loss to our country," I said. "I think what we are really about is what Lady Diana had, real girl power," Geri added.

Madonna was also performing at Radio City Hall that night and she gave a speech about Princess Diana, the tabloids, and the effect our own insatiable need for gossip can have. We sat next to our old pal Lenny Kravitz and his future film-star daughter Zoë, who was about nine at the time.

It was a sombre ceremony, but we were happy to be there and pleased (if not a bit confused, given the category) to have won an award. It was also another big acknowledgement from the US, too.

The best bit though was being invited to Madonna's dressing room to meet the Queen of Pop herself. I say invited; we were summoned! "Madonna wants to meet you," we were told, so off we scampered down the hallway and into her dressing room, my heart pounding.

"Melanie better sit down before she falls down," laughed Geri, trying to embarrass me. It was very, very brief, just hugs and hellos really. Madonna was very lovely, so engaging and funny and very complimentary about our success. She told us she loved our album, and that "Mama" was her favourite track.

For me, it was another incredible full-circle moment. From watching Madonna at Live Aid, to hanging out with her, as a fellow artist.

Madonna also came to see us in 1998 on our *Spiceworld* world tour when *so many* people came to watch us perform. We set it up theatrically with two halves so people would drop in and see us in the interval. Madonna came, as did Prince, when we played Minneapolis at the end of July. He arrived all in purple with a purple cane. We bundled into our dressing room at half-time, where we found him sitting, perfectly still and looking totally regal. Geri was really into astrology, so decided to ask him, "Prince, what's your star sign?" He said, "I go by the day I die", which felt very poignant when he did die, on 21st April 2016.

I can still see him, sitting there in that chair with his cane.

Bruce Willis came with Demi and his girls, who were all little. Full disclosure, I was a fan of Bruce Willis's music and I *loved* him, not to mention the eighties TV show *Moonlighting* with him and Cybill Shepherd. I used to watch it on a little black and white portable telly that I had in my bedroom in Ireland Street on the end of my bunk bed. I also had both of his albums. "What?", I hear you say! His version of "Under The Boardwalk" was great!

Anyway, it was so random, but I said, "Oh, I've got your records," and he said, "You should come and sing with us," and that was when Bruce invited me to go and sing at the Planet Hollywood opening in Montreal *the very next night*! As you do! He sent his private jet for me and off I went to Canada with Mum, Den and Paul. I was encouraged to take the opportunity by our wonderful US publicist, Elizabeth Freund. She is still a dear friend – my New York buddy. It was Elizabeth who first made the introduction between me and Anthony too. We always catch up if I'm on the East Coast or when she's here in London. We reminisce about those crazy days and the adventures we had.

Bruce was so famous back then, a huge movie star. As he walked the red carpet, he ripped off his t-shirt, like a true Hollywood hunk! Luckily, he'd found a new top by the time we played a couple of tracks together. We had "a jam" – accompanied by Andrea Bocelli on piano – and then after the show, we met Wesley Snipes, Sylvester Stallone and Cindy Crawford. That night, I think we flew to Milwaukee for the next Spice Girls show on the 29th July.

It was so bonkers. Being a Spice Girl was (and still is) so ridiculous in such a brilliant way.

· · ·

Our next focus after the 1997 MTV Video Music Awards in New York was our first proper full live show: *Girl Power! Live In Istanbul.* We would be doing two nights in Turkey's largest city, sponsored by Pepsi.

For me, this was everything I'd worked towards. We'd spent months miming, pretty much, and doing thousands of interviews, red carpets, photoshoots, etc., which wasn't for me at all. I love the studio, I love writing songs, and, most of all, I love being onstage. For me, it's what it's about.

There was massive pressure on us. Initially the press had tried to write us off as a "one-hit wonder". Well, we proved them wrong. Then they came at us with sleazy stories from our exes, they ran opinion pieces about whether we were corrupting young children, and they'd offer bets on how long we'd last. They did really try to bring us down but, sadly for them, it wasn't working. Their next line of attack was going to be, "Spice Girls Live: Proof they can't sing."

Not on my watch, no way.

We had proven ourselves with live performances at a recent Prince's Trust concert and over in America on *Saturday Night Live.* But this was a full show, with costume changes and a 15-song set. It was far beyond anything any of us had ever done. But it was time. Time for the Spice Girls to put on a show.

And we did.

We spent a month rehearsing in a beautiful and very expensive nine-bedroom chateau in the South of France, in a little village called Biot, near Cannes.

It became known as "Spice Camp" and later, "Alcatraz". Because of everything going on around us, we were sort of prisoners really. Security prowled the huge walled garden as we five, plus Simon, our assistant Camilla and a chef, Cresida, rattled around inside.

On one hand, we were all in this idyllic mansion living a fairy-tale life. But individually, we were all unhappy.

A replica of the stage was built a short drive away and we spent hours each day rehearsing, going over and over the set, blow by blow. We knew we had this really short time to create a 90-minute show that was going to be closely scrutinised, and we all knew we had to knuckle down and work our arses off. Back at the chateau, there were vocal lessons and the opportunity to do various aerobics and choreography classes in the makeshift gym and dance studio that had been built in a marquee on one side of the house. It was tough, but it really suited me down to the ground. I had a perfectly legitimate excuse to exercise as much as I wanted.

It was in France that Geri tried to speak to me about my increasingly obvious issues with food and exercise. "I appreciate your concern, but honestly, I'm absolutely fine," I insisted, brushing her off immediately.

I wasn't anywhere near ready to have that conversation.

We each had our individual stresses with family, relationships, weight, fame and so on, and collectively, we were all upset about the direction Simon and 19 were taking our careers. We needed some space and some rest.

But we weren't getting that. We were on an impossible schedule. And we were starting to feel like cash machines. Sure, we were making money, although not as much as Virgin and 19 were making. But it was our faces over all this stuff, not theirs. And we could tell that we were reaching the point of over-saturation. We were everywhere on everything. If I was fed up with seeing us, surely everyone else was too.

Throughout that year, Simon struck countless merchandising and sponsorship deals, which helped propel the success of the brand. He was the first person to really do that, so on one hand, we changed the face of pop music, in terms of marketing and branding. We showed artists that there were other avenues to make money outside of the music itself and traditional merch like t-shirts and badges. And it made us more famous.

By the end of 1997, we had done deals with PepsiCo, Cadbury, Walkers Crisps (we sold 16 million bags), Polaroid and Impulse. You could literally buy Spice Girls Chupa Chups lollies for a quid. Then there was our own merch like the Spice Girls dolls (yes, I do still have mine), while our first book sold 200,000 copies on *the first day*. We had our fanclub and the *Spice Girls* magazine too. This is aside from the movie and the music. It's estimated that merch alone bought in over £300 million in 1997, rising to £800 million by the end of 1998. The five of us didn't get anywhere near all that, mind, but we did well out of it too.

We started to get criticised and ridiculed for the merchandising of pretty much everything that could be merchandised by the music industry, but also in the press and on television chat shows. The focus was veering so far away from the music. We were all feeling unhappy about the way things were headed with Simon. And we were getting a lot of stick for it.

Okay, great, you've got money, but if you hate what you're doing, what's the point? None of it sat right with me.

While we weren't entirely impenetrable before Simon came along, after his arrival the cracks between us started to widen. As I mentioned before, he implemented this divide and rule style of management, one rule for one person, a different rule for another, which was designed to keep us all separated and insecure. That really impacted on our relationships with each other, and even our families. We all started to become isolated. Any opportunity for time off, and we'd get as far away from each other as possible. While in France, the second we had a weekend free, we all flew to different places.

We were a commodity that was being sold for any old rubbish and we could see that the band was coming apart. That wasn't what any of us had gotten into it for.

Surely, you focus on building a long and lasting career that stays financially sustainable, and you try and protect the relationships within the group, try to make them better, not worse. Yet we seemed to be on a trajectory of burn bright, burn hard, cash in while you can and then, I guess, cash out. And in fact, I think we might have all handled being treated like an ATM, if we didn't feel like we were purposefully being turned against each other.

It was suggested I was too "vulnerable' to have boyfriends, but Mel B could have as many as she wanted. Victoria's parents weren't allowed to come backstage at the Prince's Trust, but because Simon was a huge football fan, he got the red carpet out for David's mum and dad. Emma could have what she wanted; Geri was told to quieten down. That was how he managed us. He had different relationships with each of us and he'd have different conversations with each of us. He'd say certain things to one person, other things to another.

We were all feeling bullied, bossed about, undermined.

I had never been sure about Simon; from the day I first met him and saw those turn-ups. But I was impressed because he managed Annie Lennox and I really respected Annie. There was just something that made me not fully warm to him.

Our relationship with Simon Fuller is complex though, because he also did so much for the band. I can't argue with the fact that Simon, 19 and Virgin helped take the Spice Girls beyond the places we'd dreamed about, back in Boyn Hill Road. He did so many great things and, for the most part, did a pretty great job of managing five people who were quite unmanageable. He was as determined as we were that the Spice Girls would be a success. He did also try to help me, and the other girls, with our issues around food. He brought in Cresida, our chef in France, to encourage healthier eating, and even prior to that he organised for a nutritionist to see us. I think he did try to have our best interests at heart.

We also had so much fun together, and he taught us so much. We had some great moments with him, but I did feel betrayed by the fact that he was favouring certain people over others. It didn't sit well with me. There were a lot of things going on that I was very uncomfortable about, but no one voiced anything. And we were all too scared that our phones were being tapped to tell our friends or parents how we felt.

Our dreams were to perform live, take our music and our message around the world. And, of course, we hoped to make money too, it would be silly to say otherwise, but we weren't driven by cash. The money was a brilliant thing to have, but it ultimately isn't fulfilling either creatively *or* emotionally. Plus, the money, as I've said, brought with it its own complexities.

It was really isolating for us all individually.

It was in France that Victoria first said to Geri that she wasn't happy with Simon. Geri immediately agreed, but the two of them agreed to keep their thoughts quiet.

For now.

CHAPTER ELEVEN

Good Enough

Something happened to me in Turkey that I've never really spoken about before. I'm not even sure if I've ever told my mum and dad, and that's because I blocked it out. It was towards the end of writing this book that I woke up in the middle of the night and suddenly remembered this incident.

The night before the big Istanbul shows began, I decided to treat myself to a massage. I hadn't had many at this point, so wasn't too sure about what to expect. I went down to the spa in the hotel and there's this huge male masseur waiting for me. I was immediately put off, because I'd expected a woman, but maybe this was normal in Turkey. I hesitantly took my robe off.

"And those too," he gestured towards my knickers. It didn't feel right but I didn't know what to do, so I complied. "Lie on your back," he said, which if you've ever had a full body massage is just never what happens. Lying there completely naked and vulnerable, he didn't even cover me with a towel, which I now know is what should happen, and I've never once been asked to remove my knickers since. I was tense and so uncomfortable.

He proceeded to massage closer and closer between my thighs until he was basically almost touching me. "Relax, relax," he kept insisting as I became more and more frozen in place. I didn't know what to do.

Suddenly I felt his erection against my arm.

That was enough. I sprang up, grabbed my underwear and my robe, and left. I went upstairs to one of the suites where I knew everyone would be and found Karin and Jennie, who I told what had happened. I was so upset. Jennie was outraged and immediately rang reception, who went to the spa, but the guy had gone.

With our first, full, filmed live performance the next day, there wasn't any time to process what had happened. We had the biggest night of our career coming up, and I think it was just expected I had to get on with it. The show must go on.

I've mentioned it to friends over the years, but I don't think I've ever dealt with it really. I buried it.

I'm including this story because I want to reiterate to people that when you think or feel that something is wrong, it's because it is. You have to trust your instincts and while you do have to weigh up each situation and the safety implications within that, the best thing to do is to remove yourself as quickly as possible. Trust yourself and stand up for yourself. I was violated that day, and nothing was done about it. I just got on with my life and this man, presumably, went on harassing women.

Sometimes unwanted physical attention isn't so easy to call out either. As both a woman, and a woman in a pop band, I often have people being overly familiar with me. Sometimes you can be almost mauled and it's so unpleasant. Know what your boundaries are and enforce them because we're all too polite sometimes, aren't we? I know I am. But it's not okay when you feel creeped out by someone running their hands down your back, or if someone gets too close, a hand almost on the bum, just not quite. Your body belongs to you, and you have every right to protect your body and not let people take advantage of it, or you.

. . .

All the hard work we'd put in during boot camp in France for Istanbul paid off; the show was a huge success and we proved, again, that we weren't a manufactured band of pop puppets. We could sing, we could dance, and we could put on a bloody good show. "Fab Five Turk 'Em by Storm", "Istanbrill", "Spices Delight Turkey" and "The crowd became total prisoners of Girl Power for ninety glorious minutes", said the papers.

As ever, we had little chance to take it all in. We immediately flew to India, then Singapore and then Japan. We were all utterly exhausted. Mel B and Geri both spoke with Simon about the relentless schedule. He gave us the odd day off here and there and it was so needed. We had been existing on a few hours' sleep a night and each day was physically and mentally draining.

It was while in Japan that Mum called me to tell me that Winnie, Carole's mum, had died. We flew back to Europe, where we shot with Mario Testino for *Vogue Paris* and attended the BAMBI awards (an annual award presented for excellence in international media and television) in Germany. Winnie's funeral was on the Tuesday, and I left the girls to briefly attend with my family. Winnie was an incredibly formidable woman, fun-loving and so independent. Her passing was a huge loss to the family, and we still miss her to this day.

The following weekend, 1st November, we flew from France to Johannesburg, South Africa, for a show for the Prince's Trust. While we were there, Nelson Mandela (then-President of South Africa) invited us and Prince Charles to the president's official residence in Pretoria. Of course, we said yes.

Nelson. Mandela. One of the most important, respected and influential people of our lifetime.

When you meet royalty and dignitaries, there's a protocol, as we'd previously learned (and ignored) when we first met Prince Charles earlier that year, in May 1997, at the Manchester Opera House for a performance at the 21st anniversary of the Prince's Trust.

Never give a Spice Girl protocol because she will do the opposite.

We were pretty excited about meeting the future King of England and we were all a little nervous, because none of us had been anywhere near royalty before now. During the pre-meet briefing, we were given instructions that included doing a half-curtsey when meeting the heir to the throne.

With us, it all went in one ear and out the other.

We did the line-up and it makes me laugh to look at us now, we all looked a right show. Geri's in some sort of bizarre showgirl/sailor dress, I've got me Kappa trackie bottoms on and I'm chewing gum, which is awful, and you can hear the fans singing "Say You'll Be There". It's total havoc. Just as it's all coming to a shambolic but polite end, Geri and Mel B planted heavily lipsticked kisses on Charles's cheeks and Geri patted HRH's bum. I guess they forgot to say "Oh, and no snogging or petting the Prince" during the pre-meet brief!

To be honest, I was mortified. Although I wouldn't have cared about curtseying, I would never have been so bold to do something like Geri and Mel B did. But I wish I had. Something about being a Spice Girl I feel very proud of, in hindsight, was that we didn't only ignore the rules, we'd break them. I love that about us now, but at the time because I was a "good girl", I'd find it so embarrassing. Regardless, Charles clearly loved it because it was the start of a friendship, of sorts, between us girls and his family.

There were the same rules and regulations around meeting Nelson Mandela. We were all briefed beforehand, and there was a similar sense of anticipation in the air as we waited for him. But when he walked out of the house to greet us, there was an immediate warmth. He made us feel very relaxed. It was noticeable, which says a lot about him, I think. You sensed this powerful, calming, positive energy and it surrounded everyone that was there. He had such a special aura; his presence dispelled the anxious energy and calmed and relaxed us all. That's what I took away from meeting this great man; you can be this formidable, impressive person but be able to emanate humanity and allow people to enjoy your presence, rather than be intimidated by it.

Sadly, on what was arguably one of the biggest days of our career, we all looked like a dog's dinner, because our bags hadn't made it from France. The schedule was so mad that we landed and got ready in the back of a van, while driving to Nelson Mandela's house. Oh, the glamour! I was stuck wearing a vest and crumpled cargo trousers, Emma had on a tiny black dress and Geri was in some sort of a kimono. Well put together we were not.

The conversation between us, Nelson Mandela and Prince Charles has been much documented. He told reporters that meeting us was "the greatest day of my life", although Charles said it was the second greatest of his, before adding: "The greatest was the first time I met them." It felt like such an honour, maybe one of the greatest, to be able to spend time with Nelson Mandela, who was such an impressive man. Growing up in the eighties, we saw footage of apartheid in South Africa and though I was unable to comprehend the situation as much then, to be next to someone who was able to change the course of history and positively impact people's lives forever really stayed with me.

It's been fun to meet pop stars, film stars and royalty, but you can't beat meeting a real-life revolutionary hero, can you?

Mel B took some toilet roll from the loo and a handful of stones out of the flowerpots, wrapped the stones in the loo roll and gave us all some as a memento.

It was all over in the blink of an eye. We weren't there long before we had to head to the show. A bulletproof truck with police and armed soldiers escorted us to the North Gate Dome, where 30,000 people had gathered to watch us perform.

We met Prince Harry backstage, who was 13 at the time. He had accompanied his dad on the trip, presumably hoping to meet a Spice Girl (Emma is my guess!). Harry was very sweet, blushing as us five fussed around him. It was his first public appearance after the death of his mum, two months before. We were sensitive to that, but also aware that it wasn't the time to be offering condolences, with the world's press before you. It must have been so terrible to lose his mother at such a young age and in such a shocking way. I hope that meeting us that day gave him a small lift and helped him feel happy for a brief time, however temporary it might have been.

Despite more kissing of cheeks (this time I mustered the courage to wipe some off Charles's cheek), we obviously did something right because the following April, Prince Charles invited us to High Tea at Highgrove House in the Cotswolds. We were picked up by helicopter from London, landing in rainy

Gloucestershire in the late afternoon. We disembarked, basically in the garden, and there's me in my trainers, striding across the soggy grass as poor Victoria lurched to the door in her high heels. I'm forever grateful that I'm the sporty one. Imagine having to wear heels all time. Horrendous!

It was very formal, initially. We sat on deeply plush sofas with Charles, Harry and William in a very grand drawing room, where we were served cucumber sandwiches and tea in the finest china.

What struck me most about that day was how normal the boys were. Harry was 13 and William 15 at the time, so there was typical teenage banter. They were both very cheeky and made fun of each other as Charles grinned along.

We ate our delicate sandwiches, but everyone was still hungry. I think Mel B was the first to say, "Hmm, this is nice, but have you got anything more… substantial?" William said, "Follow me" and led us down to the kitchens, where he made us peanut butter on toast. Pretty cool, to have the future King of England making you a piece of toast.

They then proceeded to take us on a tour, and it was so interesting to get to see behind the scenes at Highgrove. I've been lucky enough to perform at Buckingham Palace, which is ornate and beautiful and so on, but Highgrove, backstage at least, was quite modest. The kitchens, for instance, weren't like *Downton Abbey* with a fabulous Victorian set-up of copper pots and pans and so on. It was just this very basic catering kitchen really. It was an amazing, bizarre opportunity hanging out with these teenage brothers and seeing how simple their kitchens and bedrooms were – it felt more like an army barracks than a royal household.

As I know I've said before, I am so grateful for the opportunities the Spice Girls gave me; being given access to worlds that are unavailable to most people has taught me so much. We've been to Highgrove and Buckingham Palace, Nelson Mandela's home and the players' lounge at Anfield. We've played Wembley Stadium and Madison Square Garden and met Prince *and* Prince Charles. We've been around people from so many walks of life, from all over the world, people that have changed the planet, people that are trying to save the planet. Having the opportunity to meet so many incredible humans, I've learned one thing: we can be overwhelmed or inspired and impressed by our heroes but royalty, dignitaries, campaigners and activists, pop stars, actors.... people are just people.

. . .

We managed to get a short break in South Africa. I think Simon could feel there was a mounting tension between him and us, and he arranged to have our parents fly out to meet us at Phinda, a private game reserve in Maputo. We were there for just three nights, but it was a beautiful place and I've got lovely memories of that time.

There were other strange moves from Simon though. He'd booked us all separate lodges to stay in and separate jeeps even for the safari itself. We were on holiday "together" but very separated. I ended up asking Mum to come and stay in my lodge because I felt so lonely on my own. I didn't say much to her about what I was thinking about Simon at that point. I just said, "He keeps separating us from each other, which is weird," but I left it at that.

We did have one lunch all together, near the top of a mountain, which was stunning. Mum, Victoria and I really needed the loo on the way back, so we had to squat behind some bushes to do a wee. Den apparently has video footage of someone running behind us, roaring like a lion, and we all scarpered, screaming our heads off!

It was a brief respite from the workload. A couple of days later, on the 4th November 1997, we headed to Rotterdam.

. . .

It was at the MTV Europe Music Awards in Rotterdam in 1997 that the Spice Girls once more took matters into our own hands. We are the Spice Girls after all.

We'd built a career on following our instincts and not being bossed about by record industry blokes. Yet, here we were, being run into the ground and, in our opinions, mismanaged. We were not happy.

Something had to give. And it did.

We got to the hotel in the centre of Rotterdam, and checked in. Minutes later, Geri rang me and said to meet her, Mel B and Victoria in Victoria's room.

"Look, we want to sack Simon," they said before I'd barely stepped in the door. I stared as they looked cautiously at me. Victoria had already voiced her feelings to Geri in the South of France, Geri in turn had spoken to our lawyers, bringing in Mel B to the conversation. They knew it was time for us to take back control.

They were nervous about me and Emma because I was such a good girl and they thought Emma might not want to rock the boat. While the other girls were increasingly vocal about the workload and wanting a holiday, Emma and I just got on with it. We did what we were told. I had learnt my lesson at the BRITs two years ago. Keep quiet, keep your head down.

But not this time.

I paused for a beat. "I didn't get into this to advertise fucking chocolate bars," I said to them. "I want to be onstage, I want to perform. Let's fucking do it!"

They all nearly fainted! I was so unhappy with us being turned into a constant product and I didn't feel comfortable with how we were being manipulated. We brought Emma in, who agreed, and the decision was made.

When us girls are on the same page, it's powerful.

Just like we had when we decided to leave Chris and Bob, we all looked at each other... and burst into laughter. Whenever we find ourselves with huge, serious, life-changing decisions to make, we just laugh.

We realised it was a big deal to suddenly leave 19. We had a film coming out, a new album, a world tour booked, not to mention various shoots, brand deals and whatever else. Leaving Simon meant leaving behind a schedule, contracts and contacts. Pretty much the entire team around us, from hair and makeup to PR, security, our assistant, were all employed by, or via, Simon and 19. We wanted to leave, but we were wary about how we would then navigate the next few months of our career.

Scooby-Doo was back in full effect as we hatched a plan.

At this point, Geri still loved her charity bargains. She had this little red holdall, patchwork quilt style, that she carried everywhere with her.

While we were in the dressing rooms, it was Team Spice Distraction as we cornered Camilla so that Geri could grab her tan Mulberry Filofax and mobile phone. Geri popped them in her handbag, just as security walked in to tell us it was time to rehearse.

Off we go, to rehearsals, innocently performing "Spice Up Your Life" with a full band, there's a catwalk and full-on choreo. "Geri, can you put that bag down, please," came a voice over the PA. There, bobbing about on her arm, is Geri's holdall, complete with Camilla's massive Filofax and phone. Onstage with stolen goods!

We finished rehearsing, and while one of us kept Camilla distracted, Geri copied down all the numbers and information we thought we'd need and quickly replaced the Filofax back in Camilla's bag, who by that point was asking anyone who would listen, "Have you seen my phone?"

When she finally did find it, there was Simon, telling her to leave immediately. Our lawyers had called him and fired him.

We were on our own.

In the same way as we'd done with Chris, Bob and Chic three years before, we were taking our career into our own hands. We'd had enough of men controlling us and telling us what we should do, say, wear. Telling us we could or couldn't date. We had been controlled and manipulated. It put a huge barrier between us, which, although we plastered over it as best we could, I honestly don't think we got over it until our reunion 10 years later.

That's how damaging emotionally and mentally – and, in my case as well as some of the other girls, physically – that period was.

Much of Simon's approach to management was just how it was done at the time. He didn't do any worse than the multitude of other managers, but he didn't do any better either. I don't think he's a bad person, I believe the way he handled us was him trying to keep it going, to stop it from imploding. I think he was spinning plates and he thought he was doing it in the best way. Ultimately though, it became about us girls or him. We were becoming so fractured as a band that it was in danger of falling apart.

So, naturally, we chose us.

• • •

Deciding to leave Simon Fuller wasn't the only thing that happened at the MTV Awards in Rotterdam.

My fragile mental health also affected my luck with relationships. Throughout my time in the Spice Girls, I was pretty much the only single one. The other girls arrived in Boyn Hill Road either with long-term (albeit soon-to-be doomed) boyfriends (Emma and Victoria) or seemed to have a short-term thing here or there. I'd had boyfriends at school and a couple of relationships through college but had been single for a while when I joined the band.

Then it was straight into the Spice Girls and, I don't know, maybe I was just focused on getting the band going and didn't think about it. I didn't want to drink so I wasn't out socialising. We were so busy it wasn't like I could go out and meet people even if I wanted to. By the time I might have been ready to, my physical and mental health meant that, in all honesty, I was too ashamed to even try to have a relationship. I wouldn't be able to sustain anything.

It was also frowned upon.

It had become almost industry practice for managers not to let boy band members have girlfriends, the theory being that they'd lose popularity if the fans thought they didn't have a chance with Gary, Jason or whoever. And being gay just wasn't an option, or certainly it was incredibly difficult at that time. It must have been so tough when Stephen Gately was forced to come out in 1999. He was so, so brave.

Of course, the other girls had boyfriends, most notably Victoria and David, whose relationship was obsessively covered in the tabloids. But, while Simon "allowed" them to date, he took a different approach with me. He advised that I shouldn't have a boyfriend because I was too vulnerable.

But I was lonely, and I was craving attention.

Finally, I did get the attention I so badly wanted. Little did I know that it would come via a man whose poster I'd had on my wall just a couple of years before.

When Robbie Williams took an interest in me, I was taken aback, to be honest.

I first properly met Robbie in Cologne in the summer of 1996 at Popkomm, which was an industry trade show. I was there with the girls and Robbie was performing as a solo artist – I think it might have been one of his first shows without Take That. We ended up hanging out that night, purely platonically, but I went up to his room and he gave me one of his tracksuits, a white adidas one with black stripes. It was way too big for me, but I treasured it.

I found out later that Simon Fuller wasn't keen on this potential partnership and told the girls to make sure they kept me away from him. In one sense, he had a point: Robbie was a troubled lad back then and might not have been the steadiest potential partner. On the other hand, it was my life.

I ignored the frostiness towards him from the others, and we kept in touch by phone over the next few months. When we were going through it with the movie and feeling really overwhelmed, Robbie was really sweet. He understood some of the difficulties because he'd been there, and he sympathised with what I was going through.

The next thing that happened was that he sent flowers while we were away performing in America, I think it was at the MTV Video Music Awards, in September 1997. The flowers came to the hotel, and Camilla let us know Robbie had sent us all a bouquet. A little later, she pulled me aside. "I've been told to say they're to all of you, but actually they're for you," she said –

Simon was still clearly unhappy about the potential of any sort of relationship between Robbie and me – before pressing something into my hand.

"It must be difficult for you all right now, mentally sending my support. Send my love to the rest of the girls" and he'd signed it, hilariously, "Robbie Williams". Mind you, could have been Robbie Fowler, I suppose.

I found the card in an old diary while writing this book.

We performed two songs at the MTV Awards in Rotterdam: "Spice Up Your Life" and "Say You'll Be There". It was a big moment, millions of viewers, full live performance, live band, live vocals, choreography, the works, so we of course had a proper soundcheck. There we were, Geri with the stolen phone and Filofax under her arm and me giving it the full as-though-we-were-live performance. As the song finished with my "Hi, Si, Jah, hold tight", there's me, dickhead, jumping around, high-kicking like a sporty nutter despite the fact this is just a rehearsal.

I'm onstage heavy breathing, we all were after sacking Simon, we were on a *Scooby-Doo* high! As I looked out to the empty venue, who do I see, right at the front, watching me, with a big grin on his face?

Robbie bloody Williams.

I think, I guess, he must have asked me out that night. Not like, "Do you want to be my girlfriend?", but more a casual, "When you gonna come and see me play then?"

It was an exciting time, and it was lovely to get that attention. Robbie had left Take That in 1995 and launched his solo career in 1996. He'd just released his debut album, *Life thru a Lens*, and it was right before things went crazy for him. He'd put out three singles, which had done okay, and then, just after we hung out, he released "Angels", which really catapulted things for him. When we had our first dates that November, he was also on tour playing smaller venues. He was on the periphery of becoming the biggest pop star in the world, but at that point he was still unsure which way things might go.

We met up a couple of times. On both occasions I went to his gig and then saw him afterwards. There was one somewhere in Germany, maybe Munich on our day off on the 15th, and we met again in Milan a week later. We fitted it all around our schedules.

It was all very exciting, albeit short-lived. The truth of the matter was that we had a couple of dates, but he was a mess; I was a mess. Nothing came of it, and it broke my heart. We'd spent the last year talking about our lives and bonding over this shared experience; he let me know what it was like to be a solo artist and the highs and lows that came with that. I thought I'd found someone, someone of my very own.

It took me a long time to get over it because I thought I'd maybe finally got myself a partner. All the other girls were with someone, and I was so fed up with not only being single but being constantly ridiculed in the press for it.

Sadly, Robbie did behave badly – he led me on and then abruptly dropped me at a time when I was incredibly vulnerable. I don't have any bad feelings towards him now, but he did break my heart a bit. It was horrible because everyone knew about it, and I'm sure I'll be asked about it for the rest of my life.

I was hurt and I was humiliated, because it was somebody that I had admired, and *he* pursued *me* and then treated me badly. He has apologised to me publicly and privately, and of course I've long forgiven him, but I must admit, it did really hurt at the time.

I made more bad choices. Two years after Robbie, I ended up dating Jay "J" Brown from the boyband 5ive, who were managed by Chris Herbert, who we would finally publicly apologise to at one of our O2 reunion shows in 2007. I *think* he's forgiven us. Sadly, his father Bob passed away in a car accident in 1999 but I hope he'd found peace with what had happened too.

J and I met at the BRITs 2000. He'd slagged us off in the press, and so I went up to him to "have a word" and it went on from there. I thought, *"Oh, you're quite fit!"*

We ended up seeing each other for a little while. He lived with me in North London for a time. His band were touring and promoting all over the shop, as was I, so we based ourselves at mine and whenever we were both in London, we got to see each other.

J grew up in Warrington, which is right next door to Widnes, so we had this thing in common about where we grew up. He is a lovely guy, and we did really get on, but it turned out messy too. The press started reporting that an American model and "personality" called Caprice had taken a shine to him and was determined to date him.

This one day, I went to meet his dad, who was a fireman in South London, and we went to see him at the station. He was showing us around and his dad had the article *on the wall* about Caprice fancying his son. I thought, "Oh, that's really hurtful." It compounded everything, all my insecurities. I saw it as "this hot woman fancies my boyfriend so I should probably give up now". I'd never have seen it like "This lucky guy who is admired by many is dating a Spice Girl". The relationship quickly collapsed because, again, we were both in this insane pop bubble and we were both a bit of a mess. It was an dysfunctional relationship really from the beginning to the end when he announced publicly that we weren't together – before discussing it with me. Which was, as you can imagine, quite hurtful.

I don't remember saying much to him though. I wasn't assertive at that time. I didn't really become assertive until a couple of years ago, to be honest.

I got an apology from J though. I seem to collect a lot of them! He reached out to me around 2015 to ask if we could meet up. He'd had some tough times like me and went off and lived somewhere remote in Wales to have time to reflect. When he started to feel better, he messaged saying he'd like to see me. We went out for lunch. "I want to apologise for the way I behaved," he said, and it was lovely to have that apology and that closure.

Neither Robbie nor J were bad people, they just weren't good people for me at that time.

I dated a few other people, but nothing serious. I suppose I wasn't really in a place where I was able to be my true, real self. As much as I wanted somebody and wanted to be desired and to have affection and to have someone to share things with, I was hiding this big secret that couldn't be discovered.

• • •

Between 1997 and 2001, my eating disorder was particularly bad. Maybe if I'd met the right person who could have supported me through it, things might have been different, but I didn't feel confident enough to be honest with someone.

I felt unlovable and undesirable, and I wondered why I couldn't get a boyfriend like the other girls. My generation was constantly told we needed a partner to complete us, while the papers would very specifically remind me that I was single.

I never wanted to be rescued – I was fiercely independent – but I wanted someone to share my life with. I felt insecure, and I had low self-esteem, which isn't a good reason to have a boyfriend, but having a partner, having someone to share that with, could have given me the bit of confidence that I could have done with.

I spent many years living alone in my mind, internalising and burying everything that was happening to me. I shut off my feelings, but also my personality. It was shut off for so long that I forgot who I was.

The icing on the cake, the thing that really kicked me when I was down, was the press, who loved to tell me who I was: Single Spice, Plain Spice, Beefy Spice, Sumo Spice.

When I think about the press, it's such a dark shadow that hangs over me. As I said earlier, writing this book coincided with a hacking claim I'd decided to make against the British press. My story and the case quickly became interlinked. It was through looking over old press coverage that I had to revisit a lot of what was written about us, about me, back in the nineties and noughties. Reading it all over a few days, I very quickly saw this narrative that was created about me in that period of 1996 through to 2002. Seeing that now and looking through the coverage, even though it was over two decades ago, knocked me. It took me a few days to get over it.

I am an adult, and I am responsible for my actions, but I was young, and I was vulnerable, and I think it was inevitable that I would be affected by how the tabloids spoke about me. I don't blame them totally for what happened to me, but I do think they have a lot to answer for.

My fluctuating weight was often commented on, and I was called "beefy" and "chunky", especially around the year 2000 when I started bingeing.

They went on about me being single all the time. And the thing is, I was single, and I was lonely. I had no relationships of any note. I met people and dated for a short time and whatever happened, happened, but the narrative was that I was desperate and pathetic and undateable. The papers would always put me down, make fun of me, make me out to be a sad loser. When you're already in a vulnerable state of mind, it's harder to brush off cruel comments.

The narrative built around women, especially single women, is awful. In our culture, he's a bachelor and she's a spinster, he's a player, she's a slag. As we became more famous, we'd see – or be made aware of – horrible things being said about us in the papers and online, though the Internet was still quite new at that point. We were slut-shamed on one hand and called frigid on the other. It did hurt to see myself described as "the plain one". You're 22 years old, you don't want to be thought of as plain, do you? Of course, that got to me.

When I did date a few different people, I was always "dumped", or somebody else was picked over me. If I was a dude, it would be "Oh look who's on his arm now, what a player!", whereas I was sad and a loser. I'd felt vulnerable and apologetic and undesirable for a long time. For the press to compound that, constantly, just made me believe it.

Some of what was said was so dark. We did an interview with a magazine once, and the writer showed us these "games" doing the rounds online like "Slap a Spice Girl". In *The Mirror*, columnist Matthew Wright asked readers to send in jokes and it was stuff like "What's the difference between Geri and a rottweiler? Lipstick", and "Why do the Spice Girls wash their hair in the sink? Because they're vegetables".

There was even a "Spice Girls Death Site". One comment said, "The adidas bitch goes first". That was quite upsetting, as you can imagine.

I suppose we just got used to it, though. We knew some of it was being "funny" and we quickly figured out that the best thing to do was ignore stuff like that.

It was an unpleasant side effect of success. I would never, in a million years, have thought as a kid in my bedroom wanting to be Madonna that you'd get so much hate when you're in the public eye.

If I wasn't a "loser", they were telling me that I was gay. On shows like *This Morning,* they'd just outright ask me on live television. "Is it true that you're a lesbian?" said a jovial Richard Madeley one morning. In the press, they'd insinuate I was in a relationship with my hairdresser, Jennie, or my assistant, Ying, which I think was very much news to them both.

Here's the thing with the lesbian rumours (which people still love to ask me about today)…

I had zero problem with people thinking I was gay, it's that it's no one's *business* who's gay or not gay, or who's bisexual, pansexual, asexual, heterosexual and so on.

If I was gay, so what? It's not a bad thing, it's a brilliant thing. It's not offensive to me, it's offensive to the community because it was supposed to be a slur, it was a putdown, "Oh, guess what everyone, she's *gay*."

So, what if I was! Who cares? I think about the gay fans, all those years ago, reading those articles and seeing people like me being harassed or "outed" for their perceived sexual preference because of the way they dressed or styled their hair. It's so damaging to LGBTQI+ people struggling to come out. It must have reaffirmed to them that, yes, to come out is to be ridiculed.

It was so damaging on so many levels. If I'd been gay, I'd have been proud to fly that flag, and I'm very proud to be an ally and an ambassador, which I will continue to do forever. The gay community has given me so much, and it's all I can do to support the LGBTQI+ cause and stand up and made my voice heard whenever I can.

I know it's difficult to come out and, look, I can't say for certain because I haven't lived this experience, but if I was gay, I don't think I would have kept it a secret because I wouldn't have been ashamed. Also, knowing myself and how much I hate lying, I couldn't have done it. I'd have been asked about it in interviews, which I was many times, and I'd have had to lie. And I don't think I'd have been able to do that repeatedly, because I'm so bad at lying, more than anything else.

Sure, I had my hair cut short, I had tattoos, I was muscular, so therefore that means I'm gay? Why is there a stereotype? I think what's been wonderful, with all the recent conversations around gender, is that people are now questioning, why do we attach the colour pink to a girl?, why do boys play with trucks?, and so on. What do "butch" and "feminine' mean? Our ideas around gender are so based around old-fashioned and inherited ideas from way back when. But those old stereotypes are outdated and wrong.

Not to mention, at that time, I was young, I was lonely... I wanted a boyfriend and they're telling any available man out there I'm not available! Bloody bastards.

I spent some time in the US recently and it was interesting to look at our press from a distance. I would read things about other people online and feel this huge swell of criticism, envy and judgement. As a country, we have a reputation of having some of the best media in the world – the BBC, *The Guardian*, and so on

– but we're also known for how underhanded, ruthless, and cruel some of our (especially tabloid) media can be.

Wouldn't the world be a much better place if the tabloid media could be more positive and supportive? It's always said that the papers give the public what they want, and I know we all have that part of us that loves gossip and scandal. It's why we watch *Love Island*, *The Real Housewives* and *The Kardashians* and spend hours scrolling through the Sidebar of Shame. But maybe if all that wasn't there, who knows, maybe we'd... read books, watch films, think about life!

I find it upsetting when I think of my daughter and her mates. I've watched them being formed in front of my eyes and I've seen how they've gone from being open kids who loved everyone and everything to slowly becoming more cynical, more vulnerable, more susceptible to negativity. It happens to us all, but it seems to be happening to us younger.

I don't want to blame the media for everything, we all play our part. But they have a huge responsibility, and they could make a big difference.

Thankfully, I did manage to put aside what the media was telling me about myself, and I did eventually find a relationship. I met Tom, the father of my daughter, who I was with for 10 years and, although it didn't work out, we have our amazing daughter.

Anyway, all that is to come. Before we get into relationships *beginning*, we need to talk about relationships *ending*.

We had let go of Simon, but more changes were on their way.

This time though, we wouldn't get to make the decision.

CHAPTER TWELVE

Here I Am

When Geri left the Spice Girls on 31st May 1998, we were shocked and upset. But truth be told, it wasn't the first time Geri had left the band.

We shot the video for our second single, "Say You'll Be There" in the Mojave Desert in September 1997. It was a fun video featuring us dressed as our martial arts alter egos (I was Katrina Highkick) that got nominated, and won, a lot of awards, including a BRIT. But there were issues. A couple of weeks after the shoot, a row erupted over who had been given more screen time. We'd always set out to do everything totally equally; no lead singer, no spokesperson, everything split five ways, no one was more important than the other. But the edit came back with one of us featured far more heavily than the others and none of us girls were happy about it.

From the very beginning, we were all adamant that we all had equal shots, equal lines, equal time on stage, no one was to ever have more than the other. We were always very conscious that everything was very fair, down the line, between the five of us. In publishing everything was split equally and that was thanks to good advice from Simon. He told us, "Don't get into the 'you wrote this' and 'I wrote that' because it will cause problems." To futureproof the band from the beginning we said *"Let's make everything equal"*.

It's swung the other way now, mind. We did something together recently and it was very much like, "Oh, you can say that line!" "You can be in that shot on your own if you want?" We are all totally happy to have to do as little as possible. None of us ever wants to do anything now we're older and lazier!

So, we got the rushes back on the video and it wasn't a very even-handed edit, shall we say. A fight broke out, voices were raised, and in a huge huff, Geri decided she was leaving the band.

Of course, Geri didn't leave at that point, but we did wonder how seriously to take it. We were young women and things got volatile from time to time. I had almost been kicked out; Geri had threatened to go, I think Mel B had threatened to quit on a couple of occasions too.

So, when Geri first said she was off, we couldn't believe it but we were certain she'd be back. Although thoughts of life beyond the band had been discussed very briefly around the time the *Spiceworld* tour kicked off in Dublin in February 1998, I think we all assumed that we'd carry on for years to come, taking time off for our own solo projects but ensuring the band carried on for as long as possible. I've got vague memories of Geri talking about pursuing other things once the tour had ended, in September of that year. But we never thought she would actually leave, and certainly not mid-tour!

It was a hugely important time in the Spice universe. We'd sold millions of records, broken records, had a hit film, changed the cultural landscape and were halfway through a six-month, sold-out world tour. The plan after we'd played the last date was to take a bit of time out, regroup, and go from there. We were all exhausted – of the schedule, of each other, of everything. We needed a proper break to think about what might come next. Both Mel B and I knew we wanted to do solo albums, Geri was clearly thinking about that too, but that didn't mean the end of the group. We'd go off, do our own projects, and then come back and do the third album.

We all had different struggles with aspects of how crazy our lives had become. Maybe with a bit more maturity, emotional support and sleep we could've worked things out, but it wasn't meant to be.

The 97-date tour kicked off in Dublin on 24th February 1998. We played the UK, Belgium, Italy, Austria, Sweden, and several other places. In between the travel and performances, we were still promoting the record and the tour and trying to see our families and friends when we could. It was exhausting but exhilarating, sometimes in equal measure.

A few dates in, 20th March 1998, while we were in Lausanne, Switzerland, I got some terrible news. My Grandad Vincent had died. He was the only grandfather I'd known because my paternal grandfather, Billy, had died just after I was born. Grandad Vincent was a huge part of my childhood; me and Mum lived with him and Nanna when we first left Kendal Drive all those years ago. He'd been in the Navy and because of his job as a gardener he was always outdoors. He was very physically fit and strong, his sinewy arms covered in tattoos from his days on the high seas. The classic anchor, dagger, and swallows – the old black ink now faded, blurry and blue.

So, it was a surprise when he was suddenly taken ill towards the end of 1997. They thought initially it was a stroke, but it turned out to be a brain tumour. Three months after he was diagnosed, my lovely Grandad Vincent was gone. My Nanna Alice was so lonely after he went. She lived a good, long life though, passing away on 21st September 2012 at the age of 88. But she was never the same. She was so lost without him.

I went home for my grandad's funeral, and when I re-joined the girls, things were still tense, but no more than normal. As I think I've made clear, my favourite thing is performing, there's no place I'm happier. But being on tour is tough – you're performing until 10, 11 at night, you then drive to the next city, or get up early for a flight, get to the next venue, soundcheck, play a show until late in the night... It wears everyone down, even me. We were burnt out, overworked, overwhelmed.

We knew that we just had to get to the end of the tour, take a long break, and then reassess. Let's make the most of this time, give the fans an amazing experience and then we can take some time off and see how we feel.

It didn't quite go that way.

We played two shows in Helsinki on the 25th and 26th of May and we had more shows in Norway on the 28th. We also had to squeeze in an appearance on the BBC's *National Lottery Live* back in London on the 27th, to promote "Viva Forever".

We came back on a private jet and Geri was being a bit weird. A bit quiet, not really answering anyone's questions, she didn't seem to have much to say. But there hadn't been any arguments so there didn't really seem to be anything to be concerned about.

We landed in London well after midnight. When we left to get into our cars Geri gave us all quite a serious, meaningful goodbye, but we didn't think too much of it because... well, it's Geri!

Early the next morning, Victoria got a phone call from our lawyer, Andrew Thompson. He got to the point quickly. "Geri's leaving the band," he told her. "She's had enough."

An emergency meeting was called at Spice HQ, at our office on Bell Street. We still weren't taking it entirely seriously at that point, but we were a little unnerved that the lawyer had been in touch. That's what had happened when we sacked Simon. But Geri had said this before and didn't mean it. This time would be the same, surely, we thought. We all took it in turns trying to ring her, but we couldn't reach her. "We've got to perform on live television in a bit, c'mon, Ginge, where are ya?"

Eventually we got through and we tried to cajole, persuade, demand and beg that she get herself over to the BBC for the *Lottery* show.

She got quite upset at one point and we realised there was nothing more to be said for the moment. We still thought that she would return.

To buy us some time, we decided to say she wasn't well and for some reason I was nominated to tell the lie on national television, which was so stupid because I'm the worst liar in the world. I was so uncomfortable with it. I think I was nominated because the girls thought that people would trust me. "Unfortunately, Geri's not very well tonight, so get well soon, Geri," I said, smiling brightly while fibbing through my teeth.

As the days passed and there was no sign of her, the reality sunk in: Geri was gone.

We knew for sure she wasn't coming back when we heard about a documentary she was making with the filmmaker Molly Dineen. She had apparently started filming it just two days after she left. Geri clearly had no intention of being a Spice Girl anymore.

It was official. The rug had been whipped out from under our feet.

• • •

What had happened to us wouldn't have happened without Geri. She was absolutely determined to make the band work from day one, I mean we all were, but she had a sense of urgency, it was though she was on borrowed time, almost, she wouldn't, couldn't, wait around. The Spice Girls just wouldn't be the Spice Girls without all five of us, but Geri was the one who would speak to anyone and everyone to see if they could help us in some way. She was incredibly canny, intuitive and strategic. With Mel B backing her up and me, Emma and Victoria right there beside them, we pushed and pushed until we broke that door down, smashed that glass ceiling. Geri was very much a driving force in the success of the Spice Girls.

Because the band always came first, it meant we upset people. I think we crossed a line with the Herberts and certainly with Simon – but it was their line, not ours. Egos were bruised. I think we threatened them, because with this dynamic we were never afraid to question, contradict or disagree with any man that was attempting to steer our career. It worked well when we had someone to fight against, but once we were without a manager, it became trickier. Things between Geri and Mel B, which were often explosive anyway, had deteriorated further after Simon's departure.

It often felt like a battle to lead the band, but neither of them seemed to be winning.

In retrospect, it was clear Geri was unhappy and that something was amiss. She became very quiet and withdrawn, no longer that energetic young woman with loads of mad ideas and an insatiable drive to push the band to greater and greater heights. She withdrew.

There was also the performance side of the Spice Girls, which I think Geri struggled with. For me, it's my playground, it's what everything leads to. For Geri, she had to work extra hard at that, because it wasn't something she'd grown up doing. When there's five of you, there's a lot to navigate. I imagine the idea of being a solo artist and operating more within her comfort levels would have been appealing and I can totally identify with that.

Geri is very creative, we worked well together in the studio as a team and she was always writing, whether a book or a script. But she sometimes felt vulnerable onstage, even though she always pulled it off because she worked so hard to get it right. Then there was everything going on in the background, whether fallouts with us lot, the thought of another three months of touring, as well as any personal reasons that aren't mine to talk about, I think she felt it was time to do what she needed to do.

I could understand that. I was also feeling frustrated and had started to imagine what it might sound like if I did my own record. A huge part of our success is that we were able to combine our strengths into this dynamic ball of energy. But what would it be like if we made music on our own, for ourselves?

I understand now why Geri left and I don't blame her or harbour any resentment at all.

But at the time it was really hard.

We were starting to feel a real turn in the tide of public opinion, certainly via the newspapers anyway.

After we'd sacked Simon, the backlash began. We got booed offstage at an awards show in Barcelona, because we banned photographers from taking pictures of us while we played. The press leapt at that. There were all these pieces about us being over, being done. Right before she left, photographer Dave Hogan had taken a picture of Geri onstage, where it looked like she was crying. The tabloids knew something was up and were delighted to be proven right.

Geri leaving sold newspapers. Lots of them.

At the time, the four of us let our feelings about her be quite well known. There are some old interviews I can look back on now and think, *"Ouch"*. I think with hindsight we could have handled it a little more maturely, but we were hurt, we felt very betrayed. We didn't speak to Geri again for quite a while.

And it did impact our success. Post-Simon and now post-Geri, the press was very much centred on our downfall. We were painted as spoiled brats, divas, ungrateful and so on. Woe betide a woman trying to take her own career into her own hands.

It didn't help having to constantly read about how your career was over, you were done, you were old news. It's the age-old British press mentality, where they love to build you up and bring you down. We weren't the first to suffer from it, and we certainly weren't the last.

The British press have a lot of power and if they say you're over, then radio stations, magazines, record labels all start to get nervous.

• • •

In the aftermath of Geri's departure, there was a lot to sort out. Our most immediate concern was America because we had a three-month tour booked as a five-piece. Would that create a legal issue, would we be in breach of contract? Thankfully, the promoter was happy to take us as a four-piece and so it was full-steam ahead. We had a couple of hours before our next show in Oslo to sort things out. We needed to change from a five-piece to a four-piece and we had to do it fast. We quickly divided Geri's vocals between us and changed the choreography to leave no gaps.

But of course, there was a gap, figuratively as well as literally.

It was such a shame that Geri wasn't there for it because the North American shows were a real crowning glory for us. After the incredible success of the two albums and the movie, we were ending this period on a high with a sold-out North American tour. That's not something many British bands back then could say they'd done. So much that happened to us tended to pass us by because it was almost too big to take in. Now we had the opportunity to allow everything to sink in while playing to over 700,000 people around America.

From the first show in Palm Beach, we were able to see, up close, the impact we'd had, not just in the UK, but around the world. The shows were sold out, the fans were screaming and, once we had settled into it, we were able to get our families over for some much-needed catch-up time.

David came out to join us in the summer of 1998 after he was sent off in the last-16 World Cup game against Argentina and became a villain in this country. We saw similar scenes, didn't we, at Euro 2020 with Marcus Rashford, Jadon Sancho and Bukayo Saka, though this time it was centred on their race and the fact they'd missed penalties. I love football, but some of the fans make me ashamed to be British at times.

David had a tough time in 1998. When he joined us in America, he was a broken man, and we took him under our wing as best we could.

My brother Paul also came over during the tour. Paul has said since that after I left for college that he felt like he lost a part of himself. We'd been so close as kids, and there I was off to a new life, leaving him behind. Then he turns 16 and he's got this famous sister and he's stuck at home without a job, with no idea what to do with his life. Mum called me while I was in America, asking if I could invite Paul over. He'd left college by this point, and he was struggling a little bit. I called him up, "You've got Mum worried, she thinks you're losing your way. Pack your bags and get over here."

It was a bit like *Home Alone* for him staying in five-star hotels and being around us, the dancers and the crew. He not only had a great time, but inadvertently, we got his career going. I introduced him to our chef, whose brother raced cars. Paul got in touch with him when he got home, and this guy invited Paul down to a race-track and helped him get his racing licence. He went on to race in the British Touring Car Championships, MGF Cup and the GT Championships and is now a sports commentator on ITV, racing coach and all-round idiot on social media.

Funnily enough, the person he now hosts a show with, Steve Rider, was there the night we launched the McLaren Formula 1 car, back in 1997 with Jamiroquai. Steve has always championed Paul and been a mentor to him. It worked out well, with Paul and I having different surnames, as it enabled him to make his own name in motorsport without being too obviously linked to me.

Mum and Den came to join me and Paul and the girls later during the *Spiceworld* tour. We were on the West Coast, early August 1998, staying at our beloved Four Seasons in LA. We got back from a shopping trip, and my mum and Den headed straight to the bar while I popped up to put something in my room. I went into the lift and a chap got in with a guitar on his back. "*I know him*," I thought.

It was Bryan Adams. We'd met a few months before at *Top of the Pops*. He was the singer of one of the biggest singles of all time, "(Everything I Do), I Do It for You", as well as my favourites "Run To You", "It's Only Love" featuring Tina Turner and "Summer Of '69". We made a fuss of him because we were big fans of Bryan. He'd been fully Spiced up and he loved it!

We said our hellos and as the lift got to my floor, I turned back towards him. "Bryan, would you do me a favour? My mum is here and she's such a big fan. I don't suppose you'd have time to come and say hello to her down in the bar?"

I did the thing that everybody does to me.

Bryan is the loveliest guy, so of course he said, "Yeah, sure, I'm just going to put my guitar up in my room." He came down and ended up hanging out with us all evening and that was a star-studded night too: Jon Bon Jovi popped by and said hello. Hugh Grant and Liz Hurley were in the bar, as was Sean Penn.

Bryan and Mum are mates now. They have more contact than he and I do! She's got such a soft spot for Bryan... and who can blame her.

Bryan and I swapped numbers that night and a few weeks later when I was back home in the UK he called to ask me if I'd be up for duetting on a song he'd written with Eliot Kennedy, the same Eliot we'd stormed up to Sheffield to beg to work with us. I think I said yes before I'd even heard it! Well, I knew my mum would never forgive me if I didn't and knowing Bryan and Eliot, it had to be a corker – and a corker it was. "When You're Gone" did really well; it was a huge hit, going to number three in the UK and selling just short of a million copies. It's a black cabbie's favourite, they all tell me when I hop in.

It really helped establish my own voice.

Bryan has been a great friend. He really put his faith in me back then and continues to do so. He gave me so much confidence at a time when I really needed it. He's a legend.

Working with Bryan opened my eyes and made me start to think seriously about my own career. Although I was duetting with him, people saw that I could sing on other types of music, and without the girls. It was time to start putting myself first and thinking of my own future. A lot of people around me were telling me that I had the best shot at a solo career, or certainly as good a shot as any of the other girls.

It turned out that moment might be coming sooner than I thought. The next big news came via Mel B and Victoria. They were both pregnant, and due roughly around the same time.

Three down, two to go.

The four of us discussed the future. We agreed to make another record as a four-piece but in the meantime the girls that were about to have babies wanted some downtime, leaving Emma and I to explore solo music.

It was both good and bad timing. On one hand, the tour was really exciting, but backstage, things were unsettled. Me, Emma, and Victoria were close, but Mel B was quite isolated. She was having a tough time with her boyfriend Jimmy, who went on to become her husband later that year. They got together after he was chosen to be her dancer on the tour and, as she references in her second book, *Brutally Honest*, it was a very tumultuous relationship. When Mel B was seven months pregnant, they had a huge falling-out. She rang me, very upset, and came to stay with me for a few days. I never questioned anything with Mel B; if she needed me, I was always there. Come in, cup of tea, what do you want to eat? There's your bed…

She's been through some terrible times, but she's come through them and I'm so proud of her and all the work she does now to raise awareness around charitable causes and vulnerable women as a Patron of Women's Aid. I think she's a real inspiration.

That North American tour wasn't a happy time for Mel B, whereas for us other three, we were enjoying it. We'd be in the dressing room having a laugh and then we'd hear Mel B's footsteps and brace ourselves. Mel B could change the atmosphere in an instant. She mentions that period and this one specific time in her book, *Catch A Fire*. We were somewhere in the South and I had popped to the loo. Suddenly, I hear these raised voices and it's Victoria and Mel B, both a couple of months pregnant by this point, hormones all over the shop, going at each other. Like, fully at each other. I'd no idea what the fight was about, but when I stepped out of the cubicle, eyebrows raised, it broke the tension. We all burst out laughing.

But it was obviously time for a break, whether we wanted one or not.

• • •

By the time it came, I was so ready to have time out from the Spice Girls. I'd also found the last year hard, in terms of the dynamics within the group.

In January 1998, we were invited to go on *The Oprah Winfrey Show* in Chicago to promote the film and our upcoming tour. This was a massive deal, another indication of the impact we were having in America. Not only was her show watched by millions, but the Oprah seal of approval held a lot of weight.

It was bitterly cold in Chicago, and it was towards the end of a hectic two years of non-stop travel, promo and performance.

We'd had quite a long break over Christmas, but we'd started the New Year with two days promo in Australia, before flying over 20 hours to the East Coast of America. We were all jetlagged and, in my case, physically exhausted from starving my body.

Oprah came to see us before the recording and was incredibly gracious and kind. She is such an impressive woman; I think she recorded three shows that day but seemed completely in control and in charge of what was happening. Meanwhile, we were all in bits about appearing on *Oprah*. We got into such a state that someone forgot their microphone and you can see us panicking while we're performing, me hurriedly passing my mic to Emma.

Oprah was lovely, warm and welcoming and the audience was clearly made up of fans. It was a supportive atmosphere, but watching that interview now makes me cry. I can see how vulnerable I am. I'm very quiet, I barely speak and I'm clearly anxious.

By this point I was reluctant to speak too much in interviews. I can't remember when it started but there was often a drama, something that needed to be addressed immediately. Mel B would call: "You need to come to my room, now, we need to have a meeting." It could be as late as the early hours of the morning.

I would reluctantly drag myself out of bed and up the corridor of whatever hotel we were in, dreading what was in store. Normally these summits would serve to either tell someone what they'd done "wrong", among other things. As we walked along a corridor once, in a hotel I've forgotten and a city I can't remember, I felt a tap on the shoulder. "It's probably best if you don't say anything in this interview," someone said, lightly, "You'll only end up saying something silly." It was never a command as such, it would be more inferred. "Melanie, don't feel under pressure to say too much in interviews because sometimes what you say, well, it doesn't come across very well."

We've all said silly things in interviews – Geri and Mel B more than anyone. None of us were media trained (in fact, I think media training was invented because of us!), but we did instinctively have this ability to get our message across, even when we did all speak over each other. We never discussed beforehand what we were going to say, but we did communicate, obviously very effectively, this idea of girl power, friendship and inclusivity.

It didn't happen all the time – there are lots of interviews when I'm on form, chatting and having a laugh. I suppose it was whatever the vibe was on the day. But somewhere along the way, I started to become silenced. After what had happened at the BRITs, I tended to capitulate very quickly, not wanting to risk my place in the band or get into trouble. If I was told not to do something, I wouldn't do it. The truth is I hate upsetting people or letting them down, it makes me feel sick, I'm talking actual nausea and feelings of anxiousness. I think it increased with my time in the band, but I do remember having those feelings as a kid.

It made me question myself all the time. I'd think I was doing okay, and then someone would say something about me being too "vulnerable" to have a boyfriend or point out I'd said something "stupid" in an interview and I'd think, "*Oh shit, am I not okay?*" I was made to believe there was something wrong with me.

Comments by the media, the girls and management made me feel increasingly insecure. I felt incredibly vulnerable and stupid. And confused.

Around this time, there was a lot of self-policing and politics going on. I completely lost myself and became totally insular. It became so intense that I was the last one of us to get a mobile

Performing 'Spice Up Your Life' at the Royal Albert Hall, while filming the final scenes for *Spiceworld: The Movie*.

The Royal Premiere of *Spiceworld* with two of our stellar cast, Sir Bob Geldof and Richard E. Grant.

Elton John covered in lippy after being showered with kisses in *Spiceworld*.

"Maestro": our first meeting with Luciano Pavarotti before performing with him in Modena, where Geri was sadly missing.

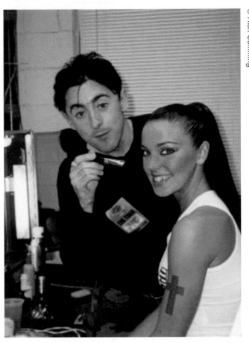

A quick rehearsal backstage at the Planet Hollywood opening in Montreal with Bruce Willis.

Messing about with the lovely Alan Cumming
behind the scenes on the movie.

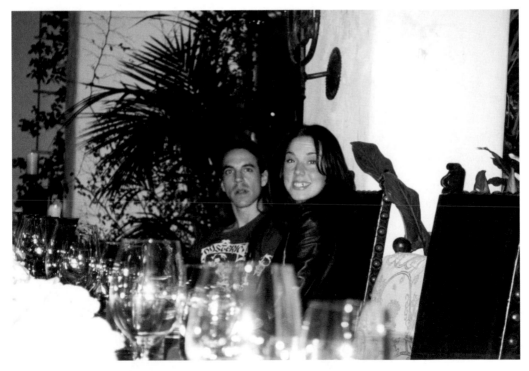

Anthony Kiedis and I at a dinner party in LA thrown by Nancy Berry for the Spice Girls.

Bryan Adams and
I backstage in
Germany promoting
'When You're Gone'

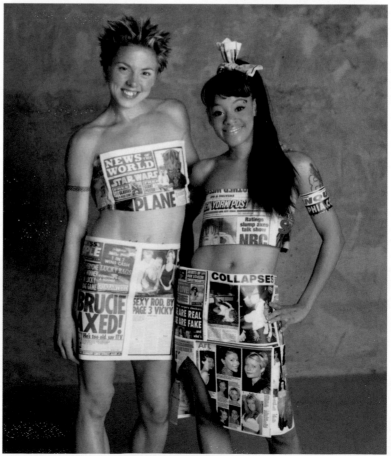

Lisa 'Left Eye' Lopes
and I wrapped in US
and British tabloids
on a promo shoot in
LA for 'Never Be The
Same Again'.

Sex Pistols guitarist Steve Jones after he joined me on stage at the Mayan Theater in LA in 1999.

Showing my love for the Sex Pistols on stage.

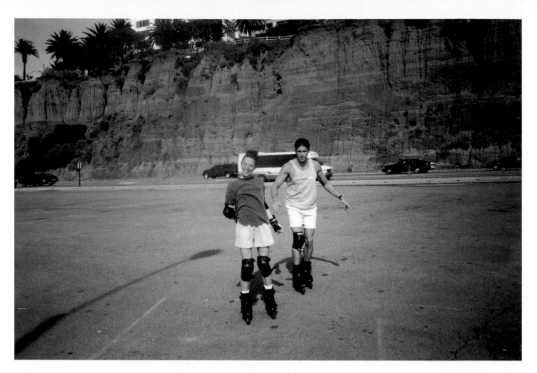

My beautiful friend Greg. Happy times in LA. I'll never stop missing him.

Early recording sessions for *Northern Star* in LA.

Shockingly thin at my mum's. The car didn't last long!

Not one of my finest moments. The *Forever* album launch November 2000.

Our lovely spice mums: Jackie, Mum, Pauline, Ana and Andrea.

Me and Mum on stage
at her 70th in Liverpool.

Celebrating my
lovely Nannie Kay's
90th Birthday.

Macca and me backstage at Glastonbury 2022 ahead of his historic headline set.

Spice Girls reunion tour 2007-2008. Head to toe in Roberto Cavalli... well, apart from my trainers!

2012 Olympics London.

Spiceworld 2019 stadium shows, 'Wannabe' finale.

Uber sporty, performing 'Holler' at the stadium shows.

Back in the game, at the Blenheim Triathlon. I really am Sporty!

Sink The Pink Pride World Tour. Proud ally flying the flag.

My incredible drag queens spicing up Times Square at World Pride 2019: Margo Marshall, Joan Oh, Asttina Mandella, Le Fil, JonBenét.

Some of the incredible artists that have spoken about their love of the Spice Girls: Adele, Charli XCX, MØ, Olly Alexander, Billie Eilish, Icona Pop, HAIM and Emma Stone

My happy place. Sharing the stage with my wonderful musicians touring *Melanie C*
Ayo Oyerinde and MD Ricci Riccardi.

phone. People still laugh that I had a pager for so long, assuming it was because I feared technology or something. I had a pager because I just didn't want the girls to ring me. At least with a pager it's on your terms to look at the number and see if you want to ring the person back. I still hardly answer my phone. Is it a hangover from those times? I automatically feel like I'm in trouble.

The day after *Oprah*, I found time to get to the hotel gym. There was a huge mirror in front of the treadmill, and as I ran my 10 kilometres, I looked at myself and repeated, over and over again, "You've just got to be a robot, no feelings, no excuses, no pain, you're a robot."

That's how I got through it.

I shut down emotionally. I controlled the things I could control, namely my physical body. I knew I had to look a certain way to be worthy of having success and to do that, I had to exercise like a demon; I had to eat the way I ended up eating. Being in the gym was also my safe place. No one could get to me there. If I was on a treadmill, I didn't have to answer to anybody.

It became such an unhealthy cycle.

After many years of therapy, I can rationalise a lot of what happened back then. We were young, we were all vulnerable and insecure, we all had our issues. I believe some of the band were threatened by me and wanted to keep me in my place. I'd always been confident of my ability, but I felt like certain things that were said or done went towards knocking that out of me. But I was so confident on stage. As soon as I'm in front of an audience, I'm invincible. I know I can perform, I can sing songs, I can run around, I can build a rapport with the audience, I can be strong, I can be inspiring.

So, ultimately, no one can keep me down because when we're onstage, I'm in my element.

The girls all trust me up there, it's where we work best. Whenever we sing a capella, all eyes are on me. The girls look to me on stage if they question themselves.

There's so much healing that's gone on. Mel B mentioned in *Catch A Fire* that she has apologised to me several times, including that time in Las Vegas that I spoke about earlier, and it is proverbial water under the bridge. Throughout the years, I've shown up for her, and I'll continue to do that. She's been through some tough times, and I'll always be there for her. I've had my own mental health issues, you know. I don't judge. I don't have an agenda and she knows that. She's a pain in the arse, but I love her.

There was and still is a lot of love between us all. We had just been so taken aback by it all: the success, the mania, the schedule, the fame. Simon hadn't helped either. And we were so jumpy about the press, about being watched and recorded. It all created an environment that was clearly not conducive to good mental wellness. Without a manager, we were rudderless and becoming uncontrollable. Boundaries were no longer blurred but broken.

As 1998 began, I was no longer trim, I was bordering on being dangerously skinny. I was completely single-minded in how I dieted and exercised, especially now we had a tour coming up. I would often use live shows and tours as a reason to be extra hard on myself.

It was as though I had two voices in my head – the angel and the devil, the light and the dark. They had always been there, but I didn't analyse things too much when I was younger. There was a sensible, caring voice telling me, *"This isn't good, you can't do this"*, but the other voice was so much louder, saying, *"This is the way it has to be."*

I didn't feel I had a choice. The angel tried her best, but the only voice I seemed to hear was that devil.

. . .

The North American leg came to an end in August 1998, with four more dates over in the UK in September.

With a couple of weeks free, I decided to stay in the US a bit longer to go and see my pal Alan Cumming, who was reprising his role of the Emcee in *Cabaret* on Broadway. I flew from Dallas, where we'd played our last US show, to New York. I went to see Alan in the show and had dinner with the cast and his friends that lived in the city.

After the intensity of the tour and being surrounded by the three girls and the hoopla that was our lives at this point, it felt amazing to slip back into the crowd. In the mass of noise and chaos that is New York City, I quietly melted into the background.

Back in my Four Seasons suite early one evening, I decided to run myself a bath. Just as I was about to get in, the hotel phone rang. "Miss Chisholm," said the voice at the other end, "I have Madonna on the line for you."

I burst out laughing, amazed that the girls really thought I'd fall for this one.

"Oh really, yeah, okay great – oh hi, Madonna," I laughed, waiting for Victoria or Emma to burst into giggles.

That unmistakable voice came down the end of the line: "Melanie, hi, how are you? I heard you were in town. Would you like to come to dinner this evening?"

I nearly fell on the floor. To this day, I have no idea why Madonna invited me to hang out. I presume she somehow knew I was in town and because we'd met before, she thought she'd see what I was doing for my tea that night. I didn't need to be asked twice.

She invited me to the Mercer, a new hotel, and *the* place at the time. What was I going to wear?! I tipped my suitcases all over my bed and spent hours figuring out what clothes would be right for dinner with Madonna. Can you imagine that kid watching Live Aid knowing that one day she'd get to hang out with the person playing on that stage?

I've still got the high-waisted suit trousers from Alexander McQueen I wore with a white vest and Nike Air Max. I turned up to dinner a bit early and there was only one other person there. At the time Guy Oseary worked at Madonna's label Maverick. As an A&R guy, he had signed Alanis Morissette and The Prodigy, before later becoming Madonna's manager and more recently, U2. He is an incredibly successful person who has sold something like 100 million albums, but you would never know it. He's the most sweet, down-to-earth, charming person. Here I was, meeting Madonna in a social situation for the first time, completely on my own, so I was nervous. Guy immediately made me feel comfortable by being so calm and lovely. We're friends to this day.

Madonna arrived, and it was immediately comfortable, if not bizarre. She is both charming and really fucking intimidating. She's so cultured and educated so you have to focus to keep up with her. I concentrated on simply following what was going on.

I don't remember what we ate; I just said, "I'll have what she's having." Madonna was opposite me; Guy was to her left and the other guest was the comedian Chris Rock, who came with his then-wife. I didn't really know who he was, he wasn't on my radar at that point. Anyway, he was lovely, the whole night was very laid-back. It wasn't a rock "n" roll party night, it was a nice dinner, meeting people, and quite chilled.

Guy was staying at the Mercer so after dinner we went up to his room to listen to demos of the second Alanis Morissette record. As you do.

And then Madonna gave me a lift home back to the Four Seasons!

Surreal isn't the word.

• • •

We finished the tour with a triumphant homecoming, playing two nights at Wembley Stadium. I think back on that, playing the Mecca of venues, and I remember... nothing. Nothing at all. I have no memories, no recollection of what were the biggest dates of our career at that point. I was on autopilot, going through the motions and, while some of the time enjoying all that was happening to us (I hope), I think a lot of the pain I was going through emotionally and mentally during that time caused me to blank whole sections of my life out.

Things winding down might have been a good moment for me to rethink my life and perhaps start to address some of my issues. That wasn't the case at first though. With Mel B and Victoria both heavily pregnant as the year ended (they would give birth to Phoenix and Brooklyn the following February and March respectively), Emma and I did the remaining promo for *Spice World*.

In November, we went to the MTV Europe Music Awards in Milan to collect two awards for Best Group and Best Pop Act, one of which was presented to us by Busta Rhymes and the other by Donatella Versace, who also dressed us for the evening. We watched Madonna, who also won two awards that night, perform "The Power of Goodbye" and Backstreet Boys do "Everybody".

After the awards Donatella threw a belated fortieth birthday party for Madonna. She had it at her place in Milan, and it was huge, like a wedding. Of course, my old pal Madonna was there, and Emma and I were sat with Massive Attack. It was basically a who's who of who'd been at the MTV Awards, including Blur, The Prodigy, All Saints and so on. I went out afterwards to some random club with Damon Albarn and Alex James and things got even more messy. Thankfully, I must have come to my senses at some point because my homing beacon switched on and I headed back to my hotel, leaving Alex and Damon to it.

Early the next morning, my assistant came in to wake me up. She had someone on the phone asking if I knew where Damon and Alex were. The pair had gone missing, and I was apparently the last person to see them. "What's this shit?" she said, picking up a coat that was most definitely not the Versace coat, generously gifted by Donatella, that I'd been wearing the night before.

It seemed like I'd accidentally picked up the wrong coat when I left the club and somehow come home with some poor Italian woman's Miss Selfridge or Topshop number. I got my Versace back though; I still wear it now and then. Sadly, the other coat never found its way back home, though I think we did try to reunite it with its owner. As we know, Alex and Damon were also found safe and sound... eventually!

All fun, all games, on the surface. But I'm not sure how much fun as I was having when I was, really and truly, so desperately unhappy.

I started to focus on my solo career. "When You're Gone", my first single as a solo artist, with Bryan Adams, did well, both critically and commercially. That was a huge boost for me. Although my confidence around my talent remained relatively solid, the accomplishments of that single underscored that there was the possibility of success for me outside of the band.

I worked with Matt Rowe up at Mayfair Studios in Primrose Hill on rough ideas for a third Spice Girls album, and I was back and forth to Ireland a bit, where Emma and I recorded a B-side for "Goodbye", a cover of The Waitresses' song, "Christmas Wrapping".

Compared to our previous schedule though, things were quieter. Here was the chance I needed to reflect and recollect. But instead of that being the potential for something positive, I started to hurtle deeper into a feeling that I had no words for. I felt low, I felt guilty, I felt confused. These were supposed to be the happiest days of my life, why did I feel so sad?

I was at, or nearing, my lowest weight. In fact, I was under-weight. I didn't know how to stop obsessively exercising and completely undereating. I knew what I was doing wasn't right, I knew it didn't make me feel better, but it was the only sense of control I seemed to have in my life.

I was, quite simply, very, very lonely. I'd gone from airports, private jets, constant interviews and playing to thousands of people to... resounding silence. Here I was, living alone in my tiny one-bed flat in Finchley. Mel B and Victoria were pregnant and loved-up, Emma had all her family close by, Geri had moved on. My friends from college had long since scattered around the world. I had a few mates in the industry, but they were all part-nered up or were busy with their own frantic lifestyles of touring and recording.

I felt completely and utterly alone.

I was faced with this crashing reality where I'd gone from my life not being my own to suddenly becoming my own again. What was I going do with it? What did I have?

Back at the MTV Awards, did I really want to go out half the night with the lads from Blur? Not really, but it meant I was around people, having "fun", living life. I could escape from myself, just for a bit (plus it's a good anecdote).

The whirlwind that began with "Wannabe" and went into a succession of switching on the Christmas lights, making the movie, the second album, winning BRITs, doing a huge tour... there wasn't a second to process it at the time. We just were constantly onto the next thing and then the next thing after that.

This was the first opportunity I had to exhale and all I could think was, *"Who the fuck am I? What do I do when I'm not flying off to do TV performances or press?"*

I was left trying to figure out what my life was when I wasn't being a Spice Girl and it was then that I felt so isolated. I didn't have a social group or a partner. All of my friends and family were still in the North, and I didn't manage to get back there as much as I needed to.

It was just little old me trying to find a life outside of work, a social life, a love life.

I couldn't seem to find one, no matter how hard I tried.

I was anxious. I was depressed. I just didn't know it. There was so little information about mental health back then. I brushed it off as best I could and kept going.

I was ill and the Spice Girls seemed to be crumbling. I seemed to be crumbling. Where did that leave me? What was I going to do?

I went home to Widnes for a bit, where I lay on the sofa for a few days, crying, with Mum looking after me. I had no idea, nor did she, that this was depression. I suppose we just thought I was wiped out, exhausted, and that I needed a bit of a rest, but I'd be fine.

Everything swirled around inside me as I thought about the future. *My* future. Look what happened when the Spice Girls suddenly stopped. I was left spinning and left with the feeling that things weren't in my control. I knew, somehow, that I needed to fix this if nothing else.

Somewhere within that mess of emotion I managed to see a tiny glimmer of hope.

I had to take matters into my own hands. I had to do something I hadn't done for two years, if not longer.

It was time to put myself first. Finally, it was my time.

CHAPTER THIRTEEN

Too Much

As the plane left Heathrow towards the end of January 1999, and began the 12-hour journey to Los Angeles, where I would record my debut solo album, I felt a mixture of emotions. Mostly relief, that I was on my own and away from the girls. And anticipation of what was to come.

And anger. Real, burning anger. Listen back to "Going Down" and you'll see what I mean.

I'd started the writing sessions in London and Dublin but had decided on a three-month trip to LA to finish writing and recording the album. I'd always loved it there. I still do. The weather, the lifestyle... LA was always the front runner in health and fitness although I think we've pretty much caught up in London these days. But those endless sunny days just make me smile and get shit done!

Never had I wanted separation and a new start more. I needed to be seen as an individual, with a voice of my own. That was so important to me. I wanted people to value me and what I could do. I was more than just Sporty Spice. There was more to me. People had to see that and I needed to show myself that too.

A car collected me from LAX and I felt the thrill of arriving in LA. It was late afternoon and still warm. The sun always makes me feel good. The palm trees practically swayed in greeting to me, the sky was a perfect pastel pink, the breeze gentle.

Los Angeles.

Palm trees and golden light. Malibu, Topanga Canyon, Muscle Beach, Venice Beach and rollerblading along the Santa Monica bike path. A sunset hike to the Griffith Observatory, where James Dean so memorably played that *Rebel Without a Cause*. Jon & Vinny's Italian and the Farmers' Market. Kombucha and bee pollen smoothies. The best Mexican food you can eat outside of Mexico. The Four Seasons Beverly Hills and Crunch Gym. The Beverly Center, the Kardashians, and shopping on Melrose. The Viper Room. Amoeba Records and Tower Records. Scientology. Mulholland Drive. Katy Perry in Whole Foods and Leo DiCaprio hiking Runyon Canyon.

There's no place like it.

I arrived at the house I was renting in Beverly Glen. It belonged to the actor Anthony Andrews, who had been in the film *Brideshead Revisited*. Coincidentally, his son, Josh, worked on *Spiceworld: The Movie* and he later worked with Bill Kenwright, thanks to whom I would later make my 2009 West End debut in his production of *Blood Brothers*. Small world, once more.

The hill-set house was just what I needed. Plenty of space, a pool surrounded by a lovely garden and amazing views of the city below. There was practically a gym and a studio on every block. I felt right at home.

• • •

A few people took me under their wing pretty much as soon as I landed in Los Angeles: Guy Oseary in particular. Following my amazing dinner with Madonna, I had kept in touch with Guy and as soon as I got to LA to begin writing *Northern Star*, he was on the phone.

"Right, you're in my town, I'm taking care of you," he said and I immediately found myself on the red carpet of the Golden Globes at the Beverly Hilton, alongside Gwyneth Paltrow and Christopher Reeve.

Guy was amazing, he introduced me to everyone, including Steve Jones from the Sex Pistols and the record producer Rick Rubin, who at the time had Anthony Kiedis from the Red Hot Chili Peppers staying with him. That was my LA posse. Random but brilliant.

It blows my mind to think back on those times now. Little old me here in LA with a Chili Pepper on one side, and a Sex Pistol on the other. Steve Jones and I hit it right off. He's one of the funniest people I've ever met. He was in a band at the time called the Neurotic Outsiders with John Taylor from Duran Duran and Matt Sorum and Duff McKagan from Guns N' Roses. They had a residency at the Viper Room, a famous nightclub and live music venue on the Sunset Strip outside of which, sadly, River Phoenix overdosed and died on 31st October 1993.

One day, around early April 1999, a couple of months into recording, Steve said, "Right, you've got to get up on stage with us. We have people come up and play with us all the time. You're next." I looked at him. "Erm, yeah, okay. But what am I going to do?" He said I should do a Pistols song, so I did "Anarchy in the UK" and "Pretty Vacant". I got out there and really went for it. I looked out at this little club and saw people sticking two fingers up and spitting at me! I was like, "Oh my God, they hate me." Steve and John were laughing, telling me, "No, it's really good, that's a good sign." It's a punk thing, a badge of honour… apparently!

It was one experience after another, and what was lovely about it was that it was all unplanned. I simply lived in LA and things seemed to happen.

Those were crazy days (albeit sober, there was no partying at that time. It was not rock "n" roll in that way). I found an LA that was positive and creative and healthy, and I think that's why I have such a love of the city.

I was very used to being around celebrities by this point, but there is a part of me, the girl who went to Fairfield High School in Widnes, who's screaming inside, "This is crazy."

You're also a bit of a novelty because you're British so I lapped that up and enjoyed being constantly surrounded by positive people who didn't tell me to be quiet, or to be smaller. They encouraged me to be myself, to be louder, to be confident. They made me feel like I had every right to be there (which I did), that I was talented, that I was fun, that I had something to say.

I think that belief in myself can be felt throughout the album.

I had the world at my fingertips recording *Northern Star*. Virgin's Ashley Newton was A&R-ing the record and he really believed in me. I feel so grateful to Guy and Bryan Adams too. They were good friends; they really looked out for me and took care of me and gave me the confidence to go on and do the things I did.

When it came to the writing sessions for *Northern Star*, I had so much to express. I learnt how to write songs with the Spice Girls and Matt and Biff, the Absolute Boys and Eliot Kennedy, but it was as a solo artist that I became a songwriter. There were no dry spells or writer's block. It flowed out.

And here I was in the studio with some of the biggest names in music. It was intimidating at first, but these people really put me at ease. Whenever I think of Rick Rubin, whose catalogue at that point included Run-D.M.C., Public Enemy, the Beastie Boys, Jay-Z, the Chili Peppers, and Johnny Cash, I think about how warm he is. He never once gave it the big I am.

We did a documentary for *Northern Star,* and Rick said such lovely things. He was just like that in the studio too; he was very encouraging and warm and positive and made me feel so comfortable, which is important in that studio environment, because you can be quite vulnerable. You don't want to say something stupid or do something that's rubbish, so you're constantly on edge, but he was very encouraging. It was a very safe place where you could be creative. It was a wonderful experience.

The songwriter and record producer Rick Nowels had a studio up in the Valley. It was dead steep to get up there and because I'd been on tour and with the Spice Girls, I'd not driven much since I'd passed my driving test. Navigating the freeway in the dark as a new driver isn't something I'd recommend! It was worth it though; Rick's studio was amazing. Bryan came down and we did a couple of days with Rick. The title track, "Northern Star", was written there, as was "I Turn To You", "Closer" and "Feel The Sun". A lot of the album, come to think of it.

Ashley brought William Orbit in. Madonna's *Ray of Light* had come out in early 1998 with this brilliant electronic/pop direction and that really appealed to me. William had worked on that record so, when Ashley asked me what I was listening to, I mentioned William. You come out of the Spice Girls, and you have your pick. William and I wrote "Go" and working with him was nuts. "Just go into the vocal booth and sing anything," he would say. I sang a few different things, and he was like, "Right, great, that's that done."

He would put it all together and come up with something incredible. By this point, I was used to the structure of verse, pre-chorus, chorus, verse two and so on. William was so free. It was like how we first started out as a group, in those early sessions. And it worked. There's beauty in that chaos and magic to be found when you break the rules because you don't know what the rules are.

Next up was Billy Steinberg who wrote "Like a Virgin" for Madonna and "True Colors" – one of my dad's all-time favourite songs – for Cyndi Lauper. Like Rick, Billy is both warm and funny but also so positive, which I think does feel quite specific to LA. There's something very productive about the energy of the city and its people. It just really works for me.

When Billy is in the room, he isn't involved musically in any way. This baffled me. He's a poet and that's what informs his creativity. He gives you a pile of lyrics and you look through and respond to the ones you identify with. Rick would play chords and the mic would be up and we made it up as we went along. Suddenly there's a song. It's such a crazy way to work. We wrote "I Turn to You", my biggest hit, in that way.

As I said, I recorded some of the album in the UK too. Matt, Biff and I recorded "Goin' Down" at Windmill Lane Studios in Dublin. We went out the night before and the boys got wasted. We got in the next day and Matt was white as a sheet! Biff and I cracked on, as Matt lay on the floor trying to recover.

I told Biff I wanted to get into something guitar-based, something along the lines of Blur or Oasis. Biff came up with a riff, and we wrote it within an hour. Biff was there playing the guitar, I was screaming into the mic, letting out all that anger and rage, and Matt was passed out on the floor, somehow oblivious to all the noise. We just stepped over him and carried on.

There is no wrong or right interpretation when it comes to lyrics, which makes them incredibly interesting. There are certain songs I've written where I've thought, "*That is way too honest, Melanie*", yet people closest to me will not know what I'm talking about. They'll completely get the wrong end of the stick. But that's what I love about music. When you're heartbroken as a teenager, every song on the radio becomes relevant to your situation. I think that's how people find so much solace in music. You don't feel alone because there's somebody there who's feeling that emotion too. I feel very safe with lyrics.

People might think "Northern Star" was about the band, but it's about the media: "They build you up so they can tear you down." Meaning: you have to have faith in yourself. "I have learned my lesson well; the truth is out there." Meaning: you fuckers can say what you want and tell all your lies but this little northern star, she'll get through it.

What I find with songwriting is you often write a song and as time goes on, it has more meaning. Or sometimes the meaning shifts a little. It becomes more poignant as a lyric as life continues. I think with *Northern Star* you got to see me, the things that made me angry, or sad or happy.

· · ·

Being in LA helped me to slow down and reflect. I felt an overwhelming sense of freedom. I didn't have to worry about upsetting anybody, or compromise in any way, which was liberating. With the album flowing out of me and my confidence slowly returning, I felt compelled to look different, to change my image.

First, I decided to get more tattoos. This was before everyone, and literally their mother (including mine!), got inked up. Before it was acceptable, fashionable or cool. Ex cons and sailors had tatts. Not squeaky-clean pop stars.

I'd gotten my first one the year before, when we were over in LA. I knew I wanted a band around my arm, and I wanted something Celtic, to nod to my Irish roots. Despite the fact I was marking my body for life, I did zero research. The girls and I just walked into Tattoo Mania on Sunset in West Hollywood. This place will do. And boom, I had it done. It is a *little* bit wonky. Next up was the cross on my arm, also Celtic, and then, later, my angel, which I had done on my stomach in a hotel room in Milan during the 1998 tour. As you do!

I wonder now if the tattoos formed part of an armour. Was I creating something that protected me and protected my vulnerability by having this exterior display of toughness? I wonder too if there was a connection to self-harm. I've often thought scarring your body for life is an odd thing to do. Did it come from a form of extreme self-hatred, trying to change the way you look and therefore changing who you are? Tattoos and plastic surgery are so accepted now it blows my mind. It's so addictive – once I'd completed one, I'd have the next one planned.

I once asked Madonna if she'd ever consider getting one. She replied, "They're too permanent," which totally makes sense with her being the master of re-invention, although I think she has a few now. Just little ones though.

Towards the end of recording and mixing the album it was time to start thinking about artwork. We went out to the

Mojave Desert and did an amazing shoot with the photographer Luis Sanchis.

I'd already succumbed to blonde hair; I don't know why but whenever I spent a bit of time in LA I want to be blonde... or blonder. I decided that a new look for the new record was perfect. Sadly, my hair was so dark that the long and intense process to get my hair blonde wrecked it and I had to pretty much have it chopped off, though only up to my chin at this point.

But this was a new me, I wanted people to see me differently, to see that there was more to me than Sporty Spice.

The short, spiky cut didn't come until a little while later when we were back in LA to shoot the "Goin' Down" video. The shorter my hair got, the more liberated I felt. It's amazing the fuss it made, it's only hair! It grows back (in my case that's the painful bit!).

There was a sense of freedom, I think, being in LA and writing the music I wanted to write and expressing myself in the way that I wanted to. I could sound like me, look like me and *be* me.

I also felt ready to address some of my behaviours and issues.

I casually mentioned to my assistant, Ying, about hiring a personal trainer during the duration of my stay. She told me about someone who came highly recommended via somebody she used to work with, a pop star from the nineties called Kavana.

I knew that I needed help, and something instinctively told me that this might be the first step towards accepting it. I was exhausted with internalising this conflict within myself, my body, and my mind.

• • •

Gregory Joujon-Roche was my very first trainer and I owe such a lot to this man. I liked him as soon as we met. In fact, I absolutely adored him. He was the first person who helped take away my fear of food. Carefully and gently, Greg got me to open up about my eating habits.

"Melanie, tell me about your typical diet pre-and post-training," he asked me. I umm'ed and ahh'ed before admitting all meals consisted basically of fruit and vegetables. "So, no protein, no carbs, no healthy fats," he said. "Would you put water in your car and try to drive it?" That has stayed with me until this day. It's simple, but exactly what I needed to hear. If my body was a "machine" then I needed to care for it properly.

Greg took the time to explain about calories in and calories out and that the way I was supporting my exercise with my current nutrition was, of course, not only not useful but incredibly harmful. If I really wanted to be fit and healthy, then I needed to give my body the fuel it needed to train in the way that I wanted. It was also important to allow my body to rest and recuperate.

Contrary to what I believed, you can achieve more with a short, well-executed workout than one that's hours long. Especially when you support your body properly. You don't need to exercise excessively, or every single day. I felt comfortable and safe with Greg. Like makeup artists or hair stylists, when you get the right person, a personal trainer can quickly become a confidant, a therapist.

Inspired, I decided to spend some of that Spice Girls money and hired a chef to cook me healthy, balanced and nutritious meals. I was still being very measured, very careful with what I ate, but it was a step in the right direction. I found a healthy routine during the three months I was there. Wake up, drive down to Crunch Fitness on Sunset, and then head to the studio for whatever session was lined up that day. I was eating healthily and properly, thanks to the chef.

Being in LA gave me the space and the time to allow myself to accept I needed help and to begin to look at my behaviours. It was the start of me acknowledging and accepting that there was a problem. It wasn't as simple as getting better, but it was the start.

I told Greg that I had decided to speak to someone, and asked if he knew anyone. Aware that I wouldn't want to be papped coming out of an office that housed an eating disorder clinic, Greg arranged for a therapist to come to my house.

It was in my very first session that I admitted, out loud, for the first time, to having an eating disorder. What a relief that was. Apart from Geri and the odd comment here and there from the other girls, I'd never been asked if I was okay. Like *really* okay. To be able to say, "No, I don't think so. I think I've got an eating disorder." It was so liberating, at least at first.

Despite a great start, the experience overwhelmed me. The feeling of relief was quickly followed by rising fear. It scared me to have admitted it, to have said those words, "I think I have an eating disorder." Because now it was real, now it was true and that meant I had to challenge it and change it.

I didn't have another session. It was just a bit too much for me at that point.

LA was a huge step towards me getting better, but when I reflect on it now, I can see I just wasn't quite ready. Not yet. Rather than addressing my problems, I just found new crutches to prop myself up with.

What I did, really, was to give all the responsibility away. Because I'd been overtraining in the gym, I got a personal trainer so he could be responsible for that part of my life. I had a chef to take care of things nutritionally, so I didn't have that responsibility either. I went to therapy to "sort it all out", so I could tick that box.

I was in this fake world where I could tell myself that everything was okay, that everything was taken care of. At that time, money was no object, so I would have facials, massages, treatments. It was all about me.

I had, ultimately, lulled myself into a false sense of security.

Greg passed away in 2016 from a rare form of cancer and I was devastated. I absolutely adored him, not only because he was such a warm, lovely positive man, but because he was a big part of getting me back on the road to recovery. It's impossible for me now to be in LA and not think often, and fondly, of Greg. I really miss him. He was a wonderful human being.

• • •

Though I didn't find love in LA, I did embark on a lovely friendship. I'd met Anthony Kiedis before, on tour with the girls in 1998, via our US publicist, Elizabeth Freund. He had come to see us play at The Forum, in Inglewood, with his bandmate Flea, who brought his daughter, Clara (Balzary, who went on to become a respected photographer after Anthony bought her a camera when she was 12).

We got to talking about tattoos, and just hit it off. In fact, Anthony designed the tattoo on my lower back, the lotus flower, which I had done by his tattoo artist, Kevin Quinn. It symbolises earth and is also the Tibetan sign for grounding, which I know I very much felt I needed then.

Luckily, that one wasn't wonky.

We were just friends, though. I really liked him, but I was a bit scared. He'd been very open about his problems in the past and is a proper fucking Rock Star.

He invited me out for lunch to Real Food Daily, a famous vegan place in Santa Monica. He picked me up in his huge four-by-four truck from the Four Seasons, and we headed down to the beach. We got chatting about the weirdness of fame, and about all the free stuff you get given when you're famous. You spend your whole life skint, wanting to buy clothes, cars and all that stuff. You finally get famous, get some money, and you get given everything for free.

"It's like, I don't know what to do with it, you know," he said as we picked our way through traffic. "Well," I said, straight-faced, "you could just give it away, give it away, give it away now?"

He didn't laugh, though I suppose it was the equivalent of me being asked what I really, really want!

Nothing happened romantically although I knew he hoped it would. He would do very lovely things, like send me faxes at whatever hotel I was staying in, singing my praises. Once, I turned up to meet him, and he'd been to Tower Records and bought me a stack of CDs, including one by David Bowie. He was a great, brilliant friend.

A few months later, I was working on *Northern Star* at The Village Studios near Santa Monica. "Has Anthony played you the song that he's written about you yet?" Rick asked me. Oh my god, what? Rick smiled. "Come with me." Back then, Rick used to mix songs in his studio and then go out and play them very loudly in his Rolls-Royce. I think it came from his hip-hop days; rappers knew that most people listened to their music while driving around. If it sounded good in the car, then Rick was happy.

We went out and sat in his Roller and Rick Rubin played "Emit Remmus" about me, to me. The song spells "summer time" back-wards and it featured on the Chili Peppers' iconic 1999 album, *Californication*. Anthony mentions it, and me, in his 2005 auto-biography, *Scar Tissue*.

If you look up the lyrics, then consider this a Parental Advisory Warning because it's a bit rude! It's essentially about an American boy and an English girl but most of it has nothing to do with me – especially not the dirty bits.

I remember Rick playing it, stroking his huge beard, and shooting me these mischievous smiles.

I was really flattered by it because Anthony is an incredible songwriter and performer. He's had very difficult times in his life and yet he's such a beautiful person. He's so gentle, so interesting and interested. I mean, he's from the Red Hot Chili Peppers, one of the coolest bands that has ever existed and *he* wrote a song that was inspired by *me*, so it was a huge compliment, it was just lovely.

. . .

During the pandemic, there was a Twitter listening party and it was the first time I've gone back and listened to *Northern Star* in its entirety. I knew I could stand by every song, every lyric, every note, but I hadn't listened to the record for a long time, for years. I felt so proud of it. I think it's such a wonderful record. I was so inspired at the time. And, I had a lovely, big budget to do all the production – all those incredible Craig Armstrong string arrangements.

The experience of recording and promoting *Northern Star* enabled me to establish myself as an individual again. *That* is who I am, *this* is what I have to say. Because I'd been part of something that was so overwhelming for such a long time, I had to figure out who I was when I wasn't in that environment.

I had also felt so, *so* oppressed for so long that this was just the most amazing freedom.

I can't speak for Emma and Victoria but because Mel B and Geri were such strong characters and were written about so much,

I think I felt like a spare part sometimes. But here I was in LA, on my own, standing on my own two feet, doing my own thing, being taken seriously as an individual, as a human being, as an artist.

It was life-affirming to be able to do that.

And the album was a success. Even if that success would come very slowly.

I'd always had confidence in my ability, and I knew that that record was great and it deserved to do well. I also felt like I wasn't one of the most popular members of the band or the highest-profile member of the band, or the most interesting member of the band. I hoped it would do well, but it was not a given.

It's hard coming out of something so huge because you know you're never going to reach the heights of the band – that's pretty much impossible. Robbie Williams and Michael Jackson are rare exceptions to that rule. When you go solo, you adjust your expectations.

I had to get used to playing shows by myself too. My very first gig, at the Leadmill in Sheffield in the summer of 1999, went really well. Emma, Mel B, Victoria and David all came to support me, which was so sweet. Though I'd not performed on my own since college, as soon as I stepped onstage, I felt great. I was home again. I felt really pleased with the show and confident that I could perform just as well solo as I could in a group.

Festivals though, they were another matter. This is the time before people like Ed Sheeran, Adele or Stormzy played Glastonbury and Reading. Back then, festivals were completely dominated by rock and dance and the fans were not there to see anything even remotely pop.

The line-up for V99 included James Brown, Manic Street Preachers, Suede, Happy Mondays, Supergrass, Massive Attack and… her from the Spice Girls. Melanie C.

It was a baptism of fire, that show. I was sandwiched in-between Faithless and the Manics and it was the first gig I'd done where people weren't necessarily fans of my music. In fact, people were definitely not there to see little old me.

I started my set, and I could hear some booing. Then the bottles came flying at my head (none with wee in them, as far as I was aware, but who knows?). But you have to dig in and carry on.

"Some people might not like the idea of a Spice Girl playing V," I said to the crowd, "but I don't give a fuck – my band's wicked – if you think I'm shit." I did a rockier set, though I don't know how well my cover of "Anarchy in the UK" went down with the V crowd!

But I got through it and as soft and as vulnerable and weak as I sometimes feel, I'm quite a tough old bird in certain situations, especially if I'm onstage.

I feel grateful for that gig because it doesn't get more difficult than that. You need to have those shows to know and understand what it is to be a performer and an artist. If you want to play festivals, you've got to be prepared for a bit of shit. Mind you, just because I'd survived that one show, didn't mean I could rest on my laurels.

With V, you do two performances over the weekend: one in Essex and one in Staffordshire. Chelmsford was first and I gritted my teeth for the next one. "*Oh, it's the North, it'll be fine, they'll be much nicer,*" I remember thinking. But they were worse! Horrible bastards! I just had to dig deep and hoped that by the end of it, I'd won a few people over.

James Dean Bradfield from the Manics stopped me backstage for a chat after their set. We'd met a couple of times by that point, and he was always dead nice and friendly. He said to me, "Don't ever be negative onstage, whatever happens, remain positive." His words really stuck with me. I reminded him of them when I saw him a few years ago at a show. "Did I say that? That is good advice," he laughed. I said, "Yeah, I've carried that through my career." You can't stand there berating an audience who don't automatically love you. You've got to work for it, prove yourself and don't take it out on them if what you do isn't what they like.

Another time I was playing at Silverstone, after the F1 British Grand Prix. After the race, the drivers go onstage for an interview and then they have live music. That year it was Lewis Hamilton followed by me. I waited side of stage for my bit, but there was some delay with the interview. They said, "You go on now, do a bit of your set, and then come off when Lewis gets here."

The crowd surged forward, but when they saw it was me and not Lewis, loads of them started to leave. It's fine, I get that. I carried on singing, I had my then-tour manager, Steve, in my ear monitor telling me Lewis was on his way. Then he's not. Oh, hang on, here he is. I'm trying to do the show with all this chatter in my head! Finally, Lewis arrived.

"I know what you're all waiting for, and it ain't me," I laughed, as I left the stage and Lewis went on.

I still had three more songs to do though, so I had to get back on there. Because Lewis had been and gone, even more people started leaving. Thousands had dwindled to hundreds. The next song I was due to sing? "When You're Gone". The sweet irony.

These are all good lessons though; you've got to go through them.

• • •

Northern Star came out in October 1999 and went top ten. It was a slow climb after that. In March 2000, I released "Never Be the Same Again", which was my first solo number one, and that pushed the album up to number five.

That song is very special to me.

I was in the studio in LA with a songwriter called Rhett Lawrence, who made Mariah Carey's "Vision of Love", and we got to this point with a song that you *always* get to. It's there but it's not *there*. You've written a chorus, a pre-chorus, a couple of verses, and we arrived at the middle-eight, or the bridge, as they say in the US. I said to Rhett, "I can hear a Lisa 'Left Eye' Lopes style rap here." Rhett was like, "I know the girls, I'll put a call in."

Next thing you know, Left Eye is on the track. It was that straightforward. It was a bit like Bryan Adams, one of those amazing, successful collaborations that happened organically.

Lisa recorded her part separately, so the first time we met was at a photoshoot, a couple of days before we made the video. The photographer, Ron Davis, wrapped us in tabloid newspapers – Lisa in *The New York Post* and me in *The News of the World*. We talked about the frustrations around how you're written about in the tabloids, and the rumours and all those sorts of things you deal with. We had a lot in common and I felt connected to her. She'd also had some well-documented troubles with mental health too and had experienced the horrible scrutiny that women in the industry can come under.

She invited me to her hotel that night and she ordered a huge amount of incredible seafood and some amazing white wine – it was very sophisticated!

The video was shot in Malibu, and directed by Francis Lawrence, the same guy who shot "Cry Me A River" for Justin Timberlake, as well as three of the *Hunger Games* films. Lisa took ages to get ready. Mind you, I should be used to that with the other girls, but I am so quick. Hair, makeup, done! It was a busy day, getting ready, trying on clothes and in the middle of that working out the choreography. Again, we were aligned there, and both of us were drawn to the tai chi-inspired movement.

That song was a big part of the album's success, and I'm pretty sure that's because she was on it. It's a brilliant song of its own accord, but Lisa's presence took it up a level. Sometimes when a British artist works with an American, it can be a little… transactional. They take the cheque and get on with their lives. I've been fortunate to have had great experiences with everyone I've worked with, and Lisa in particular. She was so supportive; when I asked her if she fancied coming to London to promote the single, which I was hoping to keep at number one for a second week, she got on that plane, and we did Jo Whiley on Radio 1, *TOTP*, *CD:UK* and a bunch of other press. It was Lisa's first number one in the UK, so it meant a lot to her too.

Working with Lisa was incredible, and I feel so proud and so lucky to have had that opportunity. Tragically, she was only 30 when she died in a car crash in Honduras a few years later.

I was on holiday in Italy with my boyfriend at the time, Tom, when I heard she had died, on the 25th April 2002. It was so shocking. I couldn't believe this person I had been so fortunate to meet, and work with, was gone. When you spend time with someone like Lisa, someone who is so full of life and energy, who clearly had so much to give while she was here, it's almost like she knew she didn't have long to get it all out.

I finally met the other members of TLC at Mighty Hoopla in 2018. And I burst out crying, which yes, was weird, but I think it's because I'd had all these emotions about Lisa, which had nowhere to go, because I didn't know anyone that knew her. So, to meet

Chilli and T-Boz, it closed a circle, in a way. They were wonderful women, and I'm so glad I was able to meet that hugely important part of Lisa's life. All three of them had been such an inspiration to the Spice Girls.

In part thanks to Lisa, *Northern Star* went on to sell over two and a half million copies worldwide and was, *is*, the most successful solo album from any of the Spice Girls.

My next number one arrived in the form of "I Turn To You" and it really cemented the success of the album. It was the fourth single, and we released it nearly a year after the album first came out, but we thought we'd try it, see what happened. "Never Be The Same" had done so well, so I think it was Ashley who suggested we pair it with a few remixes to see if we could achieve similar success. Nothing to lose.

It just flew, that single, selling over 100,000 copies in just one week. The Hex Hector remix, which as soon as I heard I knew it had to be the single, was just brilliant and that helped propel the record sky-high. It was so popular that Hex won a Grammy that year for Remixer of the Year. The closest I've got to that little gilded gramophone!

Here I was, coming from the unimaginable success of the Spice Girls, and now I had achieved more than I could have hoped for with my solo record. It wasn't what I'd dreamed of as a kid – it was so much more.

In theory, I was on top of the world.

In reality, I was at rock bottom.

CHAPTER FOURTEEN

Nowhere To Run

I went home to Liverpool for Christmas 1999 feeling really low. Although the album would go on to eventually sell over two and a half million copies, at that point, *Northern Star* hadn't set the world alight. It had charted at four in the album charts while the singles "Goin' Down" and "Northern Star" had also both gone to number four. Since then, things had stalled. The label was talking about wrapping up the record and leaving it at that. Not a flop, but not quite a resounding success either.

I wasn't in a very good place, and I didn't realise at the time how ill I was. I'd gone from finishing the Spice Girls tour into making my album and then straight to promo for *Northern Star*. Now I was under pressure to get my vocals done for the third Spice Girls album, *Forever*. Instead of taking a break to assess where things were at, the band had decided we should get a new album out. In theory, I would have had a few months off between *Northern Star* promo and *Forever*, but, despite some stops and starts, *Northern Star* promo lasted nearly two years, thanks to several life-prolonging singles and remixes. It was great for the album, but it meant I was once again on a treadmill that I couldn't get off. I had to keep on, working the record, playing shows and promoting it, while recording the new Spice Girls album.

I was exhausted and doing too much. The progress I'd made in LA had started to slide. Back home, I had to be responsible for myself again, including my eating and my exercise. Very quickly, things became very overwhelming.

There was no more Greg to oversee and encourage my well-being. There was no chef to take care of my nutrition. I hadn't spoken to another soul about my disordered eating – I was alone again with what was by now a serious eating disorder. I was struggling to keep up with caring for myself. And now the energy I'd managed to maintain for the previous two years seemed to be slipping away. I felt shattered.

I also didn't want to do *Forever* at all, whatsoever. Not then, not at that point. I wanted to finish up *Northern Star,* take a break and then think about the future of the Spice Girls and my place within it.

Amid the growing pressure and knowing I could take time off over Christmas (the music industry pretty much shuts down during that period), I decided I needed something to look forward to. I was due to shoot the video for "Never Be The Same Again" in Malibu in January, so I decided to head out to the US a couple of weeks early. I knew I was always happier in California, plus it would be warmer than Widnes at that time of year.

The plan was to have Christmas at home and then me, Mum, Den and our Paul would fly out to LA together on the 27th, because we had been invited us to a Red Hot Chili Peppers show in Inglewood on New Year's Eve. We'd have plenty of time to get over our jetlag and enjoy ourselves at the gig.

Despite having this to look forward to, I still felt utterly rotten over Christmas. I don't think I showed it, or at least I convinced myself no one had any idea of what I was going through, but I was clearly unwell.

Living in such a restrictive way, things like Christmas had been stressful for me for a few years now. It was a time of indulgence, a time when everyone would eat together and enjoy over-indulging together. I wouldn't be able to sneak off and eat in my usual way. I had to go home and be around friends and family and try hard to hide my eating disorder. Of course, everyone was intent on eating, drinking and being merry, so I would relax a little bit to join in. I would balance any excess out by restricting food for the next few days and by going full throttle at the gym.

What happened at the millennium was that I became more relaxed around food, and I didn't have the energy to go to the gym. I couldn't get myself there. I think my body saw an opportunity to escape my restrictive eating and took it. I exchanged one eating disorder with another. From severe restriction, I began to binge eat.

Having had therapy and help now, I know that this was okay. It was all part of the process of trying to get well again. Setbacks are part of the story.

Despite my mood being low and my eating disorder starting to veer in another direction, I was a little more upbeat as we set off for the States. We got to the Beverly Glen house, and I felt my shoulders relax a little bit. I took a deep breath. It's okay, I told myself, it's okay.

The big day came, and I rang Anthony's manager to sort out the tickets. But there was a problem: there were no tickets. I don't know if there had been a mix-up or something, but the show was off, for us at least.

It wasn't the final straw for me, but it was close to it. I wasn't strong enough at that point to cope with any form of rejection, or any type of change in plan. I needed order, relied on it, to get me through the day.

Paul could see I was sinking and took hold of things. "Right, get your gladrags on, girl, we're off out."

We got dressed and went for dinner at an Italian place on Sunset. Afterwards, we headed towards Hollywood Boulevard to see the lights that had been set up to celebrate the millennium. They were all colours of the rainbow, and although I felt dreadful inside, it gave me the small lift I needed to get through that night. We went to an offy and wandered about Hollywood, where we somehow ended up sitting on the pavement, drinking a 40 (a 40-ounce beer) out of a brown paper bag with a homeless man.

There's me, a Spice Girl at the height of my fame, and our Paul sat on a grubby Hollywood street, drinking beer, and shooting the breeze with this lovely bloke. That was it, that was our millennium.

Despite everything, it was in its own way a sort of happy new year.

But things deteriorated for me over the next few days. I was barely able to get out of bed, let alone get up and exercise. It wasn't just a lack of energy or exhaustion, I felt wiped out mentally, physically and emotionally. I was lethargic; I couldn't exercise. I couldn't motivate myself to do anything. I was miserable and teary, and I felt frightened because I had always been so driven. I couldn't understand what was happening. LA was my safe place. I was in my favourite city, with my family, and I had a few days off. But none of that helped.

It was so alien to me to not be able to get up and go and do, do, do.

That's something that scares me the most about depression because I still have moments, I have dips like that. My biggest fear is being back in a place where I can't motivate myself, I can't drag myself out from the depths of it. And that's where I was at that point.

From having complete control to having no control was, is, the most terrifying thing to me.

Mum must have been worried about me, but I came up with one excuse after the other. And I didn't spend all day in bed, but I was certainly not getting up at 7 am to go and run 10 kilometres. To me, at the time, that felt huge. Things had been so restrictive and so ordered with food and exercise, now it was unravelling the other way.

Part of the problem was that I was in a situation I didn't want to be in. Or rather, a band I didn't want to be in. I was in emotional danger in the sense that my unhappiness at being stuck in the band was impacting severely on my mental health, and I didn't deal with it. I didn't remove myself from it. We have to truly acknowledge what we want and not feel guilty or selfish, because nobody else puts you first. Everyone puts themselves at the top of their own pile, which is how it should be. You have to take care of yourself, particularly when your mental health is in a precarious position.

For me, the most destructive thing I've ever done in my life is not acknowledge what I need. I'm still learning that.

The thing that was bothering me the most was that I did not want to be in the band anymore, but I wasn't acknowledging that's what I wanted. I couldn't tell the girls – I couldn't tell anyone – and it got to the point where I made myself really, really ill.

At that point in my life, the dynamic, the relationships in the band, that environment was dangerous, in the sense that my body's reaction to it put me in danger. I starved myself, I became anxious, and I shut myself off because I was so unhappy having to be there.

I felt completely trapped. Yet I couldn't be the one to let the band down. Not me. I couldn't be that person; I simply didn't have it in me. If I walked away, they couldn't continue. Or so I believed. If it was me who ended the Spice Girls, I would be so hated. Of course, Geri had already done that, but she seemed to have gotten away with it, in my mind at least, because we had managed to carry on. I knew I *could* leave but I was too scared. I was too scared about the backlash from the media. I feared hurting the fans. I feared the girls.

I was trapped. I didn't know where to go. I didn't know what to do.

• • •

As soon as I got home, I summoned up my courage and made the call I knew I had to make. I don't know what day of the week it was. It may have been a Monday, it might have been a Thursday. The only thing I'm sure of is that it wasn't a weekend because I got a doctor's appointment that same day.

People reach their own rock bottom for different reasons, in different ways, for different things. I simply couldn't cope anymore. I was having regular panic attacks. My anxiety was at an all-time high to the point I was becoming agoraphobic. I hated having to leave the house. But I didn't have words for these things. I knew how I was feeling, but I didn't know they were syndromes and illnesses.

I thought I was going mad.

I had moved into my Hampstead duplex apartment a year or so before, in September 1999. Throughout the height of the Spice Girls, I'd lived in my one-bed rented flat in Finchley. Whether I was at the BRITs or doing the MTV Awards, I'd come home to that modest, small place I called home. I just didn't have time, or maybe inclination, to find somewhere to buy.

While we were on the American leg of the tour, Mum and Pauline, Emma's mum, went house hunting for us and found both Emma and me apartments in the same North London complex.

I got an interior designer in to arrange everything according to Feng Shui. I got a fancy Bang & Olufsen multidisc CD player, bought a beautiful baby grand Steinway (that I still can't play!), spent lots of money on art and made sure I had the right number of goldfish in the expensive fish tank. Let's say this: I think pop stars and footballers have quite similar tastes. Though it's not what I'd have now, back then I thought it was perfect.

I had a hit album, a beautiful new home, I should have been on top of the world, but I was miserable.

People sometimes ask me how depression feels. It's different for everyone of course, but for me, being a very physical person, there's a real heaviness and lethargy. I'm someone who will always muster up the enthusiasm and the energy to get things done. But with depression, that's completely taken away. That's the hardest and the scariest part for me. I've always been optimistic, and determined, and ambitious; there's always a fire in my belly. I think that's something all the Spice Girls share; it's why we became so powerful together. But when that fire feels like it's gone out, it's very, very scary because you feel like you're stuck and that's how it's going to feel forever.

There's no joy. There's just dread.

It's a very physical, very heavy feeling, like you're dragging a weight around with you. It's an iron cloak that covers me and weighs me down.

Everything is so laboured, so difficult, such a struggle.

I felt as though I was in a catch-22 situation. I was too frightened to confront my behaviour because that meant I'd really have to face, and deal with, my problems. But then I had to keep finding the energy and the spirit and the enthusiasm to do these things I was under pressure to fulfil, whether that was a solo performance, going into the studio to record Spice Girls vocals, or doing an interview. Look at any of my interviews around 1999 and 2000 and I think you'll see, behind the mask, how I was feeling.

Yet throughout my depression, I still had my faithful robot to fall back on, so I persuaded myself, somehow, to do whatever I had to do. I told myself what I needed to hear. "Okay, this is how I'm supposed to behave, I need to go into the studio and write another album, say this, do that, sing the other," and I'd go and do it. But none of it was coming from a place that I was used to, a place of being driven and following my heart and my gut and my instinct. It was simply what I was supposed to do, so I better go and do it. I was so empty.

And that's so scary because you wonder, how do I get back to that place?

Whatever it was I had to do, I wouldn't want to do it. I'd be panicking and full of anxiety. But I'd get to wherever it was, do whatever I had to do, and then get home and turn back into a zombie.

I would lie in bed, slumped, glazed and lifeless. An empty shell.

The only thing that felt good, for a very, very, brief moment, was food. Because I'd had so much control over my consumption for so long, all I wanted to do was to go back to that feeling of when you were a kid and food wasn't an issue. You eat what you want, when you want, you don't think about it. Because my issues around food were so deeply ingrained and because I still didn't understand that I was depressed, my mind took over. It had been starved for so long that it just didn't stop.

I wanted to feel joy, to feel excited about things, to be ambitious again, and want to achieve, and create. I had to make those feelings up because I couldn't access them.

That's something an eating disorder does; it takes away any pleasure from the thing you're supposed to do every day, at least three times a day. Food becomes a place of dread, oppression, and fear, rather than enjoyment. And there's no escape. Because you have to eat, every day, at least once a day. For other people, addictions mean you stop doing that thing so you can recover. With eating disorders, you have to keep eating so you can recover.

An eating disorder is a void; it's a hole that you can't fill. I was lonely. I was unhappy. I was starved of food and affection. My body was broken. I hadn't had a period in over a year. I hadn't had a serious relationship, really, ever. I would seek out men who were unavailable or unreliable and then be heartbroken when they proved themselves to be unavailable and unreliable. When I did start to date people, I was so ashamed of my eating that it made it impossible for anyone to get close to me. I'd still only eat, pretty much, fruit and vegetables, maybe the odd bit of protein like fish. I was so embarrassed, so ashamed.

And my body had had enough.

Left to my own devices, my bingeing spiralled, and I was barely conscious that it was even happening.

I'd go downstairs at 3 am to the kitchen, and it would always be carbs. I would eat cereal and bread, to the point of sedation. When I was finally diagnosed, I learnt that it's a symptom of depression, to wake up at those hours and to eat to self-soothe and to sedate yourself, because carbs do that. I was in the habit of doing this because it's a cycle, it's an addiction, it's a drug.

I'd be in situations, whether social, work or family, feeling unhappy and uncomfortable and just be desperate, thinking, "*I've got to get out of here, I've got to go, I've got to eat.*" I needed to get my fix, to get away from people, so I could eat. I couldn't do it with anybody around – it was a very private thing. I would go to the shops, avoid bumping into anyone, get the food, get home, lock the door, and then eat and eat until I felt sick.

I would binge until I was unconscious.

I never, ever made myself sick, but I tried, I felt so disgusting. Thank goodness I couldn't do it as I fear bulimia would have been an even harder illness to recover from.

Eventually, I could barely get out of bed. The days would pass and unless I had to be at a shoot or a session, I'd lie in bed with the telly on, staring at the ceiling.

I was full of self-hatred, but I'd tell myself, "Tomorrow's a new day." And then I would start being super-restrictive again until the next time.

As my weight increased, I became increasingly isolated. I didn't invite anyone over, and I didn't go anywhere, unless I had to. I was now pretty much agoraphobic. I was paranoid and utterly miserable. I thought I was going mad.

One day, I had the telly on, Sunday morning, Channel 4. "Here's the new video from Mel C, it's called 'Never Be the Same Again' and it features Lisa 'Left Eye' Lopes from TLC."

I sat and watched as the video played, me and Lisa doing our tai chi-inspired moves, and shots of me, all in white, on a treadmill. *"God, I wish I was in LA right now,"* I thought.

The video ended and the voiceover returned. "Looks like Mel C could do with spending a bit more time on that treadmill."

You can imagine, can't you, how much that would hurt. How humiliating it would be. To be ridiculed in public for your weight, even at the best of times when you're happy, confident and secure. To hear that then when I was at rock bottom was just… devastating.

At that point, I had probably put on half a stone and was a healthy weight, finally. Still slim, but healthier.

As the months went on, I started to gain more weight. I was drinking and eating more, dieting, and exercising less. The more I tried to forget about life and "have a good time", the worse I felt.

Other symptons began to manifest. I was so filled with self-hatred that I would throw myself around the room, banging my head on the walls and the floor, hitting myself. I felt possessed. I was tortured with a destructive inner dialogue that would taunt me, reminding me how pathetic and disgusting I was. I was stuck in a cycle of eating to self-soothe, trying to fill a hole that food could never fill, then hating myself for having no self-control.

I would of course eat again to feel better, and it would all start once more.

I still have to work hard at times to keep that nasty inner voice at bay, I think it's something a lot of people struggle with. I now literally speak *to* that nasty voice; *"I hear you"*, I say, *"but you're not being very helpful right now."*

If anyone reading this knows what I'm talking about, I promise you life changes so much for the better when you're able to firmly stand up to that negative aspect of yourself. It's not easy but it is well worth the battle.

All in all, I was in a dreadful, dark, harmful space. And while I haven't ever been, thank goodness, truly suicidal, as I struggled most nights to get to sleep, this one recurring thought would go round and round in my mind:

"It would be a lot easier if I didn't wake up tomorrow."

I didn't want to die. I just didn't want to wake up and face another day.

I did wake up the next day, of course. I lay still for a moment considering my options, knowing that really there was only one. You could say on the surface that what drove me towards seeking help was vanity more than anything. I couldn't control how I looked anymore. I was overweight and I didn't know how to change it.

It was simply the biggest cry for help that my body could muster at that time.

It was time to make the call I knew I had to make.

I picked up the phone and dialled the number for the doctor. "I need to see someone, I think I'm going mad. I'm scared I'm going to die. I need help."

I was given an appointment for that afternoon.

Pulling my hood up and chucking on some shades, I made my way to the surgery. I had no reason to think the paps were following me or that someone in the surgery might spot me and call the tabloids. Or that I was being listened to and a tabloid might send a photographer to the surgery to snap me.

But even if they had, at this point, I wouldn't have cared. I so desperately needed help.

The waiting room was quite narrow, with two lines of chairs facing the other. I kept my head down until I was called in.

A deep breath.

"I've not been eating properly for a while. For years. I can't sleep and if I do, I wake up at 3 am and I can't go back to sleep. I'm scared to leave the house; I'm scared to have anyone over. I'm losing my mind," I said, in a tumble of words. Once I started opening up, it was like I couldn't stop. "There's something seriously wrong with me."

The doctor took a pause and nodded, very calmly. "Okay, Melanie. The first thing we need to address is your depression."

Depression? Me, depressed? Wait, is that what this was? This horrible, heavy, unbreakable dark cloud that filled every inch of my body, dragging me down each day to the point where I was constantly exhausted yet totally wired. I didn't know anything about depression. I don't think many people did back then. Our experience of depression came through films and television, where depressed people were "mad" and needed to be locked away. It was never spoken about unless it was an older relative murmuring about somebody having "the Black Dog".

I couldn't put together the idea of depression with my own behaviour.

He explained that many of the things I was experiencing were clear signs of clinical depression: lethargy, insomnia, low self-esteem, anxiety, feelings of guilt and helplessness, tearfulness, difficulty making decisions, weight gain.

The doctor was so calm, so reassuring, so decisive. It was exactly what I needed to hear.

I felt a massive weight lifted off my shoulders because it had a name. I wasn't going mad, I was ill.

Maybe, just maybe, I could be helped.

• • •

Going to the doctor was a huge step in the right direction for me. It helped me enormously just to know that I could get help. I didn't have to live with this forever, my illness could be treated.

I saw the doctor early in 2000, and the first thing he did was talk about therapy, and antidepressants. I also started to investigate other forms of therapy, like acupuncture, which helps me to this day.

As people who have taken antidepressants know, it can take a long time to work out which combination of medication is best for the individual. It took a while to find what worked for me.

Although I was finally on the road to getting better, there were still months to go before I would find the right antidepressants and before I started to get any sort of handle on my eating disorder.

Years before I have a vague recollection of an appointment at the Nightingale, a private mental health hospital in central London. I believe Simon Fuller was the person to make that happen, which I am grateful for. They did several blood tests, weighed, and measured me and gave me a bone-density scan.

My BMI results showed that I was medically anorexic, which shocked me.

Every eating disorder is different for each person – there are so many nuances, so although I did eat (albeit incredibly restrictively) and I thought I wasn't starving myself, I wasn't getting the nutrition I needed. On top of that, I was overexercising, so my body fat, my BMI and my body weight qualified me as anorexic.

My periods also stopped. I'd always wanted to be a mum and here I was risking not only my own health but my chances of that happening in the future. People with anorexia can find it more difficult to conceive, and then later in life you can be prone to things like osteoporosis because your bone density is also impacted by the disease. It still wasn't enough to stop me.

I had these serious diagnoses: clinical depression, anorexia, later binge eating disorder, severe anxiety. I do regret not getting help sooner. With hindsight some professional intervention would have avoided a lot of pain, for not only myself but my family. Maybe I should have taken a break or been heavily advised to take one if I didn't seem willing.

Instead, and I've got no memory of it, but it was during this period that I started to act out. The combination of workload and awful mental health problems didn't make for a good combination. I'd slag off other bands and give the paps a hard time. On the surface I was a gobby "diva" (I hate that word), sounding off and getting herself in the papers. I would go out to work events, and binge drink and say silly things. Antidepressants and alcohol are a terrible mix. I thought if I looked like I was having fun, then maybe I was having fun.

The wheels were falling off a little.

And the tabloids gave as good as they got. I was probably a size 14 when they first called me Sumo Spice. Someone's throw-away joke, a silly pun, but again, it devastated me. I was called fat and "beefy", and the lesbian insinuations were rife. I'd been to Barbados with Ying to do a recce ahead of a family holiday later that year and it was all "close friends", who "shared a room". We didn't share a room, but the message was clear. I was a fat, ugly, boring, unpopular, single (yet also in a relationship with a woman) loser.

"If I don't wake up tomorrow, that's okay. Don't let me wake up tomorrow."

A size 14 is below the average weight of most British women. Many of us know how it feels when we put on weight; you feel self-conscious, you think people are talking about you, commenting on how you look. I had all that, but then I had the newspapers telling me, *Yes, you are fat, you need to lose weight. Call yourself Sporty Spice?*

I should have taken a few months off work and focused on my recovery, but instead, I went through it all in the public eye. I tried to continue to work at a ridiculous pace, not only promoting my debut solo record but recording and promoting the third Spice Girls album. I felt like I had to work. I had to carry on. I had to put myself back in the environment that had been the catalyst for my eating disorder, my anxiety, and my depression.

Geri was long gone, Victoria and Mel B were new mums... wouldn't it be better if we just called it a day?

The feeling of being in an environment that I didn't want to be in began to grow. We had started recording *Forever* as a group, all in studio sessions together, but the way the rest of the girls worked was very different to me. I liked to go in, get my work done, work hard and go home. That didn't align with the other three. We were at a point where everyone's lives had changed. Victoria and Mel B had babies. Geri had left. The hunger and the passion that had made us so successful in the first place wasn't there. The dynamic had shifted dramatically. We'd also never been in the studio without Geri before, so that made it a very different experience.

It got to the point that it gets to for many bands: we'd all arrive and depart in separate cars and very rarely bother with each other away from the working environment. We were past sharing dressing rooms. We'd grown up and grown apart. It's sad but inevitable too. You can only stand other people for so long when you're all under so much pressure. Going on a work trip is fun the first few times. But imagine if that work trip lasted for two years with the same five people. And you rarely saw your partner, your family, your friends. My whole life existed solely with the other four. The only times we weren't together was when we went to bed.

No matter how much you like or love someone, when you spend that much time together, you start to like each other less.

Having done *Northern Star*, I realised how much I enjoyed doing things my way. And that started to get me down because I couldn't just walk away. Or I didn't feel like I could walk away. I tried to record the album in a way that felt comfortable.

Nancy Phillips was our unofficial manager at that time. She had worked in the music industry for a long time, and we all liked how she was both straightforward but thoughtful too.

I confided in Nancy about how I was feeling, how I was struggling to work with the other three, that I didn't want to be in the studio at the same time as them. "I don't want to do that session. Can we say that I'm busy or can I be busy, and I'll fit it in? I don't mind if I don't have a writing credit for publishing, I'll just go in and do whatever vocals they need me to do." I did what I had to do. I went to sessions before the others so I could do my vocals at separate times.

I went to America to do some promo for my solo record, and while I was there, I did some vocals for *Forever*. Because of our past success, we were in with these huge American producers. The plan was this album would be less pop, more R&B, because artists like Destiny's Child, Whitney and Brandy were selling so many records then. Virgin were keen for us to repeat our success in the US.

I got to Miami to work with Rodney "Darkchild" Jerkins who made "Say My Name" for Destiny's Child, "If You Had My Love" for J.Lo and "It's Not Right but It's Okay" for Whitney.

He's one of the biggest producers in the world, and I did not want to be there. I just turned up and sang. Numb. I went to Jam and Lewis's studio in LA. These were the guys behind some of Janet Jackson's biggest hits, and they had been in The Time – the pop-funk group put together by Prince. I tried to record my vocals, but I barely had a voice.

I was an absolute mess.

It was too hard and too painful. I didn't have the strength to do it anymore.

There was another reason I didn't want to be around the girls. I didn't want to be called out or questioned by them, or to have to explain or defend myself or face the truth. That was my biggest fear. I didn't want to be in a room with them.

They knew me so well. There was an obvious physical change, but I was also so withdrawn. It terrified me to think of seeing them because I knew they'd want to know what the hell was going on.

I couldn't face that conversation. Not yet.

• • •

Towards the end of 2000, while promoting my solo album and *Forever*, I was booked to go on *The Frank Skinner Show*. Frank had been the person to present us with our first BRIT. He's a lovely bloke and I'd done his show before, so I felt quite at ease. Maybe too at ease. I was very candid in that interview. Watching it back all these years later, it's probably a good indication of where I was at, emotionally, at the time. I can almost hear myself calling for help. I was so focused on the tabloids. I took every opportunity to bring them up because it was during a time when they were being particularly brutal.

Frank asked me about my solo career, and I said the one positive thing about being solo was that there was a bit less tabloid attention. "I've been a bit luckier since I left… well, since I've been doing my own thing," I said, quickly correcting myself. Had I just accidentally said I'd left the Spice Girls?

I left the studios down on the South Bank in Waterloo and headed back home, my stomach in knots. I hadn't left the band; it was a genuine slip of the tongue but there was no way that the tabloids would let me get away with it.

Sure enough, when I left my flat the next day to go to the gym, there were film crews and paps outside the gates.

"Is it true you've left the Spice Girls, Melanie? Melanie!" "Have the Spice Girls broken up, Melanie?" "Melanie! Why have you left, Melanie?" And on it went.

I jumped in my car and sped off towards the gym. The faster I went, the faster they went.

I turned left onto the Finchley Road and – bang – I clipped another car. I pulled over and put my head on the steering wheel. By the time I looked up, the papps had scarpered. They had their shot. The people whose car I'd scraped were thankfully very sweet and understanding; we exchanged details and it was all fine. I was really shaken though. It was far from the chases that some celebrities must endure, but it was enough to give me a glimpse into how horrific accidents, thanks to the paps, can (and do) happen.

Of course, I got a phone call the next day. The tabloids had covered my interview and speculation was rife that I'd left, and the band was breaking up.

The girls were furious.

It happened to coincide with Emma releasing her solo record, so Nancy persuaded me to do some damage control. I called into

CD:UK where Emma was appearing and said that the rumours were false, we weren't splitting up.

But, between me and the girls, there needed to be a conversation. I couldn't avoid them anymore.

. . .

I went home to Widnes for a few days, where my bingeing escalated further. In the middle of my time there, the call came that I had been dreading. It was the girls. They wanted to talk to me.

I got up early the next day and drove down to the office.

The details of that conversation are so hazy. It was a difficult conversation. I was unhappy, and I wanted them to leave me be, but they were confused about what my problem was. Why had I said I'd left the band? What was I doing, trying to be a rock star?

We couldn't communicate with each other.

The one thing to come out of the conversation was that we saw the enormity of a story like that. We decided pretty much then and there that we didn't want to ever actually split up. Despite everything – Geri's departure, me refusing to do a reunion for a number of years, Victoria going her own way into fashion – the Spice Girls have never officially split up.

And we never will.

But relations were hostile, hitting a real low in November, which was back-to-back, non-stop promo. I had my solo show at Wembley Arena on 5th November, then *Forever* was released on 6th November and we had a launch party that night at Red Cube, in Central London.

We got ready at the Sanderson, a hotel in Fitzrovia. We were having a few cocktails and I obviously wasn't in a good state of mind. I didn't want to be there; I was very unhappy. I think Victoria and I might have had a fall-out, or a disagreement about something, I don't remember. We got to the party, and I drank more. At the time, there was a "rivalry" being built up between us and Westlife, who were releasing their second album the same week as *Forever*. I ended up talking to a bunch of journalists and apparently called Westlife a bunch of tossers, which I don't remember saying, but it blew up into a "thing". It was so out of character for super-careful me.

I would never normally drink to excess in a working environment, I'm ordinarily very conscious of that, especially after the BRITs in 1996. I mean, I was a bit mouthy at times, I could be opinionated about other bands, but it was out of character to be consciously hurtful to people. I hate hurting people's feelings – it kills me.

A week or so later we had the MTV Europe Music Awards in Stockholm, where I was up for Best Female, Best New Act, and Best Song, and where I performed "Holler" with the girls.

I looked terrible. I was so, so sad by that point. I just don't know how I did all this when I was in that much of a state. And, how people let me.

I was visibly unhappy and having a hard time. I didn't just have a few drinks; I'd drink until I blacked out because I didn't want to feel anything anymore. Alcohol on top of antidepressants, anxiety and depression are not a good mix.

The end of that year was dark and miserable, and I have very few recollections about it. But slowly, painfully slowly it felt at the time, the antidepressants started to work, the album came out, the workload tailed off, I started going to therapy, and I started eating better and exercising more.

Unfortunately, the worst days were played out in front of cameras, so it's there online to remind me forever.

But I don't look back on those times with shame or regret. I've spent long enough feeling embarrassed and ashamed of myself.

I look back on those times now and I think, *"Bloody hell, girl, you're a warrior."*

I was so strong; I was a warrior to get through all that.

. . .

As 2000 turned into 2001, things started to improve. I was eating healthily, getting out of the house for walks and I cut out the drinking. It would take time, but as 2001 went into 2002, life very slowly started to get better.

Despite my obvious improvement, I didn't really speak about my struggles with my family and friends until years and years later, even though I'd spoken about some of what I was going through in the press.

In the nineties and noughties, nobody talked about mental health. I was one of the first people, publicly, in the world of pop, to speak about what I was going through.

There were many reasons why I did speak about it, not just because I wanted to, but also because I thought I had to. I felt like public property, like I had an obligation to bear my soul because of all the personal information about me that was, somehow, finding its way into the tabloids.

I do regret talking about it so soon because I was still so vulnerable. There's an article in one of the Sunday tabloids where I was so open. I am too honest, sometimes.

For someone to comment on my weight gain, at that time, was the most mortifying thing to me. Why? Because it meant I was weak, that I wasn't the person that I'd presented myself as being. I'd succumbed to something. I had anorexia. I had binge-eating disorder. It felt embarrassing.

It's not embarrassing, I can't stress that enough, but I felt embarrassed of it, because we have been told that we should be ashamed about these issues. I've heard people say similar things, the shame that we attach to addiction and mental illness. As though it's our fault and that we should be ashamed of ourselves. I spoke to the press because I wanted to control the narrative. And I wanted to let them know what they'd done; you've been calling me fat, well, you know what, I've got an eating disorder. I am depressed.

We didn't have Twitter then and I think one of the benefits of social media is that you do have a voice, you can answer back, you can tell your side.

In retrospect, I wish I'd not spoken to the press, but spoken to my loved ones instead.

I think the people around you who love you, they just don't know what to do. Or they certainly didn't then. If we think back to Amy Winehouse, who was very clearly unwell, she was called a druggie, a drunk, crazy Amy. We all laughed at her "rock 'n' roll" antics, as she shuffled around Camden literally battered and bruised. That was in 2011. Even then we didn't have the language to say, "*This woman is ill, this woman is unwell, this woman needs help*". Kurt Cobain was perceived to be a "druggie" who went mad and killed himself. Kurt Cobain was an unwell young man who felt unable to cope with life. He needed help.

I don't think Mum, Dad, our Paul or my friends knew what to do. I'd be away for long periods of time and when I'd get back,

I didn't let them in. I didn't know how to. And they didn't know how to ask to be let in, either.

Even those who did try, Geri for instance, couldn't get through. I just wasn't ready to be confronted about what I was going through.

As a kid I thought that being famous was the coolest thing. People adored you, people wanted to talk to you, people saw you as a person of value, of talent, of substance, of interest. It wasn't until I experienced fame myself that I realised that those of us that seek attention, affirmation and applause are often the least equipped to deal with it. Many musicians, actors, artists, creatives, and so on tend to struggle with mental health problems that can include addiction, anxiety, depression and disordered eating. Our vulnerability is perhaps key to our ability to unlock creativity but it's also the part that can let us down when the going gets tough. Which, when you become "famous" it always does. Robbie Williams, Kurt Cobain, Amy Winehouse, Caroline Flack, Sinéad O'Connor, Jimi Hendrix, Janis Joplin, Karen Carpenter, Britney Spears… the list goes on.

I wish I'd had some understanding of the realities of fame before I set off down that path. Would I still have made the choice to become a pop star? I'm certain that I would have, but I might have been a little better equipped to deal with it.

Does anyone survive fame unscathed? Does aspiring to be famous make you the least equipped person to deal with it? Those of us that follow that path are seeking the warmth of that spotlight, the adoration we get from the applause. When you come off stage and the room goes quiet, what do you do then to fill the hole? For some people it's alcohol, for others it's drugs. For me, it was about controlling how I looked, what I ate, how I felt. I disconnected from myself in order to survive.

Success was wonderful but there was so much around it that made me unhappy at a time when I should have been on top of the world. I imagine it's the same for anyone in a bad situation at work or at home. You get that promotion, but with it, there are bigger expectations. Someone gets promoted over you, and you're filled with a sense of inadequacy. A relationship ending, a death, difficulties in getting a job, anxiety of exams can trigger something you weren't prepared for. Or sometimes, you're just walking down the road, living your life, and it gets you. Whoever you are, and whatever you do, depression, illness and addiction can come for you, and it will take no prisoners.

As we've seen, the implications of lockdown have had a serious impact on our mental wellness. A 2020 study by Mind revealed that more than half (60%) of adults and over *two-thirds* of young people (68%) say their mental health declined during lockdown. A report by Roehampton University, early on during COVID, revealed a "staggering" rise in mental health issues among NHS staff. A 2021 study by the brilliant charity Help Musicians revealed that 87% of artists said their mental health had deteriorated during lockdown.

Whoever you are, whatever you do, we are all impacted.

Things have changed a little in the British music industry. Universal Music has implemented a mental health programme with a BAPC-registered counsellor, which they fund. Warner Music has also launched a similar mental health and wellbeing support programme. I think that's fantastic, but I'd like to see things progress further. Why not help manage people's finances so that therapy is available if they may need it? Why not stop creating schedules that are almost physically impossible to achieve? Explain to new artists what they might have to deal with and arm them with the appropriate tools to deal with what's coming their way. Don't pressure or persuade artists to do/say/perform/promote things that they are uncomfortable with.

Once I experienced fame and realised the downside of it, it became a negative side effect of being successful in the career that I love. People now aspire to having just that one part of it – the fame – which to me is the worst bit.

What puzzles me now is that fame, since the Spice Girls and maybe in part *due* to the Spice Girls, has changed in a way that many people we consider celebrities are simply famous for being famous. It's their *lives*, or rather, their *phones* that make them famous. They're famous for sex tapes; for their ability to use Instagram filters; for their plastic surgery or for appearing on a reality show. There's nothing wrong with that, but we're no longer celebrating people's talent, just their existence. There's no sense of scale with fame. Anyone can become famous. And we've seen how quickly those same people come crashing down. Reality TV stars seem to have suffered terribly. They go from unknown to super-famous and wealthy, to suddenly hated, forgotten and broke within a space of months. It's understandably all too much.

Watching *The World's A Little Blurry*, the Billie Eilish Apple TV+ documentary in lockdown broke my heart. You see how exhausted and worn out she is and how life becomes about survival and getting through another day. Yet you're doing the most amazing things, you're living out your wildest dreams, so you can't bitch and moan about it because that's what you wanted and you're lucky to be doing it. That creates conflict there too.

I say all this fully aware of how hugely lucky I am. I'm incredibly grateful for all that I have but I think it's important, a responsibility almost, to explain to people the realities of this "dream" that so many of us chase.

Also, people have so much more access to you now. The press was brutal to us, but at least we knew who our enemies were. Now, all of us – famous or not – can get trolled, cancelled, or doxxed within an instant. When we're not glued to our phones, we're scared of them – scared of the bullying, teasing or trolling. Scared that other people's Instagram lives are so much happier and "better" than our own.

I can't imagine being in the Spice Girls in the age of social media. I really don't know if I, if any of us, would have survived that, at the age we were and with the level of scrutiny we were already under.

Fame was just one aspect of my struggle. The pressure of the band and the press was one thing, but my struggles began from my foundations. It was a series of events, large and small, that set me on my own path to an eating disorder and depression.

The reason I decided to write this book was because I hoped that hearing my story might help someone, whether that's someone going through something like this, or someone who's worried about a friend, a family member, or a partner.

I hope hearing what I've been through might make someone feel less lonely. Because it's such a lonely place to be, when you're depressed, and you're ill.

I know it's hard to know what to do when someone you love is clearly unwell. You don't know how to help. It's so hard.

Distraction is helpful. Ask your friend if they want to go to the cinema or to an exhibition. Invite yourself over to watch a movie on the couch. Send them funny memes or voice notes to check in rather than, "Are you okay? How are you feeling?" because sometimes those questions are just too big, too hard to answer. Some of my most difficult times have been at a time when I've been very lonely. I was single, I was rarely in London, so I didn't have a social outlet. My family were all up North. I was isolated, emotionally and physically. Not having a partner, just even human touch, leaves such a huge gap. Give someone a hug, hold their hand, treat them to a massage if you can afford it. Human touch is so healing.

Mates are great. A cup of tea with someone who's going to be a twat and make you laugh can really help. People often worry, I just don't know what to say, what if I say the wrong thing? It's fine to say things like "It will pass" because it will, I am still here. But it's also so helpful to hear someone say, "I know, it's fucking shit isn't it, it's not fair." To let you wallow as well for a little bit. All these things are important.

Each person's different but finding out what works for you is vital. I have something that I call my toolkit, and maybe some, or even all of it, would be useful to you:

- **Sleep.** This is number one and I know it's the hardest to achieve because people with depression often have insomnia, it can be one of the symptoms of depression. But you have to try and rest, get your eight hours if you can, be kind to yourself. I've stopped drinking caffeine after 2 pm. A warm bath in the evening with Epsom salts is good, pop some lavender essential oil in too. Try not to eat or drink too close to bedtime.
- **Eat well.** By which I mean put good stuff into your body. It's fine to have snacks (I love crisps as much as anyone else, maybe even more) but make sure you're giving yourself the proper balance of protein, fats, fibre

and carbohydrates too. Get those leafy greens in you, a handful of nuts and seeds, some good oily fish if you're not vegan or vegetarian. I know juices are ridiculously expensive now, but crush up some ginger in a garlic press, squeeze it through a clean cloth and get that anti-inflammatory down you. You can chop it up and steep it in hot water, add honey and it makes a lovely warming tea that's great for digestion.

- **Light exercise.** For me, working out is important, those endorphins help. If you don't feel like it, go for a walk, just for 20 minutes. Do a short, free online yoga class. Don't give yourself too much of a task; small is still something. Put on your favourite tunes and have a good dance.
- **Get outside.** Get out into nature, if you can, even if that's just the local park – go and see some green, look at the sky. All the things we've learnt through the pandemic.
- **Abstain.** I'm not a big drinker these days, but if those low feelings are coming then it's no booze for me for a while.

It's my toolkit that I reach into to try and combat my feelings of depression getting any bigger than they need to.

I'd love to end this chapter by saying, look at me, I'm cured. That's not the case. I still have hard times, I still struggle. But things are infinitely, almost unrecognisably better now. Because I got help. Because I learned how to talk about what I was going through. Because I know now how to take care of myself, how to talk to myself and how to help myself.

And that's by reaching out to people and accepting their love and care.

You can't do it on your own.

I've said this before, but I wrote this book because I want people to understand that anyone, at any time, can go through similar struggles. I "had it all" but it didn't make me invincible.

There's a multitude of reasons that I ended up in such a low place around 1999, 2000 and why I've occasionally come close to the edge of those feelings again since.

It's never a straight arrow, the road from an eating disorder and depression to recovery, as I was to find out over the next few years. My journey to good, positive mental wellness wasn't quite over yet. Maybe it never will be. As a human being, I am a work-in-progress just like everyone else.

I'm not infallible. We're all of us only human.

CHAPTER FIFTEEN

Say You'll Be There

So, to the noughties.

The Millennium Dome (RIP). Britney and Justin. Brad and Jen. Paris and Nicole. Eminem and Marshall Mathers. Beyoncé, Kelly, LaTavia and LeToya. Beyoncé, Kelly, Farrah, and Michelle. Beyoncé, Kelly and Michelle. Beyoncé. Carrie, Charlotte, Miranda and Samantha. Samantha Mumba. *Pure Shores* and *Parachutes*. iPod, *Pop Idol,* and *American Idol.* Simon Cowell. Nasty Nick and *Big Brother.* Motorola Razr, Nokia 3310, Snake and The Sims. PlayStation 2 vs Xbox. Super Mario, MSN Messenger, and Top Eight on Myspace. YouTube and Broadband. Craig David taking girls out for a drink on Monday and chilling on Sundays. Adele, Amy, Duffy and Joss Stone. Heelys and Juicy Couture. "Chillax", "Fo shizzle", "That's hot", "Talk to the hand", "Crunk". Mad cow disease. 9/11 and 07/07. The Y2K bug. A man named Tom…

Napster.

My second album felt doomed from the start, not least thanks to the arrival of the peer-to-peer file sharing software that threatened to decimate the music industry: namely, Napster. The music business was seriously unprepared for the tech revolution and nearly, very nearly, went under.

The dawn of the digital age was exciting and terrifying in equal measure. On one hand, the world was being opened to infinite possibilities. On the other, the Internet seemed intent on destroying copyright, and along with that, creativity as we knew it.

Music was getting ripped and shared via platforms like Napster, MP3.com and, later, LimeWire and Pirate Bay, devastating the income of many performers, writers and musicians. The same thing was happening in the film industry. Why pay for entertainment, art or creativity when you can get it for free?

I arrived at this moment, slowly recovering from those dark years. I was a successful solo artist readying her next release. *Northern Star* had done really well, selling over two and a half million copies worldwide.

I'd managed to finally have some time out. It had been three years since I released my debut, and it was time for a new record.

I was certainly better than I had been, mentally and physically, but I was still early in the journey to recovery. There were issues that I needed to deal with, but it had been so long since my last release. I couldn't wait any longer.

I eased back into it, although my confidence was depleted. Music had always been the thing I went to, the thing I busied myself with. And, slowly, I found healing through those sessions. Being able to write and perform songs that dealt with some painful things enabled me to start to put them to bed. While I was apprehensive about the pressure on the record being commercially successful, I began to relish getting into the studio.

Working on *Reason* was the first time I met Peter Vettese, who is someone I've gone on to work with closely over the years. He was based in Battersea, at a studio called Sphere. I was back at the Strongroom with the producer and composer Marius De Vries, where I'd written "Wannabe", "2 Become 1" and "Mama" etc. with Matt, Biff and the girls. Marius played me a track he'd been working on with Dr. Robert from The Blow Monkeys. "Here It Comes Again" was the first song we wrote for *Reason*. I worked with David Arnold for the first time at the beautiful AIR Studios in Hampstead, North London. I love David, he's an extraordinary talent and so fun to be around. He's a prolific composer of television and film scores including five *Bond* movies, as well as *Independence Day*, *Sherlock*, *Good Omens*... the list goes on. He'd also worked with Björk and Massive Attack so I felt very lucky to work with him.

AIR Studios was a great place to be at that time. You'd often see the Coldplay boys milling about as they were working on *A Rush of Blood to The Head*.

David was also the Musical Director of the London Olympics in 2012 and it was good to have an old pal overseeing the music side of the Spice Girls performance all those years later. We couldn't have been in better hands.

I needed to scratch my LA itch, so I spent another three months there back in with Rick Nowels, Rhett Lawrence, Pat McCarthy, and Damien LeGassick.

It was all very good, very positive vibes. For the songs I worked on with Pat, he got the most incredible band together for me, including my old mucker, the one and only Steve Jones from the Sex Pistols as well as Abe Laboriel Jr. on drums and Rusty Egan on guitar, both of whom have toured with Paul McCartney for years. It was a really fun process because we'd rehearse as a band, so the song would evolve before we came to record it. It's a very satisfying way to make a record – the old-fashioned way!

I couldn't help but let the pressure get to me, though. How was I going to match up to my debut? I was singing my heart out, but was this music that people wanted to listen to? Would it sell?

Thanks to the success of the Spice Girls, many of the brilliant people we'd worked with at Virgin had been poached to work in America. The team I knew from Virgin were no more. I lost a level of support and understanding that I'd had with Ashley, his assistant Jane Ventom, and Ray Cooper, who died in 2018 from a rare neurological condition. Ray was such a big part of the Spice Girls' success, and I'm forever grateful to him for that. He was a warm, funny, lovely person. I remember lots of Spice shenanigans with Ray in those early days!

Except for one or two people, it was a totally new team over at Virgin. They were very excited and positive, but their expectations were high. Because *Northern Star* had sold over two million copies, they expected *Reason* to do four million.

Napster, among other things, had other ideas. By the time I was getting ready to release *Reason* in 2003, it was disrupting the whole industry. As history has shown us, clever people eventually came up with a solution to piracy via legal subscription streaming platforms and performers, writers and musicians are now better protected from their music and intellectual copyright being stolen. Which isn't to say we don't face other issues, but that's another story for another day...!

We've managed to survive thus far and at times by the skin of our teeth, but at that moment we were in the eye of the storm, it was a very real issue. It was uncertain if there would be a music industry left by the time Napster was done with it.

I can't blame *Reason*'s lack of success entirely on people downloading music for free. There are some beautiful songs on there, but it isn't a strong album. It lacked clarity and the ear of an A&R like Ashley. It was also the "difficult" second record. Many artists have fallen on that sword, and I was one of them. There had also been a three-year delay between the two records. Because *Northern Star* had done so well and for so long, I was touring and promoting that record well into 2001. Because *Northern Star* had made so much money, Virgin allowed me to spend a ton of cash on the follow-up and they wanted that money back.

With various factors working against me, I think we "only" sold around half a million copies (most artists, including me, would give their eye teeth for that today!).

At this point, I turned to my friend Ashley Forbes, who was head of A&R admin, nervous about what was going on.

Ashley, who we also very sadly lost in 2021, was described by David Joseph (the Chairman and CEO of Universal Music UK, the parent company of Virgin) as the heart of the label – and that she was. Ashley was amazing, one of those people everybody loved, and she really cared. Ashley worked at Virgin/EMI for 32 years; she quite literally kept the place going and helped me out throughout my career, long after my relationship with Virgin had ended. It's hard to think she's not at the back of my gigs looking on proudly, ready to greet me with, "Well, that went rather well there, Flossie," (which for some reason was what Ashley called me). Maybe she is. I like to think so.

Ashley reassured me that there was too much history for Virgin to drop me over one underperforming album. I had a team that cared about me, they were invested. But other people at the label had different ideas.

The tabloids, as you can imagine, were predictably supportive. There are these stairs in Santa Monica that people run up and down. It's a "thing". I got photographed there doing a stretch and the headline the next day was, "Mel C praying for another hit". They also happily pointed out that my weight was still fluctuating, which it was at this point. I was out cycling one day, again in Santa Monica, and some paparazzi "happened" to find us. I was wearing padded shorts, as you do for cycling, and there was a comment about my shorts being too small because the fabric was stretched. Basically, I've got a fat arse. This was around 2002, so, yes, the climate in the papers hadn't changed at all by that point.

There was one more thing that conspired to get in the way of that record's success and it was called *The Games*, a new reality sports game show on Channel 4. It featured 10 celebrities competing in various Olympic sports. Virgin had received an offer for me to do it and they were keen for me to take part because they thought it could help with album sales.

I'm not a reality TV show person, it doesn't suit me, I'm not comfortable with it in any way. "No, I don't want to do this," I told them, very emphatically.

Yet, they persisted, and I started to crumble. The sports aspect appealed to me; we were to train with ex-athletes and Olympians. But there was a reality angle; and people like me, James Hewitt, Gail Porter, Harvey from So Solid Crew, comedian Bobby Davro and Terri Dwyer from *Hollyoaks* would be in a dormitory where we would be filmed all the time, and so on. I had it written into my contract that I wasn't sleeping in a dorm; I wasn't having a camera in my bedroom.

Despite the stipulations, my instinct was that I shouldn't do it. But with the pressure on me, I agreed to join the show.

In fact, I really enjoyed a lot of it; I loved the training, I met some great people and was really into the challenges of learning new skills like speed skating, judo, sprinting out of the blocks, and so on. But then the competition began, at Sheffield's Don Valley Stadium. I turned up the first day and we were mic'ed up the whole time, even in the toilet. I hated it. I was so uncomfortable; I was so unhappy. It was only a week, but it felt like an eternity to be mic'ed and filmed for the whole time.

The first event we did was swimming, and the second night was 100-metre hurdles. When we were training for the hurdles, I noticed my right knee, my trail leg, was becoming increasingly painful. But we did the hurdles, and all was well. The third event was judo, for which we had to do heats and then the finals. The first heat wasn't live, but it was being filmed. I was competing against Azra Akin, who was Miss World at the time.

She threw me. I fell awkwardly and…

…there was a massive crack, crack, *crack*. I can still hear it now.

I had ruptured my cruciate ligament and damaged three others in my right knee.

I'd never had a serious injury or accident. I was lying on the mat, completely dazed. There was excruciating pain for seconds and then nothing. The whole medical team rushed to me. I was woozy. I ended up in the back of an ambulance with a doctor who I'm sure was called Doctor England, a fabulous name. I asked, "Is it bad?" "Yes," he said softly.

It was so weird because I was petrified at what the long-term impact of the injury might be, but I was also so relieved to be out of the show. They took me to what I like to call "a hotel" but was actually a private hospital, and I was given an MRI. I remember lying there with all that noise of the MRI around me, still in shock. I kept replaying what had happened, hearing this really loud cracking noise reverberating around my head.

I was taken to my hotel room (hospital suite). A nurse sat down with me and told me I was very lucky because "Mr Bickerstaff is here, he's one of the best knee surgeons in the country and you're going to go into knee surgery tomorrow." My phone went and it was Jamie Redknapp; someone had told him about my accident. "I've been operated on by Mr Bickerstaff, so I want you to know you're in really good hands," he told me. That was sweet of him, such a lovely thing to do. I went in, had the surgery, and then went to my mum's because I couldn't look after myself. I was in a cricket-pad splint for two weeks; I couldn't put any weight on it, and I basically had to learn how to walk again.

When they took off the splint a fortnight later, the muscle wastage meant the leg was really withered. I was shocked, it was half the size of my left leg. I had physio for six days a week, beginning with tiny movements. I've still got the scars. My poor right knee. I was at Mum's for a couple of months in the end, until I could bathe myself, and then I came back home to London.

It took two years for me to fully recover and after all that, it didn't help sell any more albums.

What happened next was that I was "released" from my contract. Which means that I was dropped. That's the cold, hard truth. On 1st January 2004, when I was on my arse – literally on my arse, I couldn't walk – Virgin dropped me. Three months after busting my knee, two weeks before my thirtieth birthday, on the first day of a new year. Happy New Year! Happy birthday!

A few years before, something like that could have set me back. Thankfully, I was in a far more emotionally stable place at that moment. I wanted to keep making music and I decided not to dwell on it too much. Nancy, who was now officially my manager, told me that we had options: "We can try and sign with another major but that could be tricky. We could look at an independent, which is an option. Or you could start your own label, which you have the finances to do. You self-finance and you have complete freedom, and you make the album you want to make."

Because it was so different to what I'd done before, having my own label felt the most appealing to me. I felt so betrayed by Virgin Records after all the money I'd help make for them, with the Spice Girls and my first album, to be dropped at the first hurdle. I didn't want to be in that position again, so I set up my own label to ensure I wouldn't be.

I wanted to do things very differently and I decided to do it the old-fashioned way.

Four months after being dropped from Virgin, I set up Red Girl Records (inspired, of course, by the colours of Liverpool Football Club).

Having my own label gave me the opportunity to rethink everything.

When I began thinking about my third album, *Beautiful Intentions*, I decided to tear up the rulebook. We enlisted independent A&R Morgan Nelson and for the first time I worked with just one producer across the record. I had a lot of anger to express on this album, which inspired me to go into more of a rock direction. I had loved routining (rehearsing the song you'd written with a live band, tweaking and changing things before you record them) with Pat McCarthy in LA on the *Reason* sessions, so why not do a whole album like that? I worked with the wonderful Greg Haver, good Welsh stock, who'd previously worked with The Manic Street Preachers and Super Furry Animals. It felt exciting.

Being a live performer, you realise how songs can change and grow once you get them in front of an audience, so we took the brave decision to tour the record before recording it. It was really fun; we did a run of smaller venues, mostly pubs. Glamorous it was not! But it did the job.

Greg came to my show at The Fleece in Bristol, sweat dripping off the low ceilings. The crowd went off and he was in, he was sold.

I've always felt a little bit apologetic about my solo career because when you've had a career like the Spice Girls, nothing else quite measures up. We were so fortunate with the Spice Girls. We did work hard, but we were so successful so quickly and I'm the kind of person who likes to earn my stripes. This was an opportunity for me to start again. I got out and gigged at dirty little pubs, I was driven around in a little Toyota Previa, I got changed in the loo, it was the same experience that Mum always talked about. I'd started out doing live TV and performing at the BRITs. With the Spice Girls, I'd skipped the musician's rite of passage, the place where you cut your teeth and find out what you're made of. Gigging. After playing the album to a small audience, I went back to the studio with the band to record the album. I felt like I was making music the "proper" way, like bands like The Beatles used to do.

Talking of whom, Paul McCartney's daughter, Mary, shot the cover of *Beautiful Intentions*, and she directed the video for "Better Alone" too. By this point, I'd met her dad. Imagine what it's like when a Scouser meets a Beatle, and that was basically me. I couldn't wait to tell Mum, Den and my dad. The first time I met

Paul was at Radio 1. After being shell-shocked for a few moments, I managed to make conversation. We were chatting away, and someone came and grabbed me, so I had to say, "Sorry, Paul, I've got to go!", which I loved, because who doesn't want to be too busy for a Beatle?!

The second time was June 2016, when we both played at an event called *Dine and Disco* that Chris Evans does every year for charity, which he used to hold in a marquee in a beer pub garden. I popped into Macca's dressing room after my set. "Alright, girl, how's it going?" he greeted me. When you meet another Scouser, even though neither of you have lived there since your teens, there's an immediate connection and a shorthand too. And as a Scouser, once you've met a Beatle, your job in this world is basically done.

Beautiful Intentions did okay here but it went on to do well in Europe. I had a deal with Warner Music in Germany, who were distributing my music over there. They had an idea for me to record a song written by Guy Chambers and Enrique Iglesias called "First Day of My Life". They wanted to use it as a theme tune for a telenovela called *Julia – Wege zum Glück* and that ended up being my first German number one, in October 2005. "I Turn to You" only ever got to number two in Germany so to have a number one there was great. It was also used on a telenovela in Portugal, which gave the album success in two territories. It helped to keep me very busy.

We had a fun year in Germany and Portugal doing TVs and touring.

I need to own my wins so much more, as we all do. My albums might not have always been huge in the UK, but in their own way, they've bought me success on so many levels. I'm proud of that.

• • •

During all this, it seemed like I was finally ready to see some success in my romantic life.

As part of my recovery, I decided to spend a couple of Christmases outside of the UK. In 2001 and 2002 a load of us went to Barbados, including my oldest, closest mates Ali, Steph, Si and Rach, Ali's mum and dad, Hazel and Dave, and my mum, Den and our Paul. I rented a big house in Saint Peter, on Mullins Bay. It was bliss, lots of laughing, playing games and lounging by the pool.

The first year we went, I bumped into Simon Moran in the Virgin Lounge at Heathrow. Simon runs SJM Concerts and has been my concert promoter for most of my career. I was with a load of mates and family and he was with a load of guys, and we all ended up hanging out on that holiday. He's a Warrington lad, so although he's one of the most powerful people in the music industry, he's a local boy to me. We became a bit of a holiday posse, and there were a few dinners and nights out. I've got so many special memories of that beautiful island.

The second year they were in Barbados again, and so we arranged to meet up on New Year's Eve, in an outdoor bar. It was lovely, drinks, outside, beautiful Barbados, etc., but then an older guy started bothering me. I was uncomfortable, and Simon's friend Tom was just... there. I thought, *"He's quite cute."* He came to my rescue when I needed it, and it grew from there. We started chatting and seeing each other a little bit on that holiday. I came home and he went off to Mexico for a bit. Tom was a quantity surveyor by trade and is now a partner at a construction firm, but he had connections to the music industry and sort of understood my job and that I didn't work nine to five or have a set schedule. My life was unpredictable at times, and he was okay with that. He got it.

It was a bit of a holiday romance at first. I didn't know if it would continue when we got home. I returned to London first and then when he came back, he called me. We started spending some time together and things blossomed. I almost couldn't believe that I'd met someone, and he was sticking around. I'd had so many doomed relationships that never got off the ground. But for some reason, this guy didn't seem to be going anywhere. It made me feel more secure.

While most of the time we did very normal things – cooking, cinema, bike rides – Tom very quickly found himself in the deep end. Two months after we met, I took him to New York to the wedding of David Gest and Liza Minnelli. As you do.

Before Barbados that Christmas, I'd done a charity event at New York's Madison Square Garden. David Gest was the producer of the show. Performers at the event included Whitney Houston and 98 Degrees, and Michael Jackson was there – there was a big orchestra, and I performed "I Turn to You". It was all very grand.

Being a kid of the eighties, I was of course a huge Michael Jackson fan back then. He was supposed to be performing but he was ill. However, he apparently still wanted to attend the show, so they set up a tent for him in the wings. I'll never forget performing "I Turn to You", sneaking looks to the side of the stage where Michael Jackson was crouched in his tent!

The finale was supposed to be all of us singing "Shake Your Body (Down to The Ground)" by the Jackson 5, accompanied by a full band. I remember Whitney pushing past me to the stage as the band started up. "Stop, stop, stop," she said, and asked them to change the key, right in front of a live audience.

There's Whitney barging about and Michael stuck in a tent. It was all very strange. Those were the sort of moments when I wished the other girls were there. See what I mean? My life? Far from normal.

At the end Michael did a line-up, where we all got to shake his hand. It got to my turn, and I stepped up to him, looking him in the eyes, determined to make the most of this quick meeting. He took my hand and he looked just so frail. He was really pale and with the amount plastic surgery he'd had, he didn't really look human. It was so sad, really. It was quite a shock.

Fast forward a few months, not long after Tom and I had met, and I saw that David Gest and Liza Minnelli had gotten engaged. I was out in a West End club, either Sugar Reef or Chinawhite. I'd been out for dinner before and was a bit tipsy. We looked for a seat and I spotted a table. "Sorry," said the waiter, "but we've got David Gest and Liza Minnelli coming in later, this table is for them." Being pissed, I didn't let that stand in my way. "Oh, David Gest, I know him, I'll just sit here and wait until he gets here." David and Liza arrived and seemed perfectly fine that I'd stolen their table.

Liza looked amazing, like true Hollywood royalty. I congratulated them both on their impending nuptials. "Thank you so much, you must come to the wedding," said David, and I said, "Yeah, I'd love to," as you do. I wrote my address down on a scabby old receipt (this was before smartphones) and headed off home. I woke up the next morning, very hungover, and remembered what had happened. *I'll never hear anything,* I thought.

Lo and behold, a couple of days later a very heavy envelope lands on the floor and it's an invitation to David and Liza's wedding in New York on 16th March 2002.

It was the first trip Tom and I did together and he must have thought, "What on earth is going on?" We got to New York the day before the nuptials and stayed in the Four Seasons in Manhattan. The ceremony was held at the Marble Collegiate Church, which is this very austere Protestant church in midtown Manhattan. The bridal party featured 36 people, including Michael Jackson as best man and Elizabeth Taylor as the maid of honour. And, bizarrely, Martine McCutcheon was one of the bridesmaids.

We went in just behind Mickey Rooney and sat near Lauren Bacall. Nat King Cole's daughter, Natalie Cole, sang "Unforgettable" as Liza walked down the aisle. It was just all on another level.

The reception afterwards was held at the Wall Street Regent Hotel, in downtown Manhattan, where a few months before, terrorists had brought down the Twin Towers.

There were over 800 guests, which included everyone from Lionel Richie and Donald Trump to Diana Ross and Mia Farrow. Performers included Stevie Wonder, Tony Bennett and Donny Osmond, who sang some of their biggest hits in front of a 60-piece orchestra.

It was this lavish affair and one of the weirdest things I remember, among all this, was watching Michael Jackson just pop to the loo. I suppose even the King of Pop has to pee, doesn't he?

It was totally and fantastically flamboyant. Even now, that wedding is compared to the Oscars, it was so star-studded and over-the-top. It cost something like $4 million.

We sat on the "European" table with Helena Christensen and her then-partner Norman Reedus, Graham Norton, Carrie Fisher and Martine McCutcheon. It was really fun; Carrie Fisher was so funny and she and Graham had us laughing all night. We then ended up going to a club, where we were invited to a private room with Michael Stipe. What a night!

Tom tended to take everything in his stride. His way of dealing with it was just to not be overly impressed by it, which is probably the best way to be because people are just people at the end of the day. Even *those* people!

Sadly, we didn't get our Hollywood ending – David and Liza divorced a couple of years later and then David died a few years after that in London, at The Dorchester hotel.

. . .

Not long after the wedding, I went to LA to finish *Reason*, leaving Tom in London. It was still quite early in our relationship, but we spoke every day and it was clear this was a thing. I got home and Tom quickly moved in. I was in my first serious relationship.

We managed to avoid the press, mostly. We got photographed occasionally but we never courted the attention. It got to the point where they lost interest in me, whether that was because they thought I wasn't interesting or because I wasn't playing the game, I'm not sure, but either way it suited me fine.

2002, 2003 and 2004 weren't my most successful years commercially, but I was emotionally in such a better place. I might not have had a hit album, but I felt creatively satisfied. I was getting to tour, play my music and write new songs with producers I loved and admired.

Over the next few years, my relationship with Tom settled in. My mental health was slowly improving. I wasn't "cured" by any stretch, but I was trying hard to keep on top of things, by going to therapy, taking my medication, and upholding a healthier attitude to eating and exercise.

Before long, maybe, just maybe, I'd be able to entertain a conversation about a Spice Girls reunion.

. . .

There were two things that helped me become healthier and think about my body in a much more positive way. The first was after my knee injury. I stopped beating myself up because I realised my body was incredible and I put it through so much that I wanted to start taking better care of it. The second was when I was making a human being inside of me. I realised that I *am* amazing, despite what I sometimes told myself. It began a period of being so much kinder to myself, in every way.

I've skipped ahead a bit here, haven't I? Let me back up a bit.

It was 2007 and I was still with Warner Music Germany. They were keen to get another record out quickly on the back of the success of *Beautiful Intentions*. This would be the first album where lots of the songs were written or co-written by a good friend of mine, a great songwriter called Adam Argyle. We first worked together on "Next Best Superstar" on *Beautiful Intentions*.

Where *Beautiful Intentions* had been quite rocky, "First Day of My Life" was a big old traditional ballad with strings. Warner were quite keen to go with a ballad-driven album for the German market, and they wanted to do it quickly. This suited me at the time, because I realised I really wanted to have a baby, so my mind was elsewhere. But there was no heart and soul in the album, which is called *This Time* – I found some great songs and put them together but it wasn't a record I devoted my heart and soul to.

And so, of course, the album fell on its arse, although "First Day of My Life" was a big hit in Europe.

I also knew there was a Spice Girls reunion on the cards. I saw that as a great platform to push my solo record, but Warner were annoyed about me going off to do the reunion, so they pulled the marketing budget. They felt if I was doing Spice Girls, I wouldn't have time to promote the record. They saw it as a clash rather than a great opportunity for the two projects to feed each other.

So, what did it take for us girls to get back together in 2008?

When reports of my illness emerged in 2000, conversations were had, apologies exchanged, tissues offered. But I think the girls still didn't quite understand, at that time, how sick I was. Once *Forever* was done, I had to step away from the Spice Girls for a good, long time, both literally and emotionally. It took time for what I'd been through to sink in for them. Over the years, I've had separate conversations with Mel B, Geri, Emma and Victoria about my illness, my eating disorder and the depression and anxiety that ultimately led to a breakdown at the end of '99.

I wasn't the only one who had gone through a lot, and while their stories are their own to tell, we all needed time apart from each other.

By the time the idea of a possible reunion had been put forward, by Simon Fuller (yes, he was back), we weren't best friends, but we were getting on. We'd reached an age where we were much more respectful of each other and of each other's space. All the other girls were mums, and having children completely changed their priorities. I think that was part of our problem in the nineties, the sheer intensity of us, as five women, and nobody could infiltrate that. Not even a relationship. But having children changes things, and while your career is always important, nothing comes above the kids.

Through having that space and time, our relationships began to repair. I would see Emma quite often, we'd rekindled a friendship, and I'd meet Victoria and Geri occasionally. I saw less of Mel B because she was living in LA, and I'd not had many opportunities to get out there. Of course, our parents all stayed in close contact, so the connection was always there. They all formed relationships independently of us, and although each parent will always have their own kid's back, they have helped smooth things out, here and there.

We all had our different reasons for wanting to do the reunion; for some it may have been money, for others it was to repair old wounds and put the past to bed, to rewrite a new ending for the Spice Girls.

And me, why did I do it? Having been so unhappy for so long, why did I agree to return to a place that I knew could be really triggering for me, especially when my mental health was so vastly improved?

In 2007, I was in a pretty good place. I'd had some success with my album *Beautiful Intentions*, and things were good with Tom, I felt healthier and stronger in myself. I was also considering my solo career. Doing something with the girls would give my solo career traction in the UK, the US and other territories.

I'm always striving for the next hit and trying to find that moment to take it to the next place, but in the period leading up to 2007, creatively at least, it was one kick in the teeth after the other. *Beautiful Intentions* did okay, but then *This Time* (released in March 2007) didn't do so well. But I realised that if the Spice Girls stuff was bubbling, it could be a good opportunity to springboard my own solo stuff.

Plus, the show was pretty much done, it had been put together by Creative Director Jamie King. We simply had to turn up and perform. We learnt our part and that was sort of it.

When you're doing something Spice Girls, it's so big that people care. It's unhealthy but it's really good for your ego – it makes you feel important again; it makes you feel worthy again about your little place on the planet. It's about a bit of recognition. Sometimes I think I work so hard as a solo artist; I give some damn good performances and… not so many people care.

I've completely made peace with it, though, because it is what it is.

With the Spice Girls, it's exciting and being in each other's company is exciting. People are excited to be around us – there's something very intoxicating about it.

Sod it, I'm back in. Let's do it.

. . .

We did the launch for *The Return of the Spice Girls* at the Royal Observatory in Greenwich in June 2007, and I think we were all feeling anxious, certainly Emma, Victoria and me. It all settled in quite quickly – we found our old roles but in a way that we were comfortable with. There was no vying for position, no one wanted to be boss. We were there for our own reasons, but with age and experience, without a lot of the old baggage.

"Imagine you got divorced, and you got back together with your old husband," said Geri at the press conference, before Victoria landed with a "She just appreciates we've let her back in!" That magic had returned, albeit a bit more mature, maybe a bit beaten down, not quite so sparkly, naïve, and wide-eyed, but it was still there. In an interesting coincidence, our reunion timed with Tony Blair's departure from Downing Street. Naturally, the press were interested in our opinions on his replacement. "Who's Gordon Brown?" said Mel B.

It was around this time that we all met Mel B's new partner. She had been living in LA for a number of years at this point, and so this was the first time that we were introduced to Stephen Belafonte. As Mel B wrote in her 2018 book, *Brutally Honest*, we were all immediately a little bit uncomfortable around him. He was quite an overbearing character, and he made us all feel… unsettled.

It turned out that she had secretly gotten married not long after the press conference. She came into a meeting and "happily" announced he was her husband. We were all upset about that. We had our concerns, which we discussed with each other, but she seemed to be happy. It wasn't until a lot later that we became really worried about her, and for good reason.

It was all great and fine at the beginning, we were giving each other space, enjoying each other's company, enjoying the shows, and touring. Stephen was there quite a lot but by the end, something was going on with her and she became very difficult. She went into her shell and became spikey, and it was hard for us to reach her at that point.

The last show was in Toronto, Canada, and we arranged a party to celebrate. Mel B was adamant that she didn't want to go. We tried to persuade her, but she was insistent. I didn't stay at the party that long myself, and I went back to her hotel room to say goodbye because we were all flying off the next morning. She wasn't happy, I could see that a mile off.

We fell out about it all in 2014, just after she missed the *X Factor* show, after being hospitalised. It was another time we had gotten together to talk about stuff, to go over whatever opportunities had come up, to see how everyone was feeling.

We were discussing something and I stopped the conversation. "I'm not comfortable with your husband being there, Mel." Everyone stopped breathing. I'd said what we all were feeling. But she wasn't ready to address it at that point. We both got really upset and I ended up leaving.

I get upset writing about it because what we all feared *was* going on. She was so distant, he'd cut her off from her family, from her mates in LA, he was getting in-between our relationship. The other thing was she was doing so well professionally, she looked fabulous, *"Oh, she looks great, she must be fine"* was something a lot of people must have been saying to themselves, but the reality was very different. He was a very scary character. It was hard watching that and feeling helpless.

But this is Mel B and she of course came through it. I'm incredibly proud of her, and I was so pleased that she was recognised in the 2022 New Year Honours, when she was made an MBE for her work with domestic violence charity, Women's Aid, and other charitable causes.

So, the 2007 tour came to an abrupt end. Mel B returned home, and life settled back into a sort of routine. But being around the girls, and especially their wonderful kids, stirred something in me.

I'd always wanted to be a mum, but my career had come first. I'd never been in the right situation or the right relationship. Tom was more than ready. If anything, he was frustrated and bored of waiting; he'd have liked to have started earlier. Scarlet often says, "I wish you were younger, I wish I had a sibling." I would have liked more children, but I wasn't able to do it. You have to do things when they feel right. And I wasn't ready before then. I just couldn't have been a mum in my twenties. I wasn't well enough.

Before I got pregnant, and in those early months, I did consider how having a baby could affect my mental wellness. Because I'd been diagnosed with depression in the past, I was more predisposed to having postnatal depression, which I was really nervous about.

I had to do it though. It was time for me to have a baby. I was ready.

CHAPTER SIXTEEN

When You're Gone

I had no idea that having a baby isn't as simple as wanting one and they magically appear.

As someone that loves a schedule, I got my calendar up and planned it all. I knew *when* I was going to try to get pregnant, when I'd *get* pregnant and when we would *have* the baby.

"It doesn't work like that," friends would tell me, but, somehow, someway, it did in my case.

We got pregnant the first time. After everything I'd put my body through, it was pretty miraculous, and I was incredibly grateful. I felt like Scarlet was waiting to be born. She'd often tell me when she was younger that she chose me! I loved that idea, so I went with it.

I loved being pregnant, although, as most women find, the first few months are exhausting. I'd be walking down the street and think, *"I could lie down on the floor and go to sleep right here and now."* I constantly had the most disgusting taste in my mouth, so I sucked a lot of fruity sweets and ate crisps to get rid of the taste. But I loved those nine months. And I was ready for a break. Being pregnant and being a new mum isn't a *break* break, but for me it was. A break from the norm. A break from the treadmill. A break from myself and my ambitions.

My pregnancy gave me permission to slow down. I'm a bit of a workaholic but I think that's partly because I'm frightened to stop. I think the pandemic showed, for many of us, that perhaps part of the reason we run around like blue-arsed flies is that when we stop – or we're forced to stop – there's a bit too much time to think about things.

Having something as important as expecting a child gave me the excuse I needed to slow down without any guilt. Being self-employed, it's hard to say no to things. You worry that an opportunity might not present itself again or that the offers might go away. Especially as you get older. I make pop music, which is so youth-orientated. In music, women of a certain age (over 30, basically, which I was when I got pregnant) are subject to terrible scrutiny around their age and their looks and their marital status.

Madonna is a great example of that. Good on her for sticking two fingers up at everyone and dressing how she wants, being who she wants and dating who she wants. Women are *cougars*, men are *sugar daddies* – the one a predatory being, the other a saccharine, benign benefactor. You become a "mum in pop" and it's what a lot of the press tends to be centred around. Yet, male pop stars are rarely asked about being a dad. We obsess over women's surgery and tweakments, but barely raise an eyebrow (if we haven't had botox!) at the vanity of men. We say how good-looking 40-plus actors/footballers/rock stars are while bringing in plastic surgery "specialists" to debate over what work a 40-year-old actress might have had.

The double standards are astounding.

This was all in the back of my mind, and maybe part of why I waited to have my first child. What would happen to my career if I took time out? Getting pregnant at 34 meant I had no choice but to put everything on pause. Honestly, I found it liberating that I wasn't the focus of everything. For my entire adult life, it's always been about me and my work, so to finally tell myself, "*I'm now responsible for something growing inside of me*" was a huge relief. It meant I ate properly for the first time since before having an eating disorder. I felt very strongly that it wasn't just me anymore. I was growing another human inside me and so I *had* to be sensible, I *had* to be responsible. I ate well and I slowed down. And people were nice to me!

All I cared about was the health of my child, I didn't really think about me. It was so freeing and liberating.

Quite early in my second trimester, Bryan Adams invited me and Tom to the Caribbean island of Mustique for a holiday. The thing I remember most about that holiday is how proud I was of my (what was then pretty non-existent) bump, ooh and how my feet swelled in the heat. It's a gorgeous place, I must go again.

When we got back, I went in for my 20-week scan. They chucked all the jelly on, and Tom and I excitedly looked at the screen. Our baby! Of course, I cried at every scan. How could you not?

We didn't know the sex at that point. The obstetrician waved the wand thing about, and he said, "This babe's got a rather large head!" I thought, "*Erm, okay. What?!*" Even though the other Spice Girls all had kids, I hadn't really had a lot of experience with other people's babies. I went to a prenatal class, where it quickly became clear how little I knew. In the class I asked, "If you dilate to 10 centimetres, how big is the average baby's head?" "Ten centimetres,'" I was told. This maths did not work out for me!

The last thing I wanted to hear was that my baby's head was particularly big! What was this birth going to be like?

I did my last gig at eight months pregnant; it was a charity event on 9th January 2009 at Battersea Park alongside Robin Gibb, Lulu, Beverley Knight and Paolo Nutini. I wore a black dress, and I was very pregnant! I was ready to take time off and have this baby.

She was due on 10th February 2009, and I was in the gym that day. Don't worry, I wasn't there doing a 10k or HIIT class. The focus for my gym sessions leading up to the birth was about the birth. It was about being strong, being ready, all those things. I wasn't working out hard, I was keeping moving, keeping my lower body strong.

Regardless, the birth was hardcore. *When* Scarlet did eventually decide to show up!

My waters didn't break that day, or the next day, or five days later. My obstetrician was keeping an eye on me and wanted to bring me in to induce her, but I had a birth plan which was to do it naturally and my absolute last, last, *last* resort was to have an epidural. They tried to follow my plan as much as they could, but she got to however-many-days before they had to induce. I was eating spicy food, cleaning everything in sight, going for walks, and doing everything I could to start her off. She wasn't coming out, she wasn't interested. So off I went to the hospital to get induced.

Scarlet was born at the Portland Hospital in London. Lots of Spice babies have been born there so it felt familiar and safe. The first was Mel B's daughter, Phoenix, on 18th February 1999. In fact, Scarlet was born in the same room. I remember us all waiting outside the door for the first Spice baby. Mel B was shouting all kinds, making us all chuckle even in the throes of labour. The next to arrive was Brooklyn on 3rd March. He was actually due before Phoenix but, of course, Mel B got in there first – probably just to annoy Victoria!

I was induced at 9 am on a Saturday morning. Any woman who's been through that knows it is hideous (the inducing, that is, not the time of day). I've had quite a lot of physical pain in my life, and I think I've got a good pain threshold but there's something about somebody being up in your cervix that's a whole other level. There's absolutely nothing you can do to make it feel any better, any less intrusive, any less vulnerable. They go up in the cervix and give it a little sweep. "I want you to get up, get out, have a little walk around," the obstetrician said, so as we were at the Portland, we went to nearby Regent's Park. Later, the contractions had started but there was still no sign, and they sent us off to a nearby Italian for some supper. The contractions started to get really painful as I was eating my pasta. Maybe it was the tagliatelle, but something was happening. I tried to cover my hospital band while I was in there so no one would see it and call the papers: "There's a Spice Girl in labour eating a Carbonara, get down here quick!"

We went back to the Portland around 9 pm, and the contractions got really strong. I'd doze off a bit before the pain would wake me again. At some point, a midwife came in. "Are you okay, Melanie?" she asked. And I said, "Yeah, I think I want to have a bath so I can try and get some sleep," because the contractions were getting stronger. She looked at me very doubtfully. "Erm, okay, that might not happen, but let's see, shall we?" She ran me a bath and I heaved myself in and, at some point, back out.

Tom had the sofa bed next door, and I could hear him on the rubber sheet turning about and snoring, getting a great sleep. Blokes!

I think we were moved up to the birthing suite about 11 pm. Scarlet was really long, and I could feel her bum squashed against my ribs, right up near my diaphragm, so every time I tried to breathe, it was so painful. I needed something to help with the pain, so I tried gas and air, but I didn't like it.

"I'm going to have to have pain relief, I can't do this anymore," I groaned. Tom said, "But you're doing so well," to which I screamed, "Are you in the same fucking room as me?!"

I was given the epidural so I could sleep but that slowed down the dilation. By now it was about 11 am on Sunday morning. I was dozing when I finally got to 10 centimetres. It was time to push.

I pushed for 40 minutes but I just couldn't get her out. The obstetrician said, "Okay, I've let you go as far as I'm comfortable, we'll have to prepare for surgery."

Despite my hopes for a natural birth, I had to have an emergency C-section. She'd gone down the birth canal a little bit, so they had to get her back up. They had to give me more epidural so they could operate on me. They kept giving me more and more until I couldn't feel anything. I'd had that much of it, I was itching, shaking like mad, and vomiting.

They got her out and the cord was around the neck, and she was blue, so they had to give her oxygen. It was terrifying, but in the way these amazing doctors and nurses do, they kept calm, helped her breathe, and moments later all was well.

They put her in my arms, but I was shaking so much I could hardly hold her. "She looks like Mick Jagger," I cried as I looked at this beautiful baby with these great big lips and thick mop of black hair. They took me into the recovery room, and they gave her to me, and she latched straight on and stayed there for hours.

I became a bit of a hero in the hospital. As staff changed shifts, they'd come in to see me, amazed at how long I'd persevered before having to have an emergency C-section. I was in bits, but I would do it all again in a heartbeat. It was the most magical day of my life. Since having my daughter I've heard of many women having similar and difficult experiences in labour. Women are amazing, aren't they?

After the birth, I was absolutely wrecked. I lay there for three days, out of it, in a dreamy haze, staring at my little girl as I fed her.

Here are some of the things people don't tell you about birth – the amount of blood you continue to lose, that your boobs are like rocks, and let's not even talk about toilet business. Wow! After a C-section they like to get you up and about pretty quickly. It was a day or two after having Scarlet that the midwife gently helped me stand. I was convinced my insides were going to fall out as I staggered around the room, looking like a right state. This one nurse came in, looked at me kindly and said, "You're going to have to start wearing a bra, love."

I was in the Portland for about six days, and eventually I had to go home – although I didn't want to. I wouldn't be able to press a button and get things brought to me anymore! And I didn't know what I'd do without that electric bed to sit me up and down as my abdominal wall had been sliced to bits.

That moment when you step outside the hospital, just you, your partner, and your newborn baby, it's so scary.

We left through the back entrance to avoid the media and got in the car. There was no sign of any paps. I had Scarlet in the baby seat, me in the middle and Mum next to me. Tom was driving, and Den was in the passenger seat. We got to Hampstead and stopped at the lights on the main road, where there's always traffic.

It turned out we had been followed, because a guy jumped out of a car behind us with his camera and started taking photos directly into the car. My instincts kicked in. Geri always compares being a new mum to being a lioness, and it's true. You'll do anything to protect your baby. I threw myself over Scarlet, to protect her from the lens, and in the process really hurt myself. After having major surgery, my body wasn't too happy about that.

I didn't want pictures of Scarlet in the papers, which I think is my right as a mother to decide, on her behalf. I still haven't agreed to pictures of Scarlet being printed. I have very close friends and colleagues that don't share this approach, and I respect that everyone is different.

I've found certain aspects of fame very difficult, and so, for me, it must be my daughter's decision. I don't want to make that decision for her.

Once you agree to put your child in public, then they are now in the public domain. The minute you earn money from an image of them, you've lost the right to their privacy. It's not an issue of law, it's more related to IPSO (the Independent Press Standards Organisation). A moral code, a handshake, if you like. But from the day you do put your kids on stage, or in a video, etc., they can be photographed and in the press.

The first picture of the baby is the one everyone wants – it's the one that makes them money. This is the thing with paparazzi: they want to find you in a compromising position because it's the money shot. They pursue you; they harass you. Paparazzi would shout insults at male musicians about their partners, calling them "slags" or whatever solely in the hope they'd punch them. Because then they'd get "the shot" which could make them five, 10, 15,000 pounds. We've all seen that footage of Britney getting harassed and taunted by paps; they're relentless and they will do anything to get that picture. These people prey on you for something terrible to happen, so they earn money.

To control it – to have a picture published to get the paps off your back – you have a photo with your newborn and give the payment to charity. Bryan Adams took the pictures of Scarlet and me for *Hello!*.

My instincts with Scarlet kicked in immediately. I would do anything to protect her. If being pregnant changed how I felt about my body, then being a mum changed how I felt about myself and it changed everything when it came to Scarlet. She was number one above everything, including me.

Becoming a mum changed me so much more than I ever expected it to. I felt very liberated. Being a pop star or an entertainer can be a very selfish life because it's all about you. Especially being in something as successful as the Spice Girls. You are completely looked after. Everyone is making sure you're okay and you're getting a lot done for you (albeit you pay people to do it). But it becomes all about you. A lot of my personal issues, whether self-esteem or body image or the mental turmoil I've been through, well, when you have somebody else, they become the most important thing. Especially when they're new-born and completely helpless and you are the person there to protect them, to teach them and to nurture them. It was such a relief to get the attention away from myself.

I suddenly had an immediate family. Me and Scarlet, we are one. We're a family, me, and her, forever. I kept thinking, "*It's not just me anymore.*" I've always fantasised about "the family" and I think a lot of people of my generation do; to have children, a partner, a house, and pets. That whole thing. Even though I had a happy childhood, it felt complicated. I think most children want their parents to be together and so I wanted to create that later in my own life.

In short, becoming a mum was a dream come true. Not that there haven't been the occasional couple of nightmares. I mean, the things you do when you're a mum. We were coming back from Wales once, just me and Scarlet. I was busting for a wee, but she'd only just fallen asleep after screaming for hours. I pulled off the motorway towards the services, but I didn't want to get her out the car because I knew it would wake her up. I was thinking, "*Can I wee by the side of the car? No, because there's CCTV everywhere.*" So I got a couple of her nappies and I wee'd into them. Any parent will tell you once you've got that baby to sleep there's no way you'd risk waking them up. Especially when you've still got an hour and half on the M4 to go!

When your baby first arrives, you're just trying to figure out how to do it all. You have no idea at first. None. Going out with the buggy for the first time, I felt like there was a glowing neon sign hanging over my head saying, "*I don't know what I'm doing! I can't even push a buggy straight!*" You have to learn on your feet so quickly. You read all the books, and there's all the different advice but mostly they all say, routine, schedule, routine. Which works great for me, in theory, because I love schedule and routine.

But have you met my daughter?

Scarlet is so headstrong, and she's always been like that. We are so different. I've always been a good girl, do as I'm told, I like everything to be organised and ordered. Scarlet? She does what she wants! A couple of years back, me and Scarlet found these socks in some shop that said "Fuck off" or something similarly offensive. "You've got to get them for Mel B!" said Scarlet. We were up in Leeds visiting my dad and we went to see Mel and gave her the socks. She messaged me on my birthday recently and mentioned the present, saying, "Whenever I wear those socks, I think about Scarlet. She reminds me of me." Scarlet has more girl power than I've ever had!

So as a child, she didn't feed when she was supposed to, she didn't sleep when she was supposed to, and I couldn't understand why. I was always so good at making things work the way they're supposed to, but this baby wouldn't do what I wanted her to.

I was having a particularly hard time one day. I was at home with Scarlet, super tired, and she wouldn't stop crying. She was crying and I was crying, and I couldn't get her to settle, whatever I tried. Emma happened to come to visit with her now-husband, Jade. I opened the door to them in floods and Emma said, "Right! Kettle on!" Jade took Scarlet off for a bit and Emma made me a cuppa and we had a cry and I felt so much better! They really came to the rescue when I needed it.

One day not long after that, I thought, "*She's not going to be a little baby forever, you need to give yourself a break.*" I was giving myself such a hard time because it wasn't working the way the books were telling me it should. I thought, "*I need to enjoy this time and let go of routines.*" And that helped so much.

I was in no hurry to go straight back to work. Scarlet was my first child, and I didn't know how I was going to feel so I decided not to put myself under any pressure. I didn't have a plan, post having her. I'm so lucky to be in a privileged position to not have to work for a period if I don't want to. I really enjoyed that time. I went to baby classes, I had coffees with other mums, and I loved those days.

It's hard though and I know hard work. I've done gruelling, physical things like going on tour, Spice Girls promotion, flying about the world, surviving on no sleep. I thought, "*Yeah, I've got this.*" But it's a whole new world of pain. Nothing can prepare you for how exhausted and demented you can feel on such an incredible lack of sleep! You're tied to your child by this invisible string. Even now, I'll wake up sometimes and a few minutes later, Scarlet will come into me.

I don't know if dads have that – they seem to snore through most of it!

Scarlet and her dad have always had an amazing relationship. They absolutely adore each other and have from day dot. Though Tom and I are no longer together, the most important thing for me when we broke up was that Scarlet would always have a close relationship with her dad. They were close from the beginning, but I think as she's gotten older their relationship has flourished even more

I do think there's a difference between mums and dads. My personal experience is that the minute you know you're pregnant, you *become* a mother. Because you can't drink anymore, you can't smoke (if you do smoke), you can't eat certain things. Suddenly you are responsible for this human being growing inside of you. You become a mother immediately. In my experience, with the father, I think until the baby is born, they don't have that same thing, whether it's physical, emotional or hormonal.

• • •

When Scarlet was six months old, I started to feel ready to return to work and I had an inkling that I knew what I'd like to do. I wanted to get back to my first love.

I'd trained in musical theatre, and I'd always wanted to work in the West End (Broadway is still on the bucket list). It was the path I was on, the career I hoped to have, before that fateful advert changed everything. So I spoke to a few friends about seeing if there might be anything going for me. It felt like a great way to get back to work, to be in London and still be with my girl. With theatre, you have most of the days, apart from matinees, off. It seemed perfect.

As we know, the universe works in mysterious ways, doesn't it?

I'd always loved *Blood Brothers*. Willy Russell is such a brilliant playwright and it's such an incredible show. I'd studied it at school, and I had played Mrs Lyons. My friend, Zoë Curlett, who went to Laine Theatre Arts, was in the year below Victoria and went on to play Christine in *Phantom* and Cosette in *Les Misérables*, and she'd also played Mrs Johnstone in *Blood Brothers*. I'd always wanted to play Mrs Johnstone and randomly mentioned it to someone, saying, "Oh, there's a role I'd love." I put it out in the ether and forgot about it.

The following week, I got a voicemail from my singing coach, Carrie Grant: "They're looking for a 'Mrs J' (as we call it in the theatre, dahlings). Would you like me to put your name forward?" How weird is that?! I do love coincidences, so I thought, I've got to follow this one through.

A couple of weeks later, I was asked to go to theatre producer Bill Kenwright's office in Maida Vale, this beautiful Edwardian building under the Westway, and I did my first audition since

1994 with the girls. I had to stand there and sing and read. I did "Tell Me It's Not True", which is the closing song of the show.

Luckily, I got the job.

Bill was so lovely. He really mentored me and looked after me. I hugely appreciate Bill and Josh Andrews bringing me into the West End and helping to make all those dreams I'd had come true. For those that might have forgotten, the house I'd stayed in in LA belonged to Josh's dad and he was an executive producer on *Spiceworld*. Small world.

There were challenges though. I couldn't just land the part and expect everyone to love me. This was a time when on Broadway and the West End there was a certain amount of snobbery about "celebrities" doing musical theatre. There had been a lot of pop stars coming into roles that maybe didn't deserve to have them. *Chicago*, for example, had a new Roxy every five minutes. There might have been the feeling that these already successful people were swiping roles that trained musical theatre performers relied on. There was also the argument that theatres needed bums on seats and having a "name" in a show can help that.

I knew I'd have to prove myself, and I was fine with that.

I could have negotiated not doing matinees or having the odd night off, I could have chosen a slightly easier option. But I didn't want to do that. I wanted to do eight shows a week, I wanted to earn my stripes. I wanted to challenge myself. I have so much respect for people who work in theatre. It was amazing, getting to share that experience with a company who are dedicated to their job, to their craft. A lot of people, the chorus members particularly, earn very little money, especially considering the unsociable hours and the cost of living when you don't want your commute to and from the theatre to be a mission.

When it was announced that I would be playing Mrs Johnstone, people criticised my age, saying I was too young to play Mrs J. I've still got a handwritten note from Willy that he sent to me saying that he'd written the part for Barbara Dickson and she was 36 at the time. Which was the exact age I was then.

There might have been some doubters about, but I threw myself wholeheartedly into *Blood Brothers*. It was the most terrifying thing I'd ever done. We had a short rehearsal time, maybe only a couple of weeks, and I don't think I even rehearsed with a live band before the show. With theatre, it depends on the production, but budgets can be very tight. And now it must be even worse. God only knows how these theatres have survived during the pandemic. I hope they got the funding they deserved, and I hope audience numbers return to the size they once were. It's such an important part of our culture and we must preserve it.

So, anyway, the first night. I stood in the wings literally about to vomit. You know when spit comes in your mouth? I had to suck my cheeks in hard, so I didn't throw up. I went out, I did the show, I came off and I couldn't remember a thing. It was an out-of-body experience, though by all accounts it went well. I got it out the way, I got one under my belt and then I was able to get into the show.

It was tougher than expected but I went into *Blood Brothers* for *me*. I never thought about reviews or awards, or anything like that. Bill called me on the Sunday morning after press night and said, "Girl, get up, get down the shop and get all the papers cos this is never gonna happen again." We had four and five stars across the board. Even the broadsheets.

People around me started to say I was sure to be nominated for an Olivier Award, which I decided was hilarious. I thought, *"There's no way I'm going to get nominated,"* but then I was, for

Best Actress in a Musical, which was ridiculous and prestigious, and I was delighted. I started to build it up in my head, thinking, "*Oh, maybe I could win.*"

I got to the awards, and I sang "Tell Me It's Not True" wearing Victoria Beckham (a dress, not actual Victoria Beckham) and I felt very proud. By then I'd convinced myself I was going to win. I don't know why. I didn't win. Sam Spiro, who is phenomenal, won for *Hello, Dolly!* Hannah Waddingham, who's now in *Ted Lasso*, was in the running as well, so there were all these amazing theatre actresses. And it was Best Actress in a Musical, not Musical Performance. To be nominated for that *and* an Evening Standard award was brilliant enough.

When I was leaving the Oliviers, I bumped into Sir Jonathan Pryce. As a kid growing up and loving musical theatre, I adored him, he's such an incredible actor. He came up to me and said, "I never saw you in *Blood Brothers*, but my daughter told me you were just marvellous!" That really made my night. Who needs an award when you've got praise from Jonathan Pryce?

Blood Brothers was the first time I was nominated for an award since Best Female at the BRITs in 2000 (Beth Orton won). It was so lovely to be recognised. I did have belief in myself again by this point, but I went through dips. As I got older, I found I became less and less sure of myself and my ability. The reviews and the nominations were validation at a time I could really appreciate it. I was able to really enjoy the moment, to enjoy the success and the praise. My first solo album was successful, but I was in a mess. I wasn't capable of being fully present at that time.

Getting pregnant, having Scarlet, and then going into *Blood Brothers* helped me redefine and rediscover my own narrative. One that felt completely truer and far healthier.

I was a mum; I was in a relationship and things were much more stable.

Well, for now.

CHAPTER SEVENTEEN

Version Of Me

The 2010s, what a time they were. Vine, Instagram, Snapchat, Hinge and Tinder. Lady Gaga, the iPad, planking, the Ice Bucket Challenge, the Harlem Shake, the Dab, Gangnam Style, BTS and Blackpink. "Get Lucky", "Happy", "Someone Like You". Ed Sheeran, Taylor Swift, and Taylor Swift's scarf. Harry, Zayn, Louis, Liam, and Niall. Billie Eilish. Emoji and Mimoji, Pokémon Go, Marvel vs. DC, *Black Panther*, fidget spinners, Occupy Wall Street. Time's Up. #MeToo. Black Lives Matter. President Donald Trump. Brexit. Sandy Hook. COVID-19. Same sex marriage. Kimye. William and Kate. Meghan and Harry. Haiti. Isis. Pulse Nightclub, the Manchester Arena, the Bataclan. Harvey Weinstein, Jeffrey Epstein, "Grab her by the pussy". London 2012.

2012 was a complex year.

Things had been difficult with Tom. We were growing apart. He was spending a lot more time in Wales at the house we had bought there while I was in North London with Scarlet. I was becoming more unhappy, and I didn't think he was happy either.

We were beginning to live separate lives even though we were sharing a child.

I never wanted Scarlet to experience what I had as a child. Growing up, it was my biggest wish for my mum and dad to be together. The idea that I was going to repeat history was difficult. It had been hard for me, the breakup of my parents. It made me the person I am today, which isn't all bad, but some of the more vulnerable aspects of my personality have come from that experience. I didn't want to do that to her.

But when something isn't right, you have to change it and Scarlet did give me that kick up the arse and confidence to do the right thing and be courageous. Being a mum to a young girl, I didn't want her to grow up thinking that the relationship I had with her father was a happy and healthy one. Because it wasn't. We were two separate people living two separate lives.

So, I had to change it. It was such a big decision. I felt like I was mourning a future that I would no longer have. I would have liked more children, the whole 2.4-children family unit, the family home, siblings for Scarlet, and a dog, all of that. It was such a huge decision to be made, but I wasn't happy. I couldn't continue in the relationship.

The day I realised it came with such crystal clarity. I was running on Hampstead Heath one day – some of my biggest life decisions have happened there – and it happened. That moment when you've been thinking about something for so long and suddenly, something comes over and you say to yourself, *"Do it. It has to be done."*

And there's no turning back. Something shifts in your mind, and you have to do it.

I'd made the decision but like everything in my life, I had to schedule the conversation. I needed to find a time where we could discuss it properly, and not when I was running out the door to an appearance or a rehearsal or to the airport.

I planned to talk to Tom just after we announced the Spice Girls musical, *Viva Forever,* because I knew I had a decent amount of time off after that.

We launched the musical at the St Pancras Renaissance Hotel as a nod to where we had shot "Wannabe" all those years ago. It was us girls, the show's producer Judy Craymer, and its writer, the one and only Jennifer Saunders.

We were lucky to have Judy work with us. She produced *Mamma Mia!,* a show that Victoria's mum and dad absolutely love. Somehow Victoria had gotten an intro with Judy and established a relationship with her. So, when the show was mooted, Victoria knew the exact person for the job.

We all met Judy. She's a fabulous, super formidable, brilliant woman. Girl Power on steroids. For a woman to be in that position in the theatre world, to have achieved what she has, is incredible. Judy suggested bringing in Jennifer and we were all so up for that, because we'd worked with her for *Comic Relief,* she'd been in the *Spice World* movie, and Emma had worked on *Ab Fab* with her. It was perfect.

We had it all in place, all the ingredients. One of the most successful people in theatre, a leading light of comedy, a brilliant cast and, let's face it, some amazing songs.

Guys, you know the ending here. It didn't review well, the ticket sales weren't great and it went through numerous rewrites, but our Viva wasn't Forever and the show closed six months later.

We were upset because we felt like it wasn't allowed to succeed. It was bizarre that it didn't work out. You've got Jennifer Saunders, a national treasure, the incredible Judy Craymer, and so many great songs. But it didn't work. There were worse things in the theatre that do well. Maybe there were just too many women involved?

We'd all invested in *Viva Forever*, so we all lost a lot of money doing that. It was such a shame, but I guess it wasn't meant to be. Hopefully, there is a future for a Spice Girls musical because it would be great to have those songs sung every night on a theatre stage.

So, before all that, while we're all still optimistic and hopeful, we went to St Pancras with Judy and Jennifer to do the photo call and press conference. We had booked the Little House afterwards for dinner, but on the way there, Tom called me to say he was going to Wales.

I needed to talk to him, it couldn't wait: I'd made the decision.

I left the girls and headed home. Tom was busy getting his things ready before setting off to Wales.

I took a deep breath and told him, "I can't do this anymore." He was shocked. I thought he felt the same. Because I felt so unhappy, I assumed he was. Maybe he didn't want to see it. Or maybe what we had was enough for him.

It was always really important to me to make sure that Scarlet and her dad maintained their relationship because even though I didn't always see my dad as much as I might have liked as a kid, we were always close, and I adore him. I wanted the same for Scarlet. It was vital to me that they had a good relationship.

It didn't work out for me and Tom but we got the best daughter ever.

• • •

There was a period of readjustment post-Tom, but I didn't have long to dwell. Within a few weeks I was facing one of the biggest nights of my career.

We'd always said we'd wanted to do the Olympics – five rings, five girls! Though we hadn't played together since February 2008 (and had no plans to again at that point), when the call came in (quite late in the day) from the London 2012 Closing Ceremony creators, the choreographer Kim Gavin, stage designer Es Devlin, *Billy Elliot* director Stephen Daldry, composer David Arnold and the architect Mark Fisher, of course we said yes. A great, big, huge yes.

London in 2012 was the best time to ever be in the capital city. Being Sporty, of course I loved the Olympics and being part of it, and I took Scarlet to the gymnastics and to one of the Super Saturdays. It was a fantastic time. She was only three, so I had to ply her with ice lollies when she got bored.

The Closing Ceremony was designed as a celebration of British entertainment and culture and we joined everyone from Annie Lennox to Kate Moss, Naomi Campbell, Russell Brand, Ed Sheeran, Fatboy Slim, Tinie Tempah, Muse, Brian May and Roger Taylor, Liam Gallagher, George Michael and Ricky Wilson from Kaiser Chiefs who sang with The Who. Can you imagine the Green Room? It such a mad mix of amazing people. Everyone was so happy and excited to be there because no one had done the Olympics before.

One of my last, clear memories of George was at the Olympics that day. Not long before we went on, there was a knock on our dressing room door, and in he came, all in black, black leather coat and black jeans. He was still a gorgeous looking man. And I still had no chance of making him mine...!

"I'm so nervous," he confessed. "You'll be fine, you've done this a million times," we told him. There were the Spice Girls making George Michael feel better about performing.

It had been decided that we'd arrive onstage in five black cabs – what could be more symbolic of London than that – and then we'd be driven around the stadium while standing on the roofs, a wobbly gate between us and a disaster waiting to happen on live television.

Obviously, this needed some practice, and it was while we were out in Essex rehearsing in a massive car park that the papps, presumably after a tip off, got their long lenses out and caught us at it. The cat was out of the proverbial bag.

On the day itself, we were suddenly told we couldn't rehearse. There had been some sort of delay and we were told there wasn't time. "Bollocks to that," scoffed someone, probably Mel B, who said what we were all thinking: "Have you run that past health and safety because we're literally dancing on top of a taxi here." We decided if they wouldn't give us a dress rehearsal, then we wouldn't go on. As badly as we all wanted to do the show, none of us was too keen on falling over in front of nearly a billion people.

We got the rehearsal.

It was only a four-minute performance, so we knew it was going to fly by in the blink of an eye. We told each other to take it all in, the sights, the sounds, the smells, to look each other in the eye. And we did. It was incredible. I can still see the stadium, the camera lights, and the flashes, all the athletes around the track. I've no idea how we managed to stay standing on those black cabs, but we did. Afterwards, we did the thing we always do when we're in crazy situations. We huddled together and screamed: "We did it, the knobheads did it!"

It was also the first time we'd performed during the age of "social media". I will say this until my last breath: I'm eternally grateful that the Spice Girls didn't exist during the time of

Instagram and TikTok etc, but, *but* it was amazing for us to see that night, in real-time, reactions from fans around the world. We were used to people around us reassuring us with platitudes. "Oh yes this show sold-out in such and such a time" or "Oh these people are really excited to meet you," but to see the hype and anticipation with our own eyes was really a great experience.

But that was the night when Victoria decided she didn't want to perform again. She found performing so stressful, and if anything was going to make you anxious, it would be doing the Olympics to an audience of nearly a billion people. She was really freaking out before we went on. We tried to calm her down because she was *so* nervous. I think she thought, *"I can't put myself through this again."*

The rest of us though were on such a high doing that performance, and after it.

Victoria didn't stay for long following the show, but the rest of us had other plans. And they included Mr George Michael, who had invited us to his home in Highgate where he was throwing a post-Olympics party. His family and friends were all there waiting – they'd been watching the ceremony on a big screen with this huge spread laid on.

The thing is, getting in and out the stadium was a nightmare, there was all this security around it, so we were stuck inside for ages. George thought, *"Sod this I've got a party to get to"*, and took it upon himself to just walk right out. He sauntered out onto the insalubrious surroundings of Stratford High Street; I think he had a car waiting there. Somehow, George managed to get offstage just after 9 pm and got himself home to Highgate for 9.30 pm!

Everybody else, however, had to faff about for ages, boarding these special buses to get us out of the stadium. It was a very strange experience because there was us, Russell Brand, a couple of guys from Muse, Kate Hudson, and Timothy Spall all aboard. It was an odd mix, like yet another very surreal Spice Girls dream.

We finally rolled up to George's around 1 am, but we needn't have worried. The party was still going strong. Very, very strong.

After performing for nearly 700 million people, the atmosphere among us all that night in Highgate was electric. We didn't want that night to end.

George was a generous, kind, loving man. He's really missed.

• • •

After a few months of processing my breakup with Tom, I started to emerge from the other side.

I was single but far from being down in the dumps, I decided I was going to get out there and live life to the full.

I'd started to be a lot kinder to myself, which was paying off. Scarlet is a huge part of that. Becoming a mum, and to a girl, it's so important to have a healthy attitude around body image and food. The responsibility to her made it easier for me.

I started to look at and appreciate exercise differently. Rather than focusing on weight loss, I wanted to build strength and I wanted to work out in a way that benefitted my mental wellness, not damage it.

I did my first triathlon, sponsored by Virgin Money in 2011 and went on to do several more during this period.

As with *Blood Brothers*, there's always an easier route if you're a "celebrity". They offered to let me do it as a relay, so I could either swim, cycle or run and someone else would do the other bits. No offence to anyone else, but it would never occur to me to take the easy option. If I'm doing it, I'm doing it like everyone else.

I threw myself in at the deep end – literally! I was introduced to Steve Trew, a triathlon coach and commentator. Steve showed me the ropes of open water swimming in a wetsuit and taught me about the transitions between running, swimming and cycling, the transitions being the fourth discipline of triathlon (sorry I'm a bit of a nerd when it comes to the sport). That first triathlon, I did just for fun, but I was bitten by the bug.

Like many people going through a breakup, I also threw myself into work. I spent a year on tour with Jools Holland, playing various places around the UK, alongside Ruby Turner and Marc Almond.

I look forward to working with Jools and the Rhythm and Blues Orchestra again. It's such a privilege not only to perform with him and his band but with an incredible brass section too, which is so rare. Jools has become a dear friend and he will often check up on me to make sure I'm doing okay. He's been very supportive about me writing this book too.

I first did *Later… with Jools Holland* in 1999, which was a big deal for me because he only features *musicians*. Jools has got amazing taste and having his approval really meant a lot. He was important back then, and he's important now – maybe even more so with the lack of music programmes available on telly these days. He's such a champion of musicians and he continues to tour tirelessly.

There are artists that go out now that don't tour with live musicians, which I don't think should be allowed. I don't know where the Musicians' Union is when these big pop acts hit the road without a live band. It's crazy. That was an option for a Spice Girls tour in 2019, but I said, "I'm not going out on a tour, let alone a stadium tour, without live musicians." Because you save a certain amount of money? I don't care. I feel passionate about live musicians and live music. The pandemic has been terrible for the live sector, for session musicians, the techs, and the roadies and so on. I did a couple of shows in 2021 and it was hard to find crew because they'd all had to go and get other jobs. Also, it's just not as vibey performing to backing tracks. I feel the audience is getting short-changed. Sometimes for one-off gigs you have no choice but for live touring? Grrrrr.

Later… is one of the shows I actually remember performing on during the *Northern Star* era, partly because I was petrified. I had one of my favourite bands, Supergrass, opposite me and Jools and I left the studio on a motorbike, with no helmets. Where was health and safety?!

I also did a track with Matt Cardle, who had won *The X Factor* just a couple of years before. "Loving You" was a great song and it was one of the highest charting singles I'd been on since the *Northern Star* era. We had a lot of fun working on that single. I adore Matt – he's an incredible vocalist, one of the best I've had the pleasure of working with.

During this time, I had a new lease of life and decided to work on a couple of great projects that took me out of my comfort zone.

Andrew Lloyd Webber asked if I'd be interested in being a mentor on ITV's *Superstar*, a talent show to find the next Jesus. I would be joining Jason Donovan and David Grindrod, who's the biggest casting director in the West End. David is lovely, a real character. Jason Donovan is one of my favourite people in the universe. He's so naughty and mischievous. He's remained a good friend.

It went really well and both Jason and I were asked to be judges on the live shows alongside Andrew Lloyd Webber and Dawn French. We had such a laugh filming; we'd have notebooks in front of us so we could take notes and Jason would inevitably draw something very rude on there. The camera would cut to me, and he'd be there nudging me, like, "Do you like the picture, Melanie?" Andrew was the sensible one, so he'd refuse to laugh, but then you'd have me, Dawn and Jason giggling like schoolkids.

During the live shows, Andrew asked me if I'd be interested in playing Mary Magdalene on the tour. *Jesus Christ Superstar* was another great moment for me. It came just after the breakdown in my relationship with Tom, so it got me up and out and focused on something else.

The show has an incredible score, written by Andrew and Tim Rice when they were in their early/mid-twenties. It's the perfect combination of rock concert and musical theatre. This tour was in arenas, so I felt like it was an extension of the touring life I already knew. Chris Moyles played King Herod, Tim Minchin was Judas, Alex Hansen was Pontius Pilot and Ben Forster, who was the person we found on *Superstar*, went on to play Jesus. Ben is phenomenal and so versatile. Alongside Matt Cardle, he's the best singer I've worked with. He is one of the biggest stars on the West End now and he's become one of my closest friends, as has Chris.

We don't see Tim so much as he's in Australia these days, but we all became a bit of a family on that tour. It was a magical time which inspired another album from me, my sixth. I performed "I Don't Know How To Love Him," from *Jesus* on the final of *Superstar* on ITV accompanied by Andrew on piano. I'd recorded some of my favourite musical theatre songs from *Hair*, *The King and I* and *Carousel* back in 2010 with my lovely producer Peter Vettese and landing the role of Mary Magdalene inspired me to finish and release *Stages* in 2012. There was one person I knew I had to get on the record, and that was Emma Bunton. We covered the *Chess* classic "I Know Him So Well". Weirdly, I sang blondey Elaine Paige's part and Emma was the brunette Barbara Dickson.

It was wonderful to be in a hit show. More than 150,000 people went to see *Jesus* during the first run. That's a lot of people!

To work alongside Andrew Lloyd Webber was literally a dream come true. For all his eccentricities, Andrew is very lovely and he's very loyal, and he always asks me along to things. Imagine the teenage kid in my bedroom listening to the score of *Cats*, *Tell Me on a Sunday* and *Evita* knowing one day I'd be working with the man who wrote some of my favourite musicals.

It's another full-circle, pinch-me moment, something else magical I got to experience because of being a Spice Girl. And like *Blood Brothers*, I was in a much better place to appreciate this fulfilling, fantastic moment.

• • •

For a lot of people, turning 40 can be a big deal, and not in a good way. We feel the hands of time ticking, we know that our bodies are going to start doing all sorts of weird things, and there may be a sense of regret, unfulfillment or dissatisfaction about where we are in life.

Not for me.

I was feeling great. In my late thirties, I looked the best I've ever looked, I felt the best I've ever felt, and I was excited and looking forward to the future.

was totally relaxed and happy about the big four-oh. Far
ing anxious about my age or upset that I was single and

had no one to help me plan the big day, I was really excited about my birthday. Nancy asked me what I wanted to do, and I said, "Well... I'd really like to do a gig." Typical of me, I just wanted to be onstage for two and a half hours being very self-indulgent! She knew what my answer would be and had already started the process.

We held "Sporty's Forty" at one of my favourite venues, Shepherd's Bush Empire, the day before my birthday and it was immense. I had the best party ever. It was sold out, and I got loads of mates to come and sing with me. Keith Lemon introduced me and semi-hosted proceedings and then me and Emma sang "2 Become 1"; I sang "Pure Shores" with Nat from All Saints. James from Starsailor came up and we did a couple of songs. Chris Moyles got up and did "When You're Gone".

Andy Burrows, a dear friend of mine who's in Razorlight, came and sang "Northern Star", but he'd been in the pub drinking between the soundcheck and the show with Dom from Muse and came back hammered! I went to introduce him, and I could see him in the wings, looking a bit dishevelled. He had all the lyrics on his arms, and he kept pointing at me, like, you do this bit! He still apologises to me to this day, but it was great, one of the highlights of the night.

It was an exciting time for me – I'd had a great few years doing the Olympics, performing in *Jesus Christ Superstar*, and releasing an album called *The Sea* that I really loved and believed in.

The Sea was a classic pop record, but it was inspired by different genres throughout, a little bit like *Northern Star*.

One of the early sessions for *The Sea* album was down in Brighton at Biff's studio, which is incredible – it's a great space. I loved walking along the seafront before a session and the title track, "The Sea", was one of the first songs we did, written after one of those walks. The feeling of that song inspired the rest of the album.

The Sea was a tricky one because it was a return to form in many ways – it felt like the strongest piece of work I'd made in quite a while. It didn't perform very well but by then the industry had changed so much and maybe we – me and my team – didn't evolve with that. I was spending a lot of money making, marketing, and promoting my music with the mindset that I simply needed a good song. That's not how things worked anymore.

I was really happy with the album, and I was feeling good about myself. I felt like I looked the best I'd looked in my career. I was confident in my music; I was confident in myself and for it to not do as well as I hoped was tough. I am always ambitious. I pour my heart and soul into my work.

Every album since my debut, I've thought, "Is this the one? Am I going to get back to a place where I feel taken seriously or appreciated?" I really thought *The Sea* was the one. It was hard to pick myself up again after that, but I managed to get over the disappointment because whatever the reasons were that it didn't do well, I knew I'd made a good record.

All of which is to say, everything was great, I was great, life was great... great, great, great.

And then I turned 40 and it all went to shit.

Things started to slip, mentally and physically. I started having aches that I hadn't had before. Doubts began to creep in. I was trying to get some pennies in the bank, so I could make a new record.

And then the Black Dog, that heavy cloak, appeared and I started to feel very low. 2014 was a tough year for me.

When the relationship with Tom ended, in 2012, I was initially at a low ebb. But once the sadness of the breakup began to lift, I felt excited. I felt proud of myself for changing something that wasn't making me happy, and I was elated about the future.

Any mourning the loss of the future that I thought I would have, or disappointment that I was repeating the cycle of my parents, I set that aside.

I felt happy, exhilarated, high on life.

Perhaps it was inevitable there would be a crash. I'd made what I thought was a great album and still I couldn't make it connect the way I'd hoped. I didn't have doubts about myself as an artist, but I started to wonder what the future might look like for me as a solo singer. And there was my home life too. I hadn't dealt with the breakup at all. This had been my first, long-term, serious relationship and we had had a beautiful, brilliant child together. And it hadn't worked out. I started to feel a heaviness, a sense of failure, and my confidence started to ebb. I had a delayed reaction to the split with Tom. At the time, I'd thrown myself into single life and work and I was well away.

By February, March of 2014, though, I wasn't feeling very confident. I was lonely.

I knew I needed to do something about it, so I went to see someone and was referred to a psychiatrist. As I quickly discovered, psychiatry was very much about chemicals, it's based around science. We'll fix your brain with these pills. There weren't extensive conversations about how I was feeling, as far as I can remember. I was put on an antidepressant and diagnosed with Premenstrual Dysphoric Disorder (PDD), because I'd get particularly low around my cycle. It had been a long time since I'd been on antidepressants, and they'd improved a lot since I was last on them, but I ended up on the highest dosage, with another medication that enhanced the serotonin in that medication.

I was on lots of medication for several months, and I didn't really feel any better.

Antidepressants can work brilliantly for many people and were helpful for me to a point. But I don't think they are the only fix. In all honesty I've turned to them when I need extra help, when all the other stuff just isn't cutting it. If you can, if you're able to, then I think other treatments can really help. I tried everything: aromatherapy, hypnotherapy, reflexology, but I found acupuncture and talking therapies most helpful.

Therapy, of course, is important, but I'm also aware that you have to wait for months on the NHS, and even then, you only get five or six sessions. I'm so lucky that I'm able to be able to pay for therapy, natural and homoeopathic remedies, and so on. I do not take it for granted and I am aware that for many people quite literally paying the gas bill and putting food on the table is the priority.

Thankfully, there is much better awareness around mental health now, and there are some incredible places that you can get help. Of course, there's the NHS, the Samaritans and organisations like Mind. And then there are the people around you. Talk to someone, whether it's a teacher, a parent, a friend, a neighbour, or your doctor. If you feel there's no one in your world that you can speak with, then there are many helplines, like Crisis and Rethink, who will have someone there for you.

I held everything in for years, and it did me no favours whatsoever. Talking to people and telling people how you feel is the first step to getting help.

So, for me, in 2014, I did seek help, thankfully though it was decided that medication would be the best for me at that point.

I was reluctant because I felt I'd been successful at finding other methods to improve my mental wellness, but I also didn't have it in me to argue with the psychiatrist at the time. I just wanted to feel better, and I wanted it to happen as fast as it possibly could.

The first time I'd taken antidepressants the time came when I thought, "*I think I can do this.*" It was scary but with my doctor's advice I began to slowly wean myself off the medication and I was okay. Some people just suddenly stop taking them, which can be dangerous. It's important to slowly decrease your dose. Ideally, you should consult the physician who prescribed them so you can be guided exactly how to come off.

This time I just didn't feel like the tablets had been helping much at all, so I weaned myself off them slowly. I wouldn't rule out using them again. I mean I hope I don't need to, but it's good to know they're there.

For me, I've realised that acupuncture, alongside a good diet, proper sleep, exercise, no alcohol, and talking therapies work best for me. It took a while for me to see that. I have a great therapist now, who I've had for a few years; I have been lucky enough to find somebody that works for me a little bit like antidepressants; you have to find the right one for you.

• • •

Things were brighter in my personal life too. The depression had coincided with my meeting a new partner. I first met Joe just as the heaviness started to set in. Perhaps that was the catalyst for those feelings around my breakup to surface. The feeling of having to start over, or that I'd "failed" in the first place.

Coming out of a long-term relationship, it took me a long time to even be bothered or interested to have the courage or confidence to meet anyone else. I'd had a few dates and I'd had some fun but nothing serious.

It was my good friend Ben that encouraged me to get back on the horse! I had my protectors like Ben, Tim Minchin and Chris Moyles, who were like my big brothers through a period when I was quite vulnerable. They were so supportive.

Joe and I met in March 2014, a couple of months after my fortieth, at a friend's birthday party. I met another friend in the pub near me earlier that day. "I'm going to this party tonight, I don't really know anyone, but I think it's quite good to be in a different environment. I just want to meet a nice guy, you know," I said.

Joe and I were introduced through a mutual friend and ended up having a few drinks at the party. We arranged to meet again, and we hit it off. We got on from the get-go really.

Joe was a revelation; he was a wonderful addition to my life. He'd been separated from his ex for about six months and had two children. We were taking things slowly because we had kids and responsibilities, but we were spending more and more time together and enjoying each other's company.

As the year, and our relationship progressed, I was feeling more secure with Joe, I was enjoying writing, and slowly the cloud started to lift.

When we met, Joe had an animation studio, and they were doing brilliant things like music videos, TV idents and short films. He's very creative, very smart and intuitive. He would suggest things for my own visuals, and I really liked how energetic and interested he was in my work.

Joe really empowered me. It was a very different relationship to any I've had before because he had a lot of belief in me. When I mentioned I wanted to DJ, he encouraged me wholeheartedly. He always told me, "You can do that. Just do it. Give it a go." For years, I'd been told, "Oh, you can't do that", or "That doesn't work like this". I'm fully aware you can't do everything, but maybe we could have a go? I needed a bit of encouragement and he provided that.

Around this time, my manager, Nancy, had mentioned thoughts of retiring, which was very at odds with where my mind was at. I was feeling very enthusiastic and ambitious at this point, I had this new energy in my life. New friendship groups, rekindling old friendship groups, meeting a new guy. I was feeling good about myself. I'm back, baby! When she started talking about retirement, I started to realise that, for the first time, we might be in different places. We'd had a great relationship but maybe it was nearing a natural conclusion.

Nancy was great over the many years we'd worked together. She stepped in to look after things after we left Simon and it was hard for her. She wasn't on commission, she was on salary, working for the Spice Girls nearly killed her. Can you imagine, taking that on? She also did all our solo records – apart from Geri – and *Forever*. One by one, the girls all went off to do different things, but Nancy and I continued to work together because she was a real music person. She'd worked in PR, and at a label and in management. She was a pure music lover and that's where we connected. All those people became like family; Nancy, Ying (my assistant for a long time) and my band, they were dear, dear friends. It's difficult when you need to move on from things, but people change over time. In many instances, I was going in a different direction to the people in my life, and decided it was time to move on.

Ying and I worked together for 18 years, but we were really good friends too, we did everything together. I would've been lost without her when Scarlet was born. It's very, very sad but we started to see things differently and we decided things had run their course. It was hard to end that but there was complacency on both sides. I couldn't ask for what I wanted, and her heart was no longer in it. I needed a new energy.

I absolutely loved and adored my band – brilliant musicians who I had a lot of history with. I'd worked with my lead guitarist Paul since the very first Spice Girls show. But I feared the set-up wouldn't be right for the new album I knew I wanted to make. I was planning for this record to have a much more electronic feel.

I had so many great times with them all and I loved them all dearly, but it was time for a refresh. When you've worked with people for a long time it becomes difficult because they become like family. They were very difficult conversations to have.

As well as a creative gulf, there were also financial issues too. I was self-financing all these records and I was losing loads of money. *The Sea* was another huge disappointment, and another huge knock to my confidence. I'm not getting any younger, you know, and I didn't want to be haemorrhaging money, trying to have a music career. It wasn't sustainable.

I had a full-time PA, a manager on 20%, an accountant, and I was paying for office space. I didn't need it all and I couldn't afford it all. In fact, at one stage, I was even at risk of losing my home. It had reached that point.

I was financing a situation that I couldn't afford.

I had Scarlet to think about, so I had to be sensible. Fortunately, opportunities like *Asia's Got Talent* came up in 2015, and it made sense to do that. It was a great experience working alongside the Canadian musician and composer David Foster, the Indonesian-born French singer Anggun and Taiwanese American actor and singer Vanness Wu, plus it was a chance to get some money in the bank (to spend on another album!).

(Small world alert: Vanness is also a dancer and he featured in the Jason Nevins Vs. Run-D.M.C. "It's Like That" video, the very song that kept "Stop" from reaching number one and ending our consective number one streak.)

But everything is about music for me. No matter what television shows I do, it all comes back to my first love, music. Every record I think, "What if I can't do it? What if I haven't got it in me? What if that's it, what if I've done all my best work and this is going to be shit?"

It's like I can't stop because if I stop, I'm not a whole person. It's what's always driven me. The Spice Girls were such a phenomenon and so I knew, as a solo artist, that I was never going to eclipse that or even come close to it.

It's hard for – I hesitate to use the word "older" – so let's say "heritage" acts. No one is interested in their new material, but they keep going, touring and performing, because they love it. You create for art, not commerce. It never goes away, that need to perform. And people do continue to have a long and successful career with new hits as well as past ones. Elton John had an amazing 2021, he finished the year at number one. I have so much respect for him. People might say, "*Why does he still do it, he doesn't need to?*" But maybe he does. And I understand that. It's a desire to create and have people enjoy what you make, and share it, and bring a bit of light into their lives.

I do feel like there is a place for me in the world.

· · ·

I started to work on a new record, *Version of Me*, in June 2014, two years before it came out. I went to LA with Peermusic, who were my publishers at the time. I had some very bizarre writing sessions, which was good because I didn't have a direction at that time. It was lovely to be back with Rick Nowels again, after a magical time writing *Northern Star*, and I teamed up with London-based production duo Mo Samuels and Mikey Akin, who together are known as Sons of Sonix.

Instinctively I knew I would like to go in a more electronic direction. I'd always talked about loving trip-hop, bands like Massive Attack and Portishead, and I'd always planned to explore that sound. This felt like the time, the album to execute that vision more fully. I didn't just want to do me; I wanted to do – wait for it – a version of me!

I took my time with the album. We started in 2014 and were still recording into 2016.

I love *Version of Me*. It's a bit all over the place, a bit experimental in parts, and all done on a tight budget. It was an important record for me because it allowed me to take a risk. I knew that I had nothing to lose. "Room for Love" was inspired by meeting Joe, the title track "Version of Me" is about some of the troubles I had in the band and "Blame" with Peter Vettese was inspired by the breakdown of the relationship with Tom.

I've written my most personal songs with Peter, he's such an important collaborator. He has real belief in me and has always encouraged me to dig into the depths of my soul. Nothing was ever wrong or rubbish.

This was after I'd had those difficult conversations with my team, and then Joe stepped up to hold the fort until we found the right management. I was so nervous about performing the album for the first time with a new band. But when I played my first show at Glasgow's ABC in April 2017, I knew I'd absolutely made the right decision.

The first night of any tour is so daunting. Scarlet came up with me and she was so sweet, helping me relax the night before with facemasks and foot rubs. I was stressed out with everything behind the scenes.

But the show was amazing, it went so well, and it was a massive shift for me. My shoulders came down. That feeling of elation. I knew I'd done the right thing. Everything I do, it's all to get to that point, of being onstage, to have an audience in front of me and a band behind me, that's the goal, that's the end point.

With the Spice Girls, apart from showcases in the beginning, we barely performed for the first year or two, until those shows in Istanbul towards the end of 1997. It was a lot of PA's, a couple of songs performed as live on TV chat shows, but we were mostly miming. I'd gotten into all this because I wanted to perform, but all we seemed to do was mouth along to a backing track, do back-to-back press and live on aeroplanes. Don't get me wrong, we had a lot of fun too, but there was so little of what I thought I'd signed up for.

To be doing what I loved, touring an album live, was a revelation. Even though it was hard getting a foothold, getting the numbers up on Spotify – because everything's changed – and there was still a long way to go, I felt I was on the right path. I felt exhilarated and enthused and energetic from having a new team of people. I had a good team, Joe was doing a great job, I had started DJing, I'd had my introduction to Sink The Pink (the self-described LGBTQI+ collective and club night), and I would go onto make the album, *Melanie C*, which went top ten and was my most successful album in over a decade.

Before I started *Melanie C* though, there was something else on the table.

I got a visit from Geri. There was talk of a Spice Girls show. But was I ready?

You know what, girls, I think I am. I bloody well think I am!

CHAPTER EIGHTEEN

Beautiful Intentions

For years, there had been a narrative in the press that I was the one holding back any sort of Spice Girls reunion. The implication was I thought I was too big for it; that I was an important solo artist, and I didn't need the band.

That just wasn't the case. Alongside all the happy memories and success we had had, I was also very ill during those years. I was worried, terrified really, that putting myself back into that position could have implications on my mental wellness. Particularly when I'd had some tough times over the past decade. While my depression, anxiety and disordered eating is much, much better than it was, I have to work hard to ensure that I don't slip back into old habits.

I was reluctant to put myself in a space that could set me back.

There were various "secret" meetings about it; we'd all five meet, with Simon Fuller, but me or Victoria, or sometimes Geri wouldn't be into it.

It was proving impossible to get all five of us to sign on the dotted. And I was hesitant to say yes for such a long time because it wasn't all five of us. It didn't feel right.

Then an offer came in. It would be just for one night and it would be financially worth it.

You know me by now; money is never my motivation. Throughout my career, I've met people in the street, out shopping, on the tube or wherever and they'd tell me, "The Spice Girls had such an impact on my life." "Do you know how much you guys mean to me?" I'd meet young fans who told me the band gave them the confidence to come out, that they felt as though they had somewhere to belong. There are so many stories of the band having such a positive impact on people's lives. I love to hear those stories and, leading up to the shows in 2019, all of us girls were hearing them more and more.

I don't know what was in the air, but there was a momentum gathering around this time, picking up pace. There was a real appetite for us to return. It was, and remains, a golden era to be a Spice Girl because so many young artists now talk about being a fan, whether it's Adele or Little Mix, Olly from Years & Years or Billie Eilish. When I was writing *Melanie C*, I presented the singer MØ with a Danish music award in Copenhagen. She was a massive Spice Girls fan and did a cool electronic version of "Say You'll Be There". I got up onstage with her at the Roundhouse. She's phenomenal live, she's got a real punk energy, and there was crowd surfing everywhere.

I'm so influenced by this generation of musicians. When I made *Melanie C* I thought about how there are artists who talk about being inspired by the Spice Girls, and I'm now inspired by them. There's a lovely continuing cycle.

So, when this offer came in for the reunion, I felt a shift and I thought, *"Maybe this is a good time to do it."*

Geri came to my place to speak to me. I think she prides herself on being the person to talk me round, but I'd already decided. It felt right, it felt like people genuinely wanted it and it felt like a time to rewrite the legacy that we'd failed to take proper care of.

We couldn't persuade Victoria though. The last time she had performed with the Spice Girls was at the 2012 Olympics Closing Ceremony, one of my career highlights. For Victoria, that performance solidified that the stage was not the place for her. We're still hopeful she'll join us for something extra special... watch this space!

Although I knew we would miss Victoria's presence with this new show, the time was right. I was quite vocal about not wanting to do just one show and everyone agreed. Because I've continued to tour throughout my life, I know that to rehearse and to put on just one show costs a lot, it's ridiculous. You have to do more. We explored making it bigger and discussing what the routing and venues would be. Simon Moran presented us with the offer for stadiums, which for any band is amazing, but especially for pop bands because there's not many pop bands that can play stadiums. It is the pinnacle.

One show quickly turned into five shows, which then turned into eight. I was on my way to Bangkok for a solo gig when the tickets went on sale. I switched on my phone when we arrived to a flurry of messages: "Can we put another Manchester on, can we put another London on, can we put *another* London on?"

The tickets were selling out fast and Simon Moran, clever boy, had held the extra dates just in case. He knows what he's doing. We drew the line at a fourth Wembley gig, which is gutting but we knew we wouldn't give our best performance for a fourth night running at the end of the tour. Still, that one-off show offer turned into a 13-night stadium tour.

Modest, who were the management team behind One Direction and Little Mix, came onboard and introduced us to Lee Lodge, who was the show's creative director, and he brought in the designer and illustrator Aries Moross.

I brought my band and my musical director, Ricci Riccardi, on board. It seemed silly to put a new outfit together when mine was already in existence. Plus, I knew Ricci had the right temperament to handle all the dynamics and varying needs of all the band members. Ricci is amazing, nothing is too much trouble, and he really cares. He's very patient too.

We realised, through people like Lee, Aries (who created the branding, art direction and live visuals) and set designer Jason Sherwood that a lot of their generation (people now in their late twenties and thirties) were fans, they would be the ones coming to the show. They were the prime age, they've all got their favourite Spice Girl, everyone's got their Spice Girl story.

We used to get sent hundreds and hundreds of photos of kids' bedrooms covered in everything Spice Girls; they'd have the posters, the bedding, the wallpaper. There's a great photo of an 11-year-old Adele in her bedroom, which was essentially a Spice Girls shrine.

This show was for the fans, it was about being inclusive. Creatively, the starting point was the fans' bedrooms and those precious photos, and we took that into the stadiums to create a Spice World for everybody.

The setlist was important to us. We wanted to do all the hits, we didn't want any fillers, and we didn't want any new songs or solo stuff. We wanted to give the people what they wanted – nostalgia.

The other thing that made these shows different to the 2007 reunion was that back then, we came into a show that was pretty much done. We had approved things, but we didn't have a lot of creative input, except for maybe the costumes. It was an incredible show, but it didn't encompass the essence, the heart and the soul of the Spice Girls because we were less involved.

For the 2019 shows, everyone was on the same page, and it was about nostalgia and having a great time. Aries is incredible as were the visuals and the merch, and Lee's vision was brilliantly executed.

The whole team was fantastic, everyone did an amazing job. Paul Roberts, who has worked with everyone from Harry Styles to Katy Perry, was our choreographer and Gabriella Slade our costume designer. The costume department would stay up all night sticking crystals back onto costumes that had pinged off during the show. When the heavens opened and threatened to ruin our handmade "Viva Forever" look, they somehow produced see-through rain covers.

The dancers worked their socks off too and were put back together by my amazing sports therapist Pedro Phipippou, who was booked to look after us girls but ended up fixing everyone – even the truck drivers!

I've also got to mention my lovely security guard Jarv, who'd also put me through my paces at the gym and our amazing caterers, especially Claire, who made sure my protein shake was waiting for me when I got offstage. Not forgetting the ever-patient and brilliant Rachel Wood, our PA, management, therapist, referee, protector and everything in between.

Everything was in place. The stars were in alignment, and it was felt like this could just be a big and important Spice Girls moment.

There was a lot riding on the shows, and we were *nervous*. We had a huge stage, which was very technical because we had all these lifts and a B-stage, which took us out into the heart of the audience. The poor sound guys had a nightmare because it went all the way out to the halfway line. But we wanted to be there, in the heart of it, with the fans.

It was a huge production, and it's always the same – you're never going to be ready, it won't be ready in time. We were so anxious because there was so much left to do. Things weren't built, or hadn't arrived, Mel B got an eye infection, and Geri lost her voice.

There was so much going on, an upset, illnesses, a show that looked like it might not be ready on time.

It felt like everything was going against us.

. . .

The first show was at Dublin's Croke Park. You never feel ready on opening night, ever. We got there, and we were having last-minute rehearsals backstage, getting ready, building up to it. "*Is Geri's voice okay, did that part arrive, can Melanie see, how do we get under the stage when it's so low* (wheelchairs, was the answer to that one), *where's my humidifier, who's got Scarlet? I need to warm up!*" were the sort of things flying around backstage.

Finally, we're in place, the noise of the stadium washing over us. There's that moment where the audience senses the show is about to start, they see the musicians suddenly tense up, a light goes on, there's the tiniest of movements and the roar just builds. It's so magical.

We all climbed onto the B-stage lift, crouching so we couldn't be seen. We held hands as we slowly rose to the stage. We were so, so, so nervous.

As I stood on that stage on that first night at Croke Park, the sound of 80,000 people screaming and shouting, fireworks exploding, one word comes to mind.

Arrival.

I felt an overwhelming sense of arrival.

Physically, metaphorically and literally. All the -allys, I felt them all!

We were lined up in a row: Scary, Baby, Ginger, Sporty.

The opening notes of "Spice Up Your Life" blasted out.

"When you're feelin' sad and low/We will take you where you gotta go/Smilin', dancin', everything is free/All you need is positivity..."

I remember looking out across Croke Park – I'm going to cry again, I can't work out if there's more crying or weeing going on in this book – and it was just this wave of love. The nerves dissipated, the adrenaline steadied, and this massive surge of emotion covered me.

As we had with the Olympics, I took care to take it all in, to savour it, to remember it. I wanted every one of those 20 songs we were performing to matter as much to me as they did to the people watching. I don't think I've ever enjoyed performing "Wannabe", "Viva Forever", "Too Much" and "Who Do You Think You Are" as much as I did that night, and the subsequent 12 nights.

When we came offstage at Dublin, we all went off in the same car, instead of separate cars. It was important we did that because it gave us that opportunity to say, together, "*We did it!*" We were so proud of ourselves and each other. It had been 12 years since the last full, headline show, and we were just buzzing. It was such a wonderful experience.

We got that level of support and emotion and excitement from the audience at every single show. Even when we got drenched in Bristol, torrential rain the whole way through, the audience were 100% with us. Cardiff, Manchester, Sunderland, Edinburgh, Coventry, Bristol and, of course London, were one big, massive party.

Sold-out stadiums every night. It was like a movement. In every city we went to, it felt like a national holiday. We'd head out at lunchtime to soundcheck and we'd see everyone dressed up as Spice Girls, all out drinking. It was the biggest, mass hen party, an impromptu Pride.

They were the biggest shows we'd ever done, they were stadiums, but they felt so intimate. Normally at a gig you get most of your fans up but there's always a few sat down. On this tour, every single person at every single show was up, dancing, screaming, and singing along to every word. I've played loads of gigs; I've been to loads of gigs, but I've never experienced anything like it.

And we managed to get on well the whole time too! We all had loads of family and friends come to various dates and it felt like one big, happy, brilliantly dysfunctional family. A lot of old wounds were repaired on that tour.

In fact, on the last night at Wembley, Geri apologised for leaving us all those years ago, which was a bit of a moment.

"I need to say something I should have said a long time ago. I'm sorry. I'm sorry I left. I was just being a brat. It is so good to be back with the girls that I love," she said just before we played "Goodbye". It was very heartfelt.

Despite feeling the absence of Victoria's presence, it was my favourite tour. I felt like I was in a place where I could appreciate it and it felt very, very special. I realised I could be a solo artist *and* a Spice Girl. I was always frightened because when it comes to the Spice Girls, everything else is eclipsed, nothing else matters because the Spice Girls is huge.

I was nervous about becoming Sporty Spice, until I realised that, well, I am Sporty Spice, she's always in there. Two bars of "Wannabe" and I'm jumping around like a knob. It's not like I have to put on an act, it's just there. It was a huge weight lifted from me. After struggling to understand who I was throughout *Northern Star*, and beyond, I was now able to accept every aspect of myself.

In 2019, I felt so much more *me*. With a bit of age and wisdom I was able to take it in. Any of the issues us girls have had with each other, over the years, we're so much more relaxed with each other now. We appreciate each other and we've always known that without each other we wouldn't have what we have, the lives that we've had. We give each other space we need now.

. . .

The last night of the tour was brilliant. We had great people come to see us play; Emma Stone came over with HAIM. Sam Smith, Nathalie Emmanuel, Lily Collins, and Lily James. The American artist Aminé, who I met after he wrote a song called "Spice Girl", he came to one of the Coventry shows. We also had Adele and some of her pals come to that final show.

I first met Adele sometime around 2011 or 2012. She came over to me and said, "I'm a really big fan of the Spice Girls and I'm a really big fan of yours too. *Northern Star*, I love that album." I was like, "Oh, that's so lovely, thank you!" A few months later I was at a Christmas party at James Corden's house, and she came over again: "I just want to say, I meant it, I wasn't being a dick. I am a really big fan of *you* as well as the Spice Girls." It was a lovely thing for her to say and for me to hear.

The next time I saw her was after the last Spice Girls show, when me, Emma and Mel B were up until six in the morning. It was the first time I'd had a drink since January, nearly six months – I think I deserved it! That final night was so fun. It was mayhem. We had everyone in the bar afterwards, including Jess Glynne, who supported us – we had a lovely time with Jess – and I really let my hair down that night. I went back to my dressing room to grab something, and in my room was Melanie Brown, Jess Glynne and Adele, drinking my rider. We had a laugh. And polished off a bottle of coffee Patrón.

At one point, security came over. "Right, girls, this isn't your stadium anymore. Fleetwood Mac is in tomorrow night, and you need to get going."

We were like, "Oh, they'll be fine, they won't mind!" Fleetwood Mac must have turned up, all of them in AA (Alcoholics Anonymous) and NA (Narcotics Anonymous), to find backstage stinking of cigs and booze. "Those bloody Spice Girls!" Sorry about that!

. . .

My relationship with the girls was better, I felt better about myself, I felt more confident. The shows became symbolic of everything positive in my life. Not that we'd ever taken it for granted, but the legacy we'd created, it was a real thing.

For the first time we really took in that we had an impact on a generation of young people. It was such a realisation to see, to understand, what we had achieved and to realise that it's not only about music, it's not only about breaking America, but it was also about impacting people's lives and changing history, culture, music. It was a moment in time.

And more than that, it showed what longevity we'd had. The main arc of our career was, pretty much, over and done in two years. "Wannabe" came out July 1996, Geri left in May 1998 and shortly after that... Well, you know the story now. Rather than us fading into the distance and becoming some sort of nostalgic memory, we somehow managed to outpace even newer, bigger bands with this tour. BTS, for instance, also toured during the same time that we did, albeit in different places. BTS are probably the biggest band in the world right now, they're just huge. And their tour did make more than our tour. By 1%. I believe it was $78.9 million to our $78.2 million dollars. And we only did the UK. *And* we didn't have Victoria with us. *And* this was our second reunion tour.

I think that speaks volumes, that we have a fanbase comparable to today's biggest bands.

I feel like we'll be spoken about long after we're gone. How lovely is that?

• • •

I didn't have much time to soak it all in. I left Wembley that night around 6 am and staggered into bed. Three hours later I became vaguely aware of something, or someone, standing over me. "Mum. *Mum*. Get up! I've got drama rehearsals." I half opened one eye to see Scarlet stood over me, an exasperated look on her face.

No rest for the wicked. I stumbled out of bed, still drunk, made her some sort of breakfast, and walked her down the road to her rehearsals. "Bye, Mum!" she grinned and ran off to join her friends as I dragged my poor body back home. Because all my family and friends were down for the show, we did the only thing we knew how to do: hair of the dog. We had a lovely afternoon at the local pub, re-living the previous night's events and nursing hangovers with Bloody Marys. Is it just me or is the best part of a night out the dissection of it the next day with your mates?

I was still hungover the day after that when I went for a fitting (honestly, it doesn't half hit hard once you turn 40). The day after that I had a rehearsal because the day after *that* I was on a plane to São Paulo.

I'd been invited to appear at São Paulo Pride alongside Sink The Pink. I was performing, among other tracks, C+C Music Factory's "Pride (A Deeper Love)", which I found myself frantically trying to learn on the flight over.

Because the tour had been so intense, I hadn't given too much thought to what I was going to be doing in Brazil. I've performed at various Prides for years, and always have a fantastic time. I knew it would be a fabulous event, but aren't they all?

I stepped straight off the stage at Wembley in front of 80,000 people and stepped straight onto a float in São Paolo in front of three million people.

Three million.

As the float carried us through the streets, I remember looking out and seeing miles, and miles and miles of people. It was totally overwhelming, and incredibly emotional, especially because the President of Brazil, Jair Bolsonaro, is particularly right-wing and quite happy to express his homophobic views. Because of that, and because the Brazilians really, really know how to party, there was an electricity in the air. It felt like there was a real sense of defiance. It was magical.

The opening chords to "2 Become 1" started playing and I looked out at everyone and thought, *"This is on a par with*

Wembley." How lucky, to experience something like that not just once, but twice in the space of a week.

When I look back now, I think bloody hell, 2019 was crazy. Absolutely crazy.

• • •

I'd been invited to perform on the float with my good friends Sink The Pink, who I have quite a history with. I'd begun working with co-founder of Sink The Pink and lovely human being Glyn Fussell and the team in 2017 when they invited me to perform at their night at the Troxy, a beautiful former cinema hall built in the 1930s on Commercial Road, in the heart of East London.

I went down there in the afternoon to soundcheck, and I just couldn't believe how warm and inclusive everyone was. There were people dancing and limbering up, there were people sewing costumes, people putting up lights, there was activity everywhere and everybody was so friendly and welcoming. I fell in love with Glyn, and he asked me to do their festival, Mighty Hoopla, but with some of the drag queens as my backing dancers. I loved that idea and we put a show together for the 2018 festival at Brockwell Park in South London. I was joined by Margo Marshall, Asttina Mandella (who went on to appear in *RuPaul's Drag Race*), Le Fil, Jonbenet and Joan Oh.

Glyn even gave me a drag king name – Jim Bunny!

It was a beautiful day, the park was packed, there were great vibes, everyone was just up for it, and the set went down a storm. I was doing four tracks: "I Turn to You", "Never Be The Same Again", "Think About It", and "Say You'll Be There". Pretty much as soon as I stepped onstage, I was transported straight back to Doreen Bird, to college, all those years ago. There was a shift in the crowd, I felt this invisible power surge, as the audience lifted. It sounds mad, but it's the only way to explain it.

We knew we had to do more, Glyn had ideas to make the show bigger and better, so he put together a pitch for live agents. From the first Pride in São Paulo to World Pride in New York where we performed in Times Square, we played Prides all over the world, taking us right through to Brisbane, Australia, in February 2020.

It has been such a beautiful partnership, and not only creatively. It has had such a profound impact on me emotionally too. Working with the drag queens, trans and non-binary people taught me so much and it was through getting to know them that I found further self-acceptance. It was something I never expected from doing that tour.

I feel very emotional as I write this. I think there might just be more tears than wees in this book, after all.

In the nineties, in the Spice Girls, I was Sporty Spice, I was the one in trackies, the fit, sporty one, but I had an eating disorder, and I was anorexic. I felt guilty about that. I'm a very honest person, I'm an open book, but I wasn't being honest. I wasn't sporty and fit; I was ill and projecting an unhealthy image to those people looking up to me.

That was really hard to deal with. I never truly felt confident that it was okay to just be me. I felt like I was cheating, or I wasn't really representing what I was saying. The Spice Girls really celebrated being different and that being a strength, but I wasn't owning that myself.

But the shows in 2019 reinforced this overpowering realisation of the legacy of the band, how it affected a generation of people, the celebration of it, the joy of it. I got to see the positive message people took from us, from our success. People called me a (that word I don't like again) "tomboy", but Sporty Spice made girls feel like they could wear a tracksuit or cut their hair short.

In doing the tour, I also realised that I am Sporty Spice. I don't become her, she's within me. I am a solo artist and I'm a Spice Girl, a mum, a daughter, a girlfriend, a friend, an auntie, a colleague, a human. I am all these things all the time. Good and bad, amazing and shite, this really is me. And accepting myself for that was incredible.

I hope there are people out there who may feel less alone because I've been able to go through it and come out the other side, and who can begin to accept parts of themselves too.

. . .

Then, later in 2019, Sink The Pink guided me to finally and fully owning who I am.

During the early years of the Spice Girls, I started to notice we had a big gay following; we were all of us conscious of our LGBTQI+ audience. We didn't take it for granted, we were aware of it and respectful of it. It was always important to us to be inclusive.

We talked about Girl Power because we experienced sexism within the music industry, and we knew we wanted to change that, to stop the exclusion. There are so many people in this world that feel like misfits. When you feel like that, it's great to have somewhere you feel you belong, as the individual you are. There was such a connection between us as women struggling to be heard, and the LGBTQI+ community, struggling to be accepted. We were fighting a cause for women, and we'd see the same thing in the LGBTQI+ communities, so there was a kinship there.

Working with Sink The Pink made me realise the extent of this kinship. Hearing people from the LGBTQI+ community talking and learning about other people's stories, trials, and tribulations and how they became the people they wanted to be was a big discovery. They fought for it; they carved their own space in a world that was at times reluctant to allow them to. They made mistakes, and that was okay. You pick yourself up and carry on, even when it's hard, even when it hurts.

Sink The Pink believe in the idea that it *really* is okay to just be who you are, whatever that is. Hearing these empowering stories reinforced to me that I'm both feminine and masculine, Sporty and gentle, tough and soft, strong and weak. I'm all these things and that's okay. And sometimes I don't know all the answers, but you just keep trying hard and allowing people to be the person they are.

To me, being an ally is about showing up, being vocal, being outspoken and learning. Part of that learning process is understanding what can be a rapidly evolving conversation so that you can help to educate people who don't understand. Being an ally is about standing up for issues, educating yourself and others, and supporting the community as much as you can. The hardest people to confront can be those closest to you, relatives who make offhand remarks that aren't exactly homophobic, or racist, but actually are. Each one, teach one. It's uncomfortable, but we have to learn to speak out more.

And the first stage of that is accepting ourselves for who we are, so we can learn to accept others in the same way.

• • •

It's such a privilege to have had that experience touring with Sink The Pink. But also, people really responded to what we were doing. After Mighty Hoopla, we ended up getting loads of gigs, and as 2019 closed, I found myself in Brazil, New York, Cologne, Hamburg, Bristol, Brighton, Margate, and finally Brisbane in 2020.

During that time, I'd started putting together a new record, which I felt great about. Doing shows with the girls provided me with plenty of inspiration, and then travelling with Glyn and the drag queens, I couldn't wait to start writing. Which I did. By the time 2019 ended, I'd done most of my new album and I took the opportunity to start promoting it while in different parts of the world with Sink The Pink.

The plan was to start in Sydney, and then head to LA and Canada before promoting in the UK, Europe and the rest of the world. I was so confident about this record, it felt just so right. I knew I'd be able to get out there and maybe, just maybe, it would be the one to do well.

We got to Brisbane in March.

8th March 2020.

You know what's coming next, don't you? Turns out COVID-19 had other plans. Not just for me, of course, but for the whole, wide world.

Before that, though, I had one more lesson to learn.

CHAPTER NINETEEN

Who I am

Not long before the Spice Girls reunion tour in 2019, Dad rang me: "It's Nanny. I think it really is it this time. Do you want to come and say goodbye?" It wasn't the first time I'd had the call. My Nanny Kay was 94 years old and had been close to death a few times, yet she always managed to come back from the brink.

I hoped more than anything that this would be another of those moments, but there was no way I was taking the chance.

Scarlet and I drove up to Liverpool the following morning.

She was a formidable woman, my nan. She was very religious, as Catholic as a Catholic can be. She had the Holy Water by the door and pictures of Our Lord strategically placed around the house. Not only did she attend church religiously (pun intended!), but she even did the accounts for the church. She was also very involved with the local community on the estate she lived on in Kirkby. Everyone knew Nannie and Nannie knew everyone.

I really loved her, and I know she loved me and that she was proud of me and what I'd achieved in my life. She was always showing off at church and was on good terms with the priest, he was a big fan. Dad would roll his eyes sometimes because she used to parade me up and down the street when I came to visit her. I'd go in to say hello and the next thing I knew it would be, "Oh, Melanie, one minute, Ann wants to say hello." Before the kettle was on, she'd have half the estate over and I'd be signing autographs and God-knows-what-else.

She was emotionally and physically as strong as an ox until developing lung problems when she was in her mid-seventies. She had low oxygen levels in her blood and was on oxygen 14 hours a day for the last 15 years of her life. Everywhere she went, she had a portable tank next to her.

Incidences of lung cancer in Merseyside are known for being 60% higher than the national average, while Liverpool is the only city to have two constituencies in the top ten for the highest prevalance of cases of COPD (Chronic Obstructive Pulmonary Disease) in the country. Maybe it's the dampness of the city – although there are other similar cities, geographically – or other environmental factors, but living in the North West is not good for your lungs.

It seemed like my nan's respiratory system was failing. We arrived in Liverpool towards the end of January 2018 and headed straight to Fazakerley General Hospital.

She was on a small ward with about six other women, and it was a bit chaotic. There was one old lady shouting her head off (my nan said she did that all night long) and then another who just wanted to chat and kept trying to catch our attention. There were a lot of characters on that ward and my nan was one of them.

I took Scarlet with me, and my sister Emma took my nephews, Finn and Tate. Nan was lying there, no teeth in, looking very old, but still very awake. I think it might have been a bit of a shock for the kids, but I'm glad they got an opportunity to say goodbye to their great-grandmother, who was a great-great grandmother by then. It was a serious time, but there was lots of laughter and lots of mickey-taking too, in that true Liverpool way. Nanny and my Auntie Lynne were a bit of a double act, always exasperated with each other but never apart.

After a while, Dad stood up and said he'd take the kids to get a drink and so it was just me and Nanny. I looked at the woman I'd known my whole life, now near the end of hers. All the excitement of the last hour had clearly drained her. I could see she was getting very tired and that she was fading. She took my hand in hers and she squeezed with as much strength as she had. She looked small, frail. I fought back the tears as she took off her mask and had a sip of water. She said something but I couldn't hear. I leant in closer. "I said, you're too soft you are, girl," she said and smiled at me, shaking her head.

It was one of those moments that stay with you forever. Just six words really but they were six words that were not only very true and very poignant, but words I needed to hear. She was telling me to dig deep, find my inner strength, to lose that doubt that could hold me back. She was telling me to start standing up for myself. Less people pleasing and more putting myself first.

I knew I had it in me to be strong because I'd overcome so much. Sometimes I still can't believe what I have survived. But nonetheless, I could be too soft, and it didn't always serve me well. I've really held those words close over the past couple of years and when I've found myself in situations that aren't benefiting me, I've learned to start speaking up. I think Nan wanted me to hear those words and to take them on board, to toughen up a bit.

Thank you, Nan, for leaving those words with me at a time I really needed to hear them.

She didn't say much more after that. Dad and the kids came back, and we sat there, stroking her hand and her hair. A couple of hours later, the nurse took her pulse and turned to us: "It won't be long now." A priest arrived soon after to read the Last Rites.

It got late and we needed to get the kids to bed so I said a tearful goodbye, and we left the hospital. I couldn't believe I'd never see my Nannie Kay again.

Of course, the next day she started to get better. My dad was doing the morning shift and arrived, prepared for the worst. But there she was, sitting up in bed having her breakfast. "You can probably go home tomorrow, Mrs Chisholm, you're doing much better," said the nurse as Nan cracked into her egg and toast. No one could believe it.

My dad had popped out for a bit when Nanny decided to get up after breakfast. And that's when she died. Though we knew she was ill, we thought she might have turned a corner, so it was still a bit of a shock. She died of complications due to heart failure and pneumonia.

As sad as it is, I think she would have been happy with her departure from this earth. She might have been at death's door, but she was so stubborn that, even to her Holy Beloved Father, who was waiting to whisk her off to the gates of Heaven, she had said, "No, I'm not ready yet", and made Him wait until she had decided she was ready.

She was a stubborn woman, and she was a tough woman. She had lived on a rough council estate in Kirkby since 1957, and she refused to move. She feared no one, even though there would be all sorts going on. One night someone set a car on fire right outside her bedroom (and she was breathing in all those fumes – I wonder if that had gone on to affect her lungs), but she loved her home, and nothing would have driven her from that place.

I returned to Liverpool a few weeks later for the funeral. Nanny's body was in the conservatory at my aunt's, in a beautiful coffin with all these gorgeous flowers filling the room. I watched as my dad held his mother's hand and said his goodbyes. Having been brought up in a Catholic household, he was used to it, but I'd never seen a dead body before. It was shocking yet it changed how I felt about death. I looked at Nannie, lying at rest, and realised she wasn't there. She was gone, her spirit, her soul, however you see it, the thing that made her *her* was no longer there. That experience has made me feel my connection with people that I've lost even stronger. Because our loved ones aren't here physically, I've learnt the body truly is just a shell. I know they're here with me, whenever I need them.

It filled me with a sense of peace.

The time came when we had to leave for the church, and we drove around her estate in a big procession. Even though the estate was full of all sorts of characters, she was very well looked after by everyone there. They'd get her milk or the paper from the local shop and pop in now and then to see she was doing okay. As we drove through, everyone came out on their doorsteps crossing themselves.

It's been four years since I spent those last final hours with my Nan at Fazakerley General. There's not a day that goes by when I don't think of those last few words.

They continue to inspire me today.

Epilogue

So, to today and the roaring 2020s.

COVID-19, Coronavirus, SARS-CoV-2, the 'Rona, the virus. Long Covid. The pandemic. Alpha, Beta, Gamma, Delta, Omicron. The Kent variant. Variants. Lateral flow testing and PCRs. Banana bread, daily walks, bubbles, Captain Tom, TikTok, cronyism, Dominic Cummings, Barnard Castle, the NHS, singing outside on the street. The daily briefing. Wet markets, antibodies, mutations, and viral loads. Jigsaws and colouring books. Toilet rolls and hand sanitisers. Zoom, Google Hangout, Teams, and WebEx. WFH. Livestreams, social distancing, flatten the curve, stop the spread and self-isolation. Happy birthday. Pings. The New Normal. Fake News. Pfizer, Astra-Zeneca, Moderna, Johnson & Johnson. Boosters. The fourth Booster. Not another bloody quiz.

I couldn't have known, could I, standing on that stage in Wembley back on 15th June 2019, what was around the corner? None of us saw COVID-19 coming, did we? What an unwanted thing that turned out to be.

I had no idea, certainly, what the future had in store for me at that point, let alone planet Earth.

It's "thanks" to these past two very unusual years that I started to think more deeply about my story. It was part of the inspiration to write this book.

Since leaving Widnes at 16 years old, I've hadn't been in one place for as long as I had during the pandemic. That enforced time at home gave me the time and space for some serious reflection. Although London has been home for the last 30 years, I've never quite felt rooted here because I'd constantly been packing and unpacking, boarding a plane, checking into a hotel. The chaos of constant change was the routine of my life. Yet I'd always craved the predictability and safety of a home life, working Monday to Friday, and relaxing at the weekend. Like many of us during the pandemic, I was forced into that situation. I could barely leave my corner of London let alone go anywhere else.

It was a brilliant novelty at first, but the novelty soon wore off. Not only because I was so used to a nomadic existence, but because I'd been a performer since I was a kid. Not having the stage in my life was difficult because part of what I love about performing is being able to create connections with people. It made me realise that being onstage is such a huge part of who I am, my identity, and I need it to be fulfilled.

So, if I couldn't connect with people through the stage, then maybe I could reach them in another way? I began writing my eighth record in 2019 and continued it following the successful Spice Girls tour, and a few months before the dreaded words, "COVID-19" and "pandemic" became part of our everyday language.

Touring with the girls enabled me to let go of a lot of things. I was able to enjoy the experience of being a Spice Girl. It was a real celebration, and it helped me to understand what we had achieved in 1996, 1997 and 1998.

When you're struggling and searching, ill and frustrated, you become so insular, and you don't always take in the bigger picture.

We just want to do more now. More Spice Girls, more shows. It almost feels like a duty because it was so enjoyed by people. We only got to do the UK and Ireland but there's a whole world of Spice Girls fans out there. I'm constantly asked about whether we'll do Glastonbury, but I promise you, we've never been asked.

We're just waiting for that call from Emily! Hmm, Coachella would be fun too.

The combination of feeling so at peace with being a Spice Girl and Melanie Chisholm, having Joe as both my manager and my partner, and going on tour with Sink The Pink very naturally led me to want to make another album. Those girls (and I refer to all the above!) are an inspiring lot.

You only get one go with your self-titled album, don't you, and *Melanie C* felt like the right one. So many changes had occurred, and I felt like I was finally owning every part of myself. I shed my shame, shed my past, shed my guilt. It has been a real voyage of self-discovery. It's certainly meaningful that it's taken me until my eighth record, now I've finally realised who I am, to be able to put my name to my work in this way. That makes me really proud.

I questioned, briefly, if the timing was right. The record was written in such a flush of positivity and performance, of meeting new people and travelling to amazing places, and here we all were, very suddenly and very unexpectedly, locked up amid a deadly global pandemic.

But I knew it was the right thing to do because I recognised that I could offer people a little bit of positivity and entertainment.

I was happy to help lift people's spirits. You can't help having a little dance when you put that record on. I love that the album is so upbeat, so full of life and it's all about positive affirmation. I think we all needed a bit of that in 2020.

This newfound effervescence was thanks to working with newer talents like Shura, Nadia Rose, Rae Morris and Fryars and Billen Ted. They brought such great energy to me and the album. I also went back in with my lovely Biff, as I've mentioned, and industry giants like Future Cut, who have created hits with Lily Allen and Little Mix, and Johnny Latimer, who worked with Ellie Goulding on her massive debut album.

Like *Version of Me*, I made a lot of changes, including working with a new PR team: Ruth, Beth and Rob over at Toast Press. I was in *Vogue Spain*, dahlings. Via Ruth I was introduced to her husband, Frank Tope, who A&R'd the record, he was utterly brilliant. I had needed the type of insight and overview that Frank delivered for so long.

It was very much the right time, right team, right place, right vibes. The stars aligned, as I think they have several times during this book.

Melanie C was released on 2nd October 2020. The record went to number eight, my first top ten album since *Reason* in 2003. It got great reviews across the board. I felt real, genuine love for it. I had finally repeated some of that elusive success I'd chased for so long. Just like the Spice Girls reunion tour, I was also in a place to fully appreciate and enjoy it. When I finally got to take the album on tour in 2022, albeit briefly as we very reluctantly had to cancel the European dates, it was a total joy. The shows brought together fans from all over the world, old and new, and I was so happy to finally have the chance to celebrate the record properly. We had a right old dance at every gig, let me tell you!

Like everyone, I struggled during the pandemic, but I also took a lot from the experience. I had to work from home and do things online. I had to work more with social media, I had to let people into my home via Zoom and FaceTime, neither of which I'd previously been comfortable with. I discovered that having these connections with people was so important. As much as I hate certain aspects of technology, I felt grateful that it showed me how to reach my fans, my friends and my family in a different way, at a time when we couldn't be together. I felt very strongly the support and entertainment I was giving them. And it was so beneficial to me too, as a human. I also needed that connection.

There were lots of changes during the pandemic. Joe and I have achieved so much together over the last few years, but we are no longer a couple. We still care for each other deeply. It's been a wonderful few years, but a hard few years. Joe and I still work together. I am grateful to him for everything, and we remain dear friends.

I started two other projects during lockdown (because, as you might have guessed by now, I'm not very good at sitting still!). As I said, I began a phone-hacking claim into the tabloids after several people told me I had a case. It's ongoing, so I can't say too much more than I have already, but it's been both an insightful and upsetting experience.

It took ages to read the thousands of press clippings. At the end of that process, I went into a dark place for around a week. It was so painful to revisit and read what was written. Although I'd seen a lot of it at the time, to see it in one place, to see how brutal the media were about me, about the other girls, about women in general, is still very shocking. While I could say that things have changed within the British press (have they?), I think it's simply become a little more covert, a little more hidden. The language might have changed but the intention hasn't: we can't let women be, we can't let women breathe, we can't let women get too ahead of themselves.

And of course, that helped to form part of this very book, *Who I Am*. I've never claimed to have all the answers, but I hope this book, my story, can inspire other people who are struggling. Being in a depressed mind state is incredibly isolating. Depression, anxiety and eating disorders can be such a lonely place to be. When I was at my worst, knowing that I wasn't alone was so helpful for me. I hope through this book that I have offered some guidance. Failing that, then comfort – a literary shoulder to cry on.

I wanted to give people who felt they were in their darkest moments a sense of hope. Sometimes it feels like the light has gone out – I know that feeling all too well – but you can come back from that. You can find light, and through that, happiness and self-love. Just like I did. I've by no means worked everything out, but I hope this story is one that is inspiring and affirming.

I'm not sure that we ever find "utopia", but I do think you can reach a place of faith and trust in yourself that helps you to realise that the dark days will pass. Thinking back – and now reading back – over my story, I see such incredible strength and resilience, even in my darkest moments, my toughest times. Even when I've felt "weak" and depleted, I amaze myself that I have been able to survive even the worst of days.

I appreciate what I've achieved, and I've allowed myself to be proud of what I've accomplished. I'm completely self-made. I came from nothing, but I created something. The Spice Girls weren't only a part of pop culture, we *were* pop culture for a brief period. My solo career has made me among the most successful female solo singers in the UK. I can look after myself and my daughter and I don't need anyone. It takes a lot for me to be able to say that, because we always feel like we should be doing this, or we should have achieved that, or I made this mistake, and I regret that decision.

Through the course of my album, and this book, I've learnt to applaud myself a bit more.

I have been and continue to be so courageous, yet I don't always give myself that credit, like many women, especially women from working-class backgrounds. We are the first to criticise ourselves and put ourselves down, yet we rarely, if ever, pat ourselves on the back. I'm getting a lot better at owning my achievements and reminding myself of everything I have accomplished rather than berating myself for being too soft or not as successful as this person, as clever as that person, as funny as that one... I think we all do it, don't we?

Being a Spice Girl has meant I've experienced so many incredible, amazing, strange, fantastic moments. It wasn't all jazz hands and best friends. For several years, I didn't want anything to do with Sporty Spice or with the Spice Girls. It was too painful for me. Being in the band gave me this incredible career and amazing lifestyle, but it nearly destroyed me too. They are some of the best but also among the toughest years of my life.

I hope by reading this book you've gotten an idea of how I was feeling throughout the entire journey. There were moments in the band that were very difficult for me. There were dynamics between the girls that were very challenging at times. We were an impenetrable unit, but there were some cracks beneath that surface. There was a lot of self-policing and very little outside support. We were five young women who very quickly became incredibly rich and hugely famous. It's not surprising there was a fall-out from that. Add to that a punishing schedule and a very brutal British media and, of course, there were always going to be difficult times for us individually and as a group.

What you have read within the pages of this book is what I wanted people to know about me, Melanie Chisholm, because I want people to take away strength and hope from this book.

And I think we've had a laugh here and there.

I reckon there could have been a few more wee stories, but maybe I'll save them for the next book.

Which brings me to the big question – was it the right thing to do, for me to write this book?

Let me tell you, this process has been a journey. I've had wobbles throughout, questioning myself about why I was doing it and asking both "Should I be doing this?", and "What have I done?!" But you know what? I'm really, really pleased that I have. It was hard to go over a lot of what I've talked about. The first chapter got to me for a few days because it triggered a lot of stuff. Chapter 14? That was really, really hard.

I hope what I've been through can be something for people to learn from. We're not perfect, we do make mistakes. We aren't infallible and the road to recovery isn't a straight one. But it's okay to not be okay and it will be okay. Talk to people, listen to yourself, seek help.

I think this book has helped me understand me, to understand my truth. This book is my truth. It's my story.

This is who I am.

Glossary

In Liverpool, we abbreviate pretty much everything. I thought it might be handy to provide you lot with a guide to some of the words that might confuse you a bit!

Auld fella – to mean your dad or an older relative/man

Bevvy – an alcoholic drink, usually a beer

Boss – to mean really good. "That shirt is boss, mate."

Chippy – the fish and chip shop

Come 'ed – come on, let's go

Gobshite – a person who talks rubbish, and/or talks a lot

Go'ed – to encourage someone to continue or carry on, etc., but also to congratulate someone too

Goolies – A man's testicles/balls/bollocks!

Leccy – the electricity

Made up – to be really pleased for someone

Offy – the off licence

Our Paul/Our Kid – we say "our" for siblings

Pick (i.e. there wasn't a pick on me) – To describe someone very slim

Plazzy – a plastic bag but also used to call someone a fake – i.e. a Plazzy Scouser if you're from Runcorn :(

The Argos – we just like to pop a "the" in front of shops, who knows why?!

Soft Lad – Used affectionally to tell someone they're being stupid

Sound – To mean good. *See also*, **Boss**.

Acknowledgements

First of all, I have to thank my incredible daughter, Scarlet. Sorry I'm so embarrassing, I'll keep working on that. You are my proudest achievement and have more girl power than I can believe. I can't wait to see you give the world as much hell as you give me!

A massive thank you to my family and friends for being so helpful and supportive through this process. Mum, Dad, Den, Paul and Emma, thank you for jogging my memory, and thank you also to Mel B, Marc Fox and Biff for reminding me of some things I'd rather forget!

I have to also thank Melanie, Emma, Geri and Victoria for the incredible adventures, laughter and lessons we continue to share.

Thank you to all at Welbeck, Oliver Holden-Rea first and foremost, but also Annabel, Nico, James, Rob, Carrie-Ann, Vasiliki, Wayne, Rachel, Clare and Tanisha.

My brilliant writing partner Hattie Collins for helping make sense of my early drafts, laughing at my bad jokes and helping me feel comfortable and brave enough to share some of the most difficult challenges I have had to face.

And last but never least, the fans that continue to support me through the Spice Girls, my solo career and everything in between. None of this would have been possible without you.